Foreign Films
in America

Foreign Films in America

A History

KERRY SEGRAVE

McFarland & Company, Inc., Publishers
Jefferson, North Carolina, and London

LIBRARY OF CONGRESS CATALOGUING-IN-PUBLICATION DATA

Segrave, Kerry.
    Foreign films in America : a history / Kerry Segrave.
        p.   cm.
    Includes bibliographical references and index.

    ISBN 0-7864-1764-1 (softcover : 50# alkaline paper) ∞

    1. Foreign films—United States—History. 2. Motion
pictures, European—United States—History. I. Title.
PN1995.9.F67S44   2004
791.43'75'0973—dc22   2004000958

British Library cataloguing data are available

Cover image ©2004 Comstock

Manufactured in the United States of America

McFarland & Company, Inc., Publishers
  Box 611, Jefferson, North Carolina 28640
  www.mcfarlandpub.com

Contents

Preface

The struggle by foreign film producers to increase their screen presence in the United States has been ongoing for close to a century. Foreign films enjoyed a brief period, prior to World War I, when they held a place of prominence on American cinema screens. Once the American motion picture industry overcame its early, chaotic state and organized itself into a cartel, it was successfully able to decrease and to limit that foreign presence. That was one of the reasons the cartel was organized in the first place. Ever since that time offshore producers have waged various campaigns over time, all ultimately unsuccessful, to break the Hollywood stranglehold on domestic film screens.

Sometimes those foreign producers tried to enact laws at home designed to generate reciprocity; sometimes they tried to "Americanize" their product; sometimes they tried to dub their output (instead of subtitling); sometimes they tried to self-distribute their movies (instead of contracting for that service with an American firm). Yet nothing worked.

Ever-helpful, Hollywood always had advice to offer those producers and a ready answer as to why foreign films failed so dismally in America. One reason constantly advanced by the Hollywood cartel, whether in 1913 or in 2002, has been that virtually all of those foreign films were of a very low quality. Additionally, Americans had "unique" film tastes, and they didn't like subtitles or dubbed films, and the foreign stuff was often immoral. Hollywood and film exhibitors could not understand why those foreigners did not hire American actors, writers, and directors to make their foreign films—then they might have a chance. That Hollywood exercised its dominance through its oligopolistic cartel control of the world's

1

film industry, and not by some inherent magical filmmaking ability, was never mentioned by Hollywood. Many of those foreigners, however, did understand.

This book looks at attempts made by foreign producers over the past 90-odd years to increase their film presence in America, and at Hollywood's responses to those attempts and its explanations for the situation. Print and online databases were consulted with the back files of *Variety* being a particularly useful source. Research was conducted at the Vancouver Public Library, the University of British Columbia, and Simon Fraser University.

1

Foreign Films Dominate, 1895–1915

I am willing to admit that the French [films] are ahead of us ... they are encouraged by a public of higher artistic perception than ours.
—*Thomas Edison, 1908*

[Exhibitors] ask "foreign?" and if the answer is "yes" they decline [to book the film].
—*William Fox, 1914*

We cannot secure a footing in the United States ... and can only conclude it is not the desire of the Americans to encourage foreign features.
—*Unnamed U.K. film man, 1915*

Foreign films in America have had such a minimal presence for so long a period of time that it seemed to be the natural order of things. Yet it was not always that way. There was a time when foreign movies had a majority of the screen time in America. But that was only for a brief period of time, and was very long ago.

Early in 1895 the French brothers Auguste and Louis Lumière came up with a simple, multipurpose machine that could be used as a camera, projector and printer—the cinematographe. It had its debut U.S. screening at Keith's Union Square Theater (a vaudeville house) in New York City on June 29, 1895, about two months after the New York premiere of the vitascope (a U.S. rival system). The first three Lumière machines played Keith's Union venue for 23 weeks, his Philadelphia house for 19 weeks, and his Boston theater for 22 weeks. By early September new shipments had started to arrive, and over the following eight months, the Lumières' New York office was home to 24 machines and over 1,400 "views," as those very early films were called. Lumière had opened its New York City office in November 1895, and offered to sell or lease its machines. In Brooklyn it opened a storefront and utilized publicity that appealed to a more sophisticated audience by emphasizing, as historian Charles Musser wrote, that its movies "will be of special interest to those who know something of the artistic side of photography." American counterparts to Lumière favored a subject matter of dancing girls, boxing matches, bullfights, and vaudeville acts while the French firm tried to offer subjects aimed at a more elevated audience while still maintaining a wide appeal. By 1897, the American Mutoscope Company, later renamed the American Mutoscope and Biograph Company (usually just called Biograph), replaced the Lumière organization as the foremost film company in the U.S.—a dominance it would hold for about four years. One reason for the decline of the Lumières, said Musser, was that the company was slow in bringing American views to its American audiences. Exposed film shot by one of their imported photographers had to be sent back to France to be developed. Then the resultant prints would be shipped back to the U.S. for exhibition.[1]

Other reasons for the rise of Biograph included the fact it had political connections to the Republican Party and was rewarded by a new, pro-tariff administration. As a result the French concern faced legal actions for customs irregularities because the cinematographes had been brought into the United States as personal property, instead of as commercial goods. That led to the liquidation of the Lumière American inventory of machines and stock, beginning in April 1897. Lumière also followed that strategy in England at around the same time because adding to its problems was the fact that the cinematographe was becoming technically outmoded. The liquidation sale, however, "accelerated the decline of the French company on the American market," explained Musser.[2]

Although the legitimate presence of European films in America declined around 1897, that European industry exerted a greater influence in shaping American cinema because while producers from countries such as France and England sold a small number of prints to U.S. exhibitors with overseas connections, "their films generally reached American screens as dupes [pirated] by U.S. companies," wrote Musser. During the very first few years of the 1900s Frenchman Georges Méliès, "whose pictures had been

duped by every major American producer," was so unhappy with the situation that he sent his brother, Gaston Méliès, to the U.S. to represent his
interests. Gaston arrived in New York in March 1903, and discovered, for
example, "that Biograph had been paying Charles Urban one-cent-per-foot
royalties for prints of Méliès subjects. The money, of course, had never
reached the original artist." By June of 1903, Gaston had opened a New
York factory and office. In his first catalog Gaston castigated U.S. film producers who "are searching for novelties but lack the ingenuity necessary to
produce them" and "found it easier and more economical fraudulently to
copy Star Films [his brand] and to advertise their poor copies as their own
original conceptions."[3]

If those actions reduced the number of pirated Méliès movies in America, U.S. producers still had a wide choice of European films, such as those
from the French concern Pathé Frères and several English firms. British
films did not establish a solid base in the U.S. as not a single U.K. producer opened an American agency (through 1907); instead producers sold
their product through American sales agents. By around 1904 Pathé was
expanding rapidly and setting up sales offices in countries throughout the
world, from England and Germany to South America and Japan. Pathé
opened a New York City branch in August 1904. Rather than simply copy-
righting its films and hoping for the best, as Méliès had initially done,
Pathé pursued a different solution to the pirating problem: it started to
market its movies in the U.S. before selling them in Europe. That move
undercut Edison and other American producers who had been in the habit
of buying Pathé films in London and then shipping them back to America where they were illegally duped and released as their own original material. In contrast to the gain in popularity for the Pathé product, Méliès'
pictures faded in popularity, reportedly because they failed to adopt the
crime and comedy-chase genres then most popular. Pathé's approach of providing movies with a wide variety of subject matter and having a worldwide
network of branch offices had proved to be successful.[4]

One reason for the increase in the amount of foreign film released in
America in the period 1906 to 1907, and for a while longer, was the turmoil
and uncertainty in the U.S. film industry. It was a time of confusion, stress,
and anarchy. Entrepreneurs wishing to enter the film business at that time
found it easier and more profitable to become exhibitors or distributors as
the U.S. producing firm Edison once again sued all the leading American
producers and importers of foreign films between 1902 and 1905 (over
camera patents). Although the court ruled against Edison in March 1906,
the producer appealed the decision. That continuing uncertainty made
investment in equipment and studios very problematic. As Musser noted,

"The shortage of American pictures in 1906 and early 1907 opened up tremendous opportunities for foreign producers." According to one source only one-third of all the films released in the U.S. during 1907 were American-made, with the other two-thirds coming from Europe. Of that latter group, movies by Pathé were the single largest group, being responsible for over a third of the movies shown on U.S. screens. One Coney Island exhibitor remarked, in May 1906, "We rather prefer the foreign films ourselves, especially the Pathé. They're fine."[5]

Pioneering film industry methods, Pathé had by 1906 introduced such key aspects of the studio system as a stock company of actors and multiple production units, features that did not become common in the U.S. for at least two more years. Also by this time Pathé had offices in New York, London, Berlin, Vienna, Milan, Moscow, Barcelona, and Shanghai. By October 1906, it was exporting as many as 12 movies a week and up to 75 copies of each film went to America. Pathé's production reached a level at the end of that year where it released at least one new film a day. Charles Pathé remarked at the time, "The American market by itself amortised the costs, however modest, of our negatives. We sold at least as many in the rest of our offices.... The columns of American receipts represented a net profit or nearly so." The number of Pathé offices then stood at 14. American importer George Kleine emerged at this time as the leading agent for European producers. Among others, he represented Gaumont, Urban-Eclipse, and Theo Pathé. Other importers would come and go but none seemed to last very long, or to challenge the dominant position of Kleine.[6]

Film historian Richard Abel declared that by the summer of 1905, Pathé "had become the leading supplier of moving pictures on the American market." A 1907 piece in the *New York Clipper* asserted "Pathé films [were] featured on all moving picture programs." Pathé films were known to be in circulation in America as early as the summer of 1902 and as deep into the heartland as Des Moines, Iowa. During his court testimony in an antitrust case, Frank Dyer, former vice president of Edison, was asked what was the most popular brand of film exhibited in the U.S., in January 1908. He replied, "I think the Pathé pictures were the most popular of them." Asked if the Pathé films displayed a high quality, Dyer said, "Yes, sir. The Pathé pictures were the highest standard known in the art at that time. They were pre-eminent." At another point in his testimony, Dyer claimed that Pathé films made up 60 percent of the total film product then in circulation in the U.S. Abel said of this period that "the daily newspapers, scattered ads, articles, and letters indicated that most of the films shown in the nickelodeons were French (almost always Pathé's) and that they were preferred to all others."[7]

A 1907 article in *Show World* claimed that as much as 80 percent of the film footage released weekly was foreign, with most of that from Pathé and the remainder from Gaumont and Urban-Eclipse (through George Kleine's firm, Kleine Optical). An unnamed Chicago film man made a more precise claim that American film production rarely reached 2,000 feet per week while European production generally ran from 7,000 to 8,000 feet. He frankly admitted that "Pathé is universally acknowledged as the finest photographer and his subjects are world famous." Writing in *Harper's Weekly*, Barton Currie stated that "the French seemed to be the masters in this new field."[8]

Show World concluded its 1908 survey of film producers by declaring, "The popularity of Pathé product is so great that no moving picture show is considered complete without Pathé pictures." Joseph McCoy did a survey of films playing in New York in June 1908, for the Edison company. Of the 515 movies that he viewed in that one month, over one-third (177) were produced by Pathé. In an interview that same month in the trade publication *Variety*, Thomas Edison had to admit—without naming the Pathé firm—"that the French are somewhat in advance," and not just in "artistic merit." Eastman Kodak at the time supplied 90 percent of the negative (raw) film stock used throughout the world. According to figures supplied by company head George Eastman, by the fall of 1907 Pathé was selling 30 to 40 million feet of positive film stock per year on the American market, nearly twice as much as all the American companies combined.[9]

As Pathé expanded worldwide between 1904 and 1907, with more than a dozen foreign sales offices, Charles Pathé told his stockholders of plans to build factories for printing positive film stock in countries where a high volume of movies was being sold. In the spring of 1907, Pathé was preparing to construct such a facility in Bound Brook, New Jersey, when Edison made an approach. That move by the U.S. producer was made in conjunction with the initiation of a new round of lawsuits, or threatened suits, against producers for patent infringement. Then Edison moved in to negotiate a settlement by offering each major company a license to use its patents. It marked the first serious efforts by the U.S. film industry to eliminate the chaos and anarchy within this new industry by establishing a cartel. One of the goals of that cartel was to eliminate the dominance of foreign films in America.[10]

At first glance Edison made what seemed to be a lucrative proposal to the French producer, offering to print Pathé's positive film stock (from the edited, shipped negative) at its own facilities and to serve as the principal sales agent in America for those movies. Responding favorably to the proposal, the French assumed Edison would print all of its weekly negative output and that, in turn, Pathé might gain the exclusive rights to sell Edison films in Europe. However, the Edison concern told Pathé it would not accept all of the weekly output and that Edison reserved for itself the right to select which Pathé films would be released on the U.S. market. That caused the deal to collapse. Edison then went out and negotiated licensing agreements with other producers that would allow them, for an annual fee, to exploit its patents. Again approaching Pathé, Edison this time assured the French concern that its licensing agreement would discourage or disallow "foreign imports," except those, of course, from Pathé itself. It was that assurance, a Pathé spokesman later said, that persuaded Pathé to accept the deal. Thus, Pathé became an Edison licensee in December 1907. The Association of Edison Licensees (AEL) excluded from its membership George Kleine, the only other dealer in "foreign imports" of any size or importance.[11]

Until it joined the AEL, Pathé imported only positive prints; afterwards it brought in negatives and printed the positive copies in America. Film writer Eileen Bowser concluded, "It seems on the face of it that Edison must have agreed to freeze out much of Pathé's foreign competition on the American market, as that is in fact what happened, giving Pathé a decided advantage in what was the world's biggest market." Bowser added that it had been Edison's actions at the turn of the century that had resulted in giving over the U.S. market to the foreign producers: "Now the Edison's new schemes would lead to the American film industry's gaining control over all foreign competition, including Pathé Frères." Some 60 percent of subjects released on the U.S. market in 1907 were of foreign origin; by the last six months of 1909, foreign production represented less than 50 percent of films released, and the percentage was declining. If the goal of eradicating foreign competition was never openly discussed, argued Bowser, it was surely in the minds of Edison and his colleagues.[12]

A one-quarter page advertisement by Pathé in *Variety* in January 1907 advertised a 360-foot movie, *The Wrestler's Wife*, for sale for $43.20 (12 cents a foot). Two office locations in America for Pathé were listed: 42 East 23rd Street, New York, and 35 Randolph Street, Chicago. Beside it was a quarter page advertisement for Kleine Optical Company, Chicago, which offered films produced by Biograph, Vitagraph, Edison, Pathé, and Méliès, all for 12 cents per foot, except for Edison Class A product which was listed at 15 cents a foot.[13]

While the U.S. film industry cartel would be successful in decreasing the presence of foreign films, it was less successful in other ways. Cartels came and went in those early years, some short-lived and some longer lasting, before the final cartel, which rules Hollywood to this day, took hold in the early 1920s. Firms excluded from the AEL group held a meeting of their own in Buffalo, New York, in February 1908, and organized their own combine to oppose the Edison group. A full page advertisement for the Biograph Association of Licensees listed among its members Biograph, Williams, Brown and Earle, and Kleine Optical, and stated that the combine controlled the entire output of the following foreign producers: Gaumont, Urban-Eclipse, Lux, Ambrosio, Rossi, Aquila, Theo Pathé, and Society Italian Cines. The George Kleine company was reported to have done nearly $1 million worth of business in imported films in 1907. With Kleine in the new combine, said *Variety*, the Biograph Association "will command practically the entire output of the European studios and factories with the exception of Pathé Frères." The Biograph group promised it would deliver not less than 12,000 feet of new films—domestic and foreign—each week.[14]

One of the members of the Edison AEL cartel, Philadelphia film producing concern S. Lubin, advanced, at the end of February 1908, a theory as to the reason for depriving several firms of the association of the rights to import movies to America and to deal in films of foreign manufacture. Lubin suggested the American industry should be protected. As well, he maintained his business demanded "all the protection that the new association can give [us] against the inroads of foreign manufactured films."[15]

At the same time the AEL issued a warning to all members of the Film Renters' Association that any deviation from the rules for acquisition and exhibiting of movies would subject the violator to revocation of his license— and access to AEL product. According to a media account, "It is emphatically declared that every measure within law will be used to prevent the exhibition of foreign pictures or their importation"—again, excepting Pathé product. In a related move the AEL cartel sent a letter of demand to the Kleine Optical firm. Answering the demand of W. E. Gilmore, Edison vice president, to cease importing foreign films, Kleine replied, "We beg to state that we have decided not to comply with this demand."[16]

A full page advertistment by Kleine Optical in March 1908, stated it controlled exclusive American rights for the following firms: French (Gaumont, Urban-Eclipse, Lux, Raleigh & Roberts, Theo Pathé, and Aquila), English (Gaumont, Urban-Eclipse, and Warwick), and Italian (Carlo Rossi and Ambrosio). Near the end of that year Kleine advertised itself as still representing all the above named producers as well as Radios (French) and Walthurdaw (English).[17]

Foreign film producers understood what the Edison cartel was trying to do and were determined to do something about it. All of the principal European filmmakers met in conference on March 9, 1908, in Paris. It was reported they were going to start an aggressive concerted movement to protect their interests in the U.S. film markets. At their meeting they subscribed a "war fund" of $15,400 to be spent in a campaign to hold the American field. A conference was necessary, said an account, "to consider the disturbance in the American film market created by the action of a trust formed by certain American manufacturers with the object of excluding European films." Although it was not specifically named, the reference was clearly to the Edison cartel. Those attending the meeting, besides pledging the $15,400, unanimously approved the actions of Biograph and its new organization. An international committee consisting of two English, three French and two Italian producers was elected to take any steps which they thought necessary to protect the interests of European film producers.[18]

In the late summer of 1908 it was reported that the Edison Trust was trying to make trouble for the importers of foreign films by attempting to have their goods held up in the appraiser's warehouse of the customs agency. Potential purchasers of those foreign movies were told by the importers that the trust was preventing them from getting supplies quickly through the customs department. Deputy appraiser Michael Nathan denied that such was the case; he said there was no delay in releasing goods.[19]

Biograph announced, in August 1908, that the license of the Italian Cines company in its combine had been revoked. No reason was reported for that action. Cines had earlier been denied membership in the Edison cartel. Because of the power and domination of these two cartels the Cines firm, declared *Variety*, had a "precarious future" in America. Around the same time representatives of the Edison and Biograph combines met with rumors circulating that the two groups would merge into one. Speculating on what such a move would mean for foreign films in America, *Variety* commented, "That large source of supply will be narrowed for the purpose of enlarging the scope of the native manufacturer."[20]

Rumor turned into reality and by the end of 1908 the two competing combines, tired of the continuing competition and infighting that their separate groups had failed to stop, merged into one—the Motion Picture Patents Company (MPPC). As of December 18, 1908, this new trust had granted licenses to nine producers and importers of motion pictures: Biograph, Edison, Essanay, Kalem, Kleine Optical, Lubin, Pathé Frères, Selig Polyscope, and Vitagraph. A tenth member, Méliès, was licensed in July 1909. Among other things, the cartel members agreed to use only licensed films and to only lease their movies (as opposed to the then-common practice of selling items outright). Also, they pledged not to deal with distributors who handled unlicensed films or to make dupes of existing films (that is, they promised not to pirate each other's material, another common practice of the time).[21]

Commenting on the newly formed combine early in January 1909, *Variety* called the MPPC a "dictatorship." Although George Kleine was part of the new combine, he would handle only Gaumont and Urban productions as an MPPC member, agreeing to drop all the other foreign producers he represented at the time, including Lux, Italia–Rossi, Clarendon, Raleigh & Roberts, Ambrosio, Radios, Theo Pathé, Aquila, and Walthurdaw, as well as several American producers. At the time it was reported that there was little in the way of organized opposition among the independents but that if one did develop, Méliès "would form the nucleus," possibly explaining why Méliès soon became an MPPC member.[22]

Also around that time it was reported that a conference was being planned by European film producers for Paris and that it would not be surprising if, at that meeting, "the proposition to exclude certain films in France, the same as certain French films are excluded in America, will be advanced by delegates." However, that conference never happened.[23]

Some 4,800 signed applications from cinema owners had been received by the MPPC by March 1909, calling for the payment of $2 weekly from each theater for the use of the projection machines. That alone promised to generate an income of $500,000 a year for the trust. At the time there were an estimated 10,000 theaters in America. Rumor had it that if the independents showed any degree of organized strength to fight the cartel, the MPPC would order a reduction in the price of films and service. As one trust executive said, "If it comes to a show down, I think you will see that the cut price scale will take the lead in this fight, in preference to all others, if we can not drive the Independents from the field in any other way."[24]

Independents had not been idle as the MPPC was formed and organized a group of their own, the International Projecting and Producing Company (IPPC). Some 70 New York exhibitors gathered in February 1909 to listen to IPPC representatives of companies affiliated with the group, many of which were foreign producers. Will G. Barker, of the U.K. producer Warwick Trading, told the cinema owners, "The point has been brought up that the American showman has need of American subjects. We have provided for this." However, he did not explain how that would happen except to say that studios would be set up in the U.S. to turn out native films. He also said the films would be rigorously censored before being shipped from Europe to America "by men familiar with the needs and limitations of the American market." Barker traveled to various U.S. cities such as Chicago and Boston, where he held screenings for exhibitors of imported IPPC movies.[25]

At the end of February the IPPC advertised itself as controlling the exclusive American rights for the output of 19 foreign producers: five Italian (Ambrosio, Aquila, Italia, Pineschi, Comerio); four French (Éclair, Lux, Stella, Continental Warwick); two German (Bioscop, Germania); and eight U.K. makers (Clarendon, Cricks & Martin, Hepworth, R. S. Paul, Walthurdaw, Warwick, Williamson King, Wrench Film). Later in 1909 the IPPC was still promising to add American subjects to its weekly release of films. That lack—as an increasing sentiment took hold in America for domestic product—along with constant pressure from the trust caused the IPPC to soon disappear. Just one year later *Variety* reported there were two independent film organizations then active—the Sales Company (it released eight reels of subjects per week, six America, two foreign) and the larger of the two, the Associated Independent Film Manufacturers, which released 16 reels per week.[26]

When French producer Méliès was admitted to the MPPC Trust it was revealed that at the merger talks between Edison and Biograph the French concern had been "frozen out." The reason for that, said *Variety*, was that "the Méliès people had made plans to establish a Chicago studio and manufacturing plant there." Under the terms of its membership Méliès would release through the MPPC one reel of subjects per week. The Trust then issued 18 reels weekly, 19 with the Méliès contribution.[27]

As part of its continued harassment against the IPPC, the Trust launched a lawsuit in the fall of 1909 against the independent organization charging patent infringement. It was designed to "throw a little scare" into exhibitors.[28]

At the end of 1909 the rapid rise in the motion picture industry was noted. Fifteen years earlier films were unknown in America, yet at the end of 1909 the MPPC was said to have licensed 5,280 cinemas to operate with a total estimated at something in excess of 7,000. The Trust issued from 1,880 to 2,000 reels weekly (averaging 1,000 feet of film each). Added to that was an unknown amount of footage released by U.S. independent producers and foreign film importers.[29]

Méliès' tenure as a member of the Trust proved to be very short-lived as it was announced at the end of 1909 that the French producer would, for a time at least, release no more films through the MPPC. The reason given at the time was that photographically the Méliès films had not been satisfactory to the producer. A statement by Méliès declared that when they got new equipment they would again release films through the cartel.[30]

Early in 1910 an unnamed independent U.S. distributor issued a catalog of still unscreened foreign films that it offered at cut-rate terms of 6.5, 7, 8, and 9 cents a foot. Included in the offering were films from the following foreign producers: Le Lion, Italia, Ambrosia, Éclair, Comerio, Aquila, Duseks, Cines, Deutsches Bioscope, Meester, Cricks & Martin, and Raleigh & Roberts. Those foreign makers were led, said *Variety*, by an imposing roster of businessmen who had been "buffaloed by the Patents Co." That so much unscreened product was available and that "sacrifice sales" were necessary to dispose of it were strong evidence, thought the publication, of the unsettled, disorganized and unsatisfactory state of the independent film community.[31]

Foreign members of the MPPC continued to come under pressure from the cartel itself. A plant in Flushing, New York, erected and equipped by Gaumont to print positives for the American market from negatives imported from Paris, was sold by Gaumont in June 1910. Reportedly that was the first step in the separation of Gaumont (part of the cartel because Kleine Optical was a member and allowed to handle the product of two foreign producers, Gaumont and Urban) and the MPPC. That Flushing factory had been built only eight months earlier. Then Gaumont went to the Trust and asked for the right to print positives in the U.S., as done by Pathé. However, the Trust heads immediately said no, with the result that the plant sat idle from the time it was built until it was sold.[32]

In its announced fall line-up for 1910 the MPPC had 10 producers releasing 22 films per week: Selig (2), Biograph (3), Vitagraph (3), Kalem (2), Essanay (2), Lubin (2), Edison (2), Pathé (3), Gaumont (2), and Urban (1). The major rival independent organization had 14 firms releasing 17 films per week; Bison (2), Imp (2), Thanhouser (2), Champion (1), Powers (1), Yankee (1), Defender (1), Great Northern (1), Dramagraph (1), Ambrosio (1), Italia (1), Cines (1), Éclair (1), and Lux (1). The last five of those independents were foreign producers with the others being all, or mostly all, American outfits.[33]

Back when Pathé joined the MPPC it seemed to be in a favored position since the cartel intended to work to limit access to U.S. cinema screens by other foreign producers. Pathé undoubtedly did not realize that it too was a foreigner to be squeezed out. In 1914 the French firm resigned from General Film (this was the distribution arm of the MPPC) to reportedly establish its own branch offices throughout the country. No reason was given for this action. Yet a few months later Pathé was said to be releasing its output through the company Eclectic but, noted a media account, "The sales of film there have only been a very small percentage of the business done with the General Film." Pathé was understood to be reviewing its options.[34]

Pathé entered the daily release film service on April 1, 1915, with its own organization, releasing four films daily, 28 weekly. The French concern thus became the sixth daily release service in the field with the others being General Film (by far the biggest), Mutual, Universal, Kriterion, and United. Yet just one year later Pathé notified the trade that it would cease regular releases after February 1916. Thereafter, they said, they would release only one feature a month. The reason for the drastic curtailment of production was said to be "the prohibitive competition due to the surfeit of weekly feature releases" which forced Pathé to sell "expensive" product such as Madam X and The Beloved Vagabond at prices as low as $10 a day. In its announcement to the film trade press Pathé added that it would have to cease making feature films completely unless its program was supported by American exhibitors.[35]

Nothing worked for the company that had recently dominated American screens with the largest single share of the market. That Pathé had abandoned feature film production completely became apparent in April 1918, when it offered its list of stars at their current salaries (the list included Frank Keenan at $2,750 a week, Fannie Ward at $2,500, and Bessie Love at $2,000) to other producers. Pathé said it still intended to release feature films but only ones made by outside producers and handled through Pathé's releasing service on a percentage basis. It said it would also finance producers "of reputation" in the making of movies, a system used by the company prior to the time it entered the producing field. A reason given for Pathé taking up the making of features with known and high-priced stars was an attempt on its part to break in "on Broadway" at one of the three big cinemas there with its product. Pathé then had no theater outlet in New York where it could secure a week's run for its product. The sole outlet where Pathé productions were screened in the Times Square section of the city was at a cinema called the New York, where they got a one-day run.[36]

As early as 1909 a commentator was moved to write that the strength of the MPPC "lies in the fact that they have standing orders" which had the effect of tying up exhibitors for specific periods of time. It was a practice that would become known as block booking. Back in 1909, it was observed that the eight native producers in the Trust (but not the two foreign ones) had standing orders with exhibitors of varying amounts whereby cinemas took from 20 reels per week (the smallest available standing order) to 120 reels (the largest). During 1914, General Film supplied cinemas with a full program of movies for a specified sum of money and in so doing "booked up exhibitors totally." One unnamed exhibitor praised the system but found fault with a similar standing order program offered by an independent service for having "too much foreign material" in the program. The independents were also said to be getting those foreign films "for nothing" because they were inferior.[37]

General Film was then offering a standing order that cost $28 weekly per reel, while another releasing company, Mutual, provided a weekly service at $150 for exhibitors. A third releasing outfit, Universal, was said to be willing to sell "at almost any price," although its lowest known terms were said to be $112.50 a week. Acting in concert with the U.S. producer Essanay, General Film had sole distribution rights for the Charlie Chaplin comedy releases by Essanay. Then General Film issued an ultimatum to exhibitors that if they did not use its service beyond the Chaplin pictures they would not be allowed to book the Chaplin releases. With the enormous popularity of Chaplin it was said that over 99 percent of all U.S. exhibitors used Chaplin comedies, or wanted to. Because of the comedian's great popularity, block booking became an integral part of the U.S. motion picture industry and was extended to other countries, such as the U.K., by American producers initially on the broad back of Chaplin. It would be 1949 before the U.S. Supreme Court barred the practice of block booking as part of its decision that broke up the industry's monopoly control. Block booking tied up a cinema for months and even years with the result that films distributed outside of the industry cartel (as all foreign films were by 1915) had great difficulties in finding cinemas in which to be screened. Although the MPPC succeeded in beating back the presence of foreign films in America, clearing up industry piracy problems, among other accomplishments, it did not survive the challenge of American independent producers. A court challenge ruled the MPPC unconstitutional in the late 1910s but the Trust was essentially non-functional no later than 1915. The independents were more visionary and efficient and the final cartel (which rules the industry to this day) was formed in 1922—the Motion Picture Producers and Distributors of America (MPPDA).[38]

During this period there was a dramatic rise in the number of feature films produced (defined at the time as four reels or more, roughly 40 minutes and up) relative to the standard one- and two-reel films of the time. Although foreign features were largely responsible for introducing and sustaining the fad in America, ultimately the move to feature films worked against the presence of foreign films in the U.S. The first appearance in America of a feature film type of production occurred in 1907 with Adolph Zukor's distribution of Pathé's three-reel *Passion Play*. Movement toward the acceptance of the feature film began in 1911 when two European features were imported into the U.S.: *Crusaders* (four reels), and *Dante's Inferno* (five reels). It was not the length that impressed the audience but the lavish production values, and sets, costumes and crowds. Those movies were followed in 1912 and early 1913 by other imported features, including the four-reel *Queen Elizabeth* starring Sarah Bernhardt, and a number of

American-made feature films. On April 21, 1913, the Italian spectacle film *Quo Vadis?* debuted at New York's Astor Theater—eight reels, shown in three acts, with intermissions, in keeping with stage show conventions. The importer of that highly successful film was George Kleine, who somehow reached outside the system established by the Trust to find a way to release that title. Apparently the cartel applied no sanctions to the Kleine firm for its breaking cartel rules.[39]

Another Italian spectacle film, *Cabiria*, opened in New York in June 1914 at the Knickerbocker with the very high price of $1 top, yet did a very good business. In this case the producer Italia rented the Knickerbocker at $1,250 a week. With 44 men in the orchestra and a singing chorus of 28 other people it was an expensive proposition to exhibit the film.[40]

By 1915 and 1916 there was a reported glut of feature films on the market. As recently as 1914, features were rented to first-run exhibitors at a cost of $50 to $75 per day, falling to $35 or $40 and finally, at the height of the glut, to as low as $5 to $10 a day. In such a climate foreign films were hurt more than the domestic ones as they had higher initial costs. Although such costs—import duties, extra shipping costs, translation of intertitle cards, for example—were relatively minor they did put foreign features at a disadvantage.[41]

Praise continued to be lavished on foreign films, especially up to around 1910. After that conditions began to change. When Pathé moved to a larger office in New York City in 1908 a reporter observed that Pathé movies were prominent in "every motion picture display in the country," and the studio was then releasing from eight to 12 new films each week. This journalist believed the popularity of Pathé product "lies in the photographic excellence of their subjects ... and their interpretations of a moving picture [that] are invariably clever and exceedingly clear to average comprehension."[42]

During that same year Thomas Edison was taking a more direct interest in the film business. He said: "In artistic merit, I am willing to admit that the French are somewhat in advance of us. They have a natural gift for pantomime, and that is a point in their favor. In addition they are encouraged by a public of higher artistic perception than ours." However, Edison added, "They will not long maintain their supremacy. Americans in any department of effort are never content to stay in second place."[43]

A chart showing the releases of the MPPC firms for the week November 4 to November 10, 1909, appeared in the pages of *Variety*. It listed a total of 16 releases that week from 11 producers: Gaumont (1), Méliès (1), Pathé (3), Urban-Eclipse (1), Kalem (1), Essanay (1), Edison (2), Selig (2), Vitagraph (2), Lubin (1), and Biograph (1). Those films were rated by the trade publication as follows: five good, six fair, five poor. For the six foreign releases the ratings were four good, one fair, one poor; the ten U.S.-made films were rated thusly: one good, five fair, four poor. A note with the chart explained that totals for independent producers were not included because they "have been unable to find a place to display their films in New York [and] we are forced to omit them." A few weeks later another chart appeared. That one listed 14 films released that particular week by nine MPPC producers with ratings as follows: two good, nine fair, three poor. Eight foreign films had ratings of two good, five fair, one poor; the six U.S.-made releases had no product listed as good, but four fair and two poor.[44]

G. Dureau, a French film authority writing in a French publication, urged French producers to give more attention to their admittedly successful business in the U.S. He felt it was a short-sighted policy to cater only to the home market and that French producers did not keep foreign markets in mind because "they turn out reels purely of local interest and expect to sell them abroad. Little care is taken as to the subjects shipped, whereas views that will be appreciated by other countries should be carefully studied." Dureau also argued that many French producers were almost unknown in the U.S. as the MPPC Trust had admitted only three French producers into its ranks. "An independent group has been formed to fight the monopoly, but the battle is very one-sided at present."[45]

David Horsley, partner in a large U.S. motion picture company, returned from Europe in 1913 where he had been studying industry conditions. He admitted that in many ways the European producers "were ahead of this country in making films." By that date such sentiments, once the majority, were expressed much less often.[46]

Far more common was the idea that foreign films were of poor quality, as expressed by Thomas H. Ince, general manager of the New York Motion Picture Company, who remarked, regarding feature films, "Features right now are at a standstill. The tendency is to keep from deluging the market at present, as a lot of cheap, trashy melodramatics from the other side have hurt the features."[47]

When Dureau expressed the worry that French studios did not keep the U.S. market in mind when they produced their films, he articulated a theme that foreigners would utter from time to time right up to the present. A well-known (but unnamed) U.S. film director returned home from abroad in 1914. He had been impressed with German films and predicted a bright future for them because "knowing minutely the world's taste, they put aside their own national feelings and play up to the gallery with English and American subjects, mostly manufactured in the outskirts of Berlin."

Reportedly they took care to avoid using German street names, signs, and so forth, in their productions.[48]

One of the main reasons public reviews and public perceptions of foreign films nosedived at this time was the rise of public outrage at the motion picture industry in general for what many perceived to be a lack of morality in motion pictures. By the period of 1908 to 1910, it was obvious films had become big business and were going to remain an integral part of the American entertainment scene for a long time to come. Films were not a fad. More and more critics arose to attack the new medium. George Spoor, president of film producer Essanay, said, at the end of 1908, "Attacks, scurrilous, prejudiced and oft-times absolutely vindictive, aimed at the good name and moral worth of moving pictures have been crowding on the heels of one another in some of the foremost publications of this country during the last few months." Spoor argued that producers were wide awake to the moral issue and strove to the best of their ability to eliminate all situations that left them open to criticism.[49]

Such criticism quickly came to settle disproportionately on foreign films, even to the extent sometimes of blaming them for the existence of the situation. Richard Abel noted that after around 1908, Pathé films were repeatedly stigmatized and marginalized, especially in the trade press, as "foreign or alien to (in a sense 'not white enough' for) American culture." Writing in that same year, reporter Lucy Pierce branded the French output as guilty of "bad taste and immorality." And, added Abel, the reviews of French movies in *Variety* started to be "especially bad."[50]

"The foremost French makers," declared the trade journal *Moving Picture World* in 1908, "maintain a fine standard of excellence, but they owe it to American taste to eliminate some features. The frank way in which marital infidelities are carried out in Paris though a lame moral is sometimes worked in at the end, the eating of rats and cats, the brutal handling of helpless infants, do not appeal to the American sense of humor." Bowser also commented on the suddenly poor ratings to be found in the pages of *Variety*. Looking back from 1913, an exhibitor declared that foreign films "four or five years ago" were "horrible, immoral." He added that he had issued an order at the time not to show any foreign films in any of his cinemas.[51]

Rumors circulated in 1910 that New York City mayor Gaynor was personally going to investigate motion pictures and their influence on the young. After Gaynor was through, went the speculation, there would be orders to "clean up" the film industry, at least in New York. No fan of the business, this reporter grumbled the industry had been "all wrong" for the past two years with no effort made to improve pictures as the American producers did as they pleased. Foreigners, he added, had been permitted to exhibit nearly all their product in the U.S. and "some of that product should never have been manufactured, even for Europe." It was ludicrous, he argued, to expect France to turn out movies "fit for the youth of America to see." From the time French films were "necessary" to provide a sufficient amount of output for America, he declared, "the condition has evolved itself to a point where the Americans, instead of forcing the foreigners by example to improve in theme and purity, have instead leaned toward the foreign productions by producing themselves for their own people pictures, in the majority of which of late are nothing less than lewd and wreckers for the morals of young Americans."[52]

The National Board of Censorship was formed by the motion picture industry in March 1909. Worried by all the criticism, the Trust decided it was better to regulate itself—or pretend to—rather than do nothing and run the risk of the government stepping in and imposing a regulation of its own making. Abel observed that throughout 1909 and 1910, Pathé films were either rejected or returned for alteration by that board proportionately more frequently than were the movies from American producers. In one particular month, no fewer than six of 13 Pathé pictures were rejected outright or returned to the producer with instructions for alterations.[53]

From around 1910 until the onset of World War I, the presence of foreign films in America declined dramatically. Typical of that changing structure were the actions of film mogul William Fox. One of the first to handle foreign multiple-reel films when he formed the Box Office Attraction Company (with Winfield R. Sheehan in charge), Fox announced, in the summer of 1914, his company was getting out of foreign film distribution. At the outset the firm imported a large number of foreign productions. But by 1914 it was making its own films and distributing product from other U.S. studios, because exhibitors were then turning down all foreign pictures. "Now please don't misquote me. I am not against the foreign made feature film," explained Fox. "But it is the impression the exhibitor over here has obtained of the foreign picture that brought about my decision." Most of the exhibitors did not see the film before it was booked, continued Fox. "They ask 'foreign?' and if the answer is 'yes' they decline it." Fox felt that situation was purely the fault of the European producers who exercised "very poor judgment" in the selection of films for export to America. And that was because they were greedy. Those Europeans may have believed it was good business "but it has practically ruined the American market for the foreign features." When Box Office received a consignment of foreign films they, of course, looked them all over. Fox estimated the number of good ones accepted by his company for distribution was "two or three out of twenty."[54]

Foreign films in America faced increasing difficulties in the first half of the 1910s as the Trust formed up and pressured them; as domestic production increased significantly, both inside and outside the Trust; as a nativist sentiment developed; and as a disproportionate amount of criticism on the ground of morality settled on the foreign items. An early 1915 account observed that only a couple of years earlier the U.S. received the bulk of its movies from Europe but "now everybody in America is making features and the native supply is better suited to their clientele." On top of the existing difficulties came World War I. All the countries that had a film presence in America were involved in the war and soon film production in the combatant nations withered away. By the end of World War I foreign films would command only a negligible presence in the U.S.—a position they are still trying unsuccessfully to change.[55]

Another difficulty faced by foreign films was that, in the period 1910 to 1914, distribution in the U.S. was increasingly through standing orders and exclusive contracts (block booking) that tied cinemas to a particular film service and studio. Standing orders gave U.S. producers a financial base that allowed for increasing production and more standing orders, and so on. It became harder for foreigners to distribute in the U.S. as exhibitors became increasingly booked up. Trade journals abroad started to call America a "closed market" for their films. About 350 films were offered each week in Britain in 1914 with perhaps 150 of those being sold and released. By contrast, about 200 films came onto the market each week in the U.S. at that time with around 160 actually being released. Of that latter number, about 130 were sold by standing order before they were even shot. Domestic films then comprised about 67 percent of all U.S. releases. The managing director of one of Britain's largest cinema chains complained in 1915 that while England was an open market for motion pictures, the United States was not. "We cannot secure a footing in the United States. We have given the matter careful study and can only conclude it is not the desire of the Americans to encourage foreign features," he remarked. "In our opinion they figure every penny contributed toward the support of foreign productions helps to build up opposition."[56]

2

The Silent Era, 1916–1928

The actresses who appear in many of the [foreign] films are
not young and beautiful enough to satisfy Americans....
[T]he themes [of some of their pictures] are generally
gloomy and not of a character which Americans demand.
—*Anonymous U.S. film producer, 1921*

Only three out of hundreds [of foreign films] have been of
the quality demanded by patrons of American motion picture theatres.
—*Louis Auerbach, importer, 1921*

Only when one is in Europe does one realize how far
ahead our own films are. Not only from the standpoint of
technical excellence but in their cleanliness and wholesomeness, our own motion pictures are vastly superior.
—*John F. Moore, YMCA executive,*
1926

With the end of World War I, foreign films had virtually no presence
in America. Gone were the days of European dominance, or even a healthy
presence, on U.S. cinema screens. Countries that had a strong native film
industry at the start of the war, such as France and Britain, had those industries shut down by the war. Devastation to those nations meant it would

be some time before they could hope to rebuild their native motion picture industries. In the meantime the U.S. moved quickly in the aftermath of World War I to dominate the film screens of other countries with its own output. It was a position that America has not relinquished to this day.

One foreign film that did make it to America and set off a storm of fury was the German film *Passion* from that country's major producer UFA, in 1920. A private showing of that film for distributors in October found those in charge of the screening apologizing to those assembled, stating the movie was a "costume affair" and because of that it was not felt to have much of a chance to succeed in America. Perhaps not surprisingly, the film had no takers. *Passion* made the rounds for a time, always turned down by exhibitors. Finally First National signed on as the movie's distributor. It staged another general showing for the trade but there was reportedly still "no great enthusiasm aroused for the production." Eventually the Capitol Theater in New York City booked the film for a one-week run. Although no special advertising was used for the film, *Passion* went on to set a single week's record for gross receipts.[1]

Just two months later, in early 1921, the success of *Passion* stimulated film importation to the extent that it was said that 36 foreign films, from many countries, were circulating in the space of one week. However, observed *Variety*, "The invading product, in the main, doesn't interest the native buyers. The English made stories are found too slow, the German too morbid, the Italian largely mythical and allegorical." Also among the "invaders" was one Spanish production and a few Swedish films but they were all reported to be unsuitable for the U.S. market because they were "too sleepy."[2]

During a one-week period in April 1921, some 46 German features arrived in New York, still in the wake of the success of *Passion*. Those movies were said to be available at cheap prices, which caused the U.S. industry to worry as to what effect that might have on domestic production. Rumor had it that the Motion Picture Directors' Association was ready to call a special meeting to discuss "the foreign menace," while a separate U.S. film industry delegation planned to lobby Washington with a view to getting protection under a new tariff law.[3]

Soon the fight to exclude foreign films from America expanded as it received backing from the actors' union Equity, the American Legion and independent producers, all of whom wanted a tariff wall of protection. According to one account, it was acknowledged that every foreign movie brought to America meant the loss of the production of one domestic feature, which in turn meant increasing the unemployment of American actors, directors and other studio personnel. Equity president John Emerson declared, with respect to some 50 German films then being offered for distribution in America, "the dumping of this product in America will have a disastrous effect on American labor, for while these productions are being shown the American product will be crowded out of the theatres and no work will be forthcoming for American labor." He said his organization would fight to get the highest possible tariff imposed on foreign movies. Opposed to the exclusion of foreign films were many of the nation's exhibitors, led by S. L. Rothafel of the Capitol. He argued that any exclusion of foreign product would result in retaliation and, more importantly for cinema owners, any exclusion would tend to prevent a decrease in the cost of film rentals "now extremely high, according to the majority of theatre owners."[4]

Also opposed to exclusion was Export and Import Film Company vice president Louis Auerbach, who called such action ill-advised and illogical. He remarked that he, too, worried about the possibility of retaliation because time after time his firm had encountered serious opposition from other countries who complained because their movies were not being shown in the U.S. Auerbach said there were "hundreds" of pictures then in the U.S., from various other countries, but in the previous four years only three had got to the stage of actually being exhibited—the others had never found any takers—"only three out of hundreds have been of the quality demanded by patrons of American motion picture theatres." He added: "Unless a foreign picture comes up to the high standard set by our super-features it finds very little market in this country, and therefore the fear of this foreign invasion is a dream and not a reality based on facts." Over and over, said Auerbach, he had assured the English that whenever their films came up to the standard of American product, his company would bring them before the American public.[5]

So heated did the situation became that in May 1921, rioting took place in Los Angeles against the showing of German films, started by the American Legion. The Hollywood Post of the Legion organized a parade with the assistance of the local members of the Motion Picture Directors' Association and marched through the streets to Miller's theater where *The Cabinet of Dr. Caligari* was scheduled to open with a matinee screening. Continuing throughout the afternoon, the demonstration featured rotten eggs "thrown profusely." Aiding the demonstration were hundreds of sailors from the Pacific fleet and some 2,000 other citizens who joined in the melee. With the police said to be unable to cope with the rioters, theater manager Fred Miller withdrew *Caligari* and substituted an American movie, declaring his two cinemas would not play any German films in the future.[6]

Some days earlier the same Hollywood Post of the American Legion had held a parade of protest against the showing of German films in the U.S. and received the support of the Legion posts in the surrounding towns. At Long Beach during this time, the United Veterans of the Spanish War held an encampment; they passed a resolution against the "invasion" of German pictures and pledged themselves to support the work of the Legion in "combating the menace." A Hearst newspaper, the *Los Angeles Examiner*, was reported to have "undertaken an active campaign against the showing of German pictures." Venice, California, City Council was rumored to be ready to pass a law requiring a special city license, costing $50 nightly, to exhibit any German or Austrian film within the city limits. It adopted that ordinance a week later. The Legion was also checking all film booking schedules at all local neighborhood cinemas where *Passion* (then in second and third run) might play. When any such bookings were found, pressure was brought to bear on those exhibitors to cancel the booking or to face the threat of a demonstration against their house. F. J. Godsol, spokesman for the Samuel Goldwyn firm that distributed *Caligari* in the U.S., issued a denial that his company had purchased any other German films after the riot at Millers.[7]

Within a week of their successful demonstration against Miller, a meeting was held at the Hollywood Post of the American Legion at which a permanent organization was established to oppose German films in America. Every branch of the motion picture industry was lining up against the foreign product. Representatives from the following groups were in attendance at the meeting and all had representatives appointed to the new organization: American Legion, the Authors' League, the Directors' Association, Equity, the American Society of Cinematographers, the Hollywood Board of Trade, the Screen Writers' Association, the Art Directors' League, the Assistant Directors' Association and the Central Labor Council. One night earlier, the Assistant Directors' Association held a meeting at which a resolution against the screening of German movies in the U.S. was adopted. Copies of that resolution were forwarded to U.S. President Warren Harding, Los Angeles Mayor Snyder and to the Motion Picture Producers' Association. It was hoped by the Legion that the newly established organization would become national in scope. That caused a reporter to comment, "Locally it seems certain that German films are dead."[8]

An editorial in the *New York Times* about the squabble said the public should treat the whole debate with indifference since those German films, produced much more cheaply than were American ones, did not result in lower cinema admission fees.[9] Another editorial on the subject in the *Times* just one day later admitted German production costs were far

The Cabinet of Dr. Caligari (German, 1921, actors unidentified). This movie created great controversy in America as the "invasion" of German films was protested.

lower than they were in America but went on to state: "It is also true that the German feature films lately shown here are better than anything that ever came out of Los Angeles." Continuing on, the editor argued the demand for protection of U.S. films with tariffs on imports was actually a demand "for the protection of bathos and stupidity. The real German menace in the moving picture field is the menace of superior intelligence."[10]

Another against exclusion was Alfred Kuttner, spokesman for the National Board of Review of Motion Pictures. He called the attempt at exclusion "esthetic censorship" and said that Equity led a movement that really said, "We don't want any better pictures over here. We don't want the public to see them. They might become even more dissatisfied with the native product than they already are.... We want a high tariff wall to protect us in our business, so that we can go on making mediocre pictures." Kuttner further argued that it showed no respect to the motion picture art to treat it entirely in terms of a commercial commodity. Even if the situation was entirely business having nothing to do with art, a high tariff was still unsound, he said, because the film industry was then already America's fourth or fifth largest and not a small infant industry that needed to be nursed along. In conclusion Kuttner declared, "The only legitimate way for American producers to answer this threat of foreign competition is by improving the quality of their own product, not by trying to resort to artificial means to make it safe for them to continue to turn out mediocre pictures."[11]

When the general magazine *Literary Digest* summarized the situation, the article gave the impression that the livelihood of 60,000 U.S. film industry workers was threatened by 300 German pictures on the American market, although it did admit that only two films actually seemed to be involved in the controversy. It was possible—and usually the case—for a foreign film to be officially in the U.S. but not actually be screened for the general public because the title, while it made the trade rounds, could get no distributor or exhibitor to handle it. According to the *Digest* account: "Most of the editorial comment on the question admits the fact that the American film falls below the foreign one in quality." In support of that idea it cited comments from the New York *Globe* newspaper, which declared the film industry may not have then been art but it had the possibility of becoming art. The Germans had worked toward the artistic but the U.S. industry proposed to stop them from bringing in a class of films that might have stimulated American producers to do better work. "They insist on treating the movies like lumber or automobiles," said the *Globe*. "Art, they practically say, 'has nothing to do with this matter. The matter at hand is the protection of an industry.'"[12]

Many U.S. producers reportedly journeyed to Germany in the spring of 1921 to check out the situation. Reassuringly, the *New York Times* commented that it was not generally thought that German films would be serious competition for U.S. product. One of America's "foremost" film producers, unnamed, said, "Neither the plays staged by Germans nor the personality of the German actors I have seen would appeal to American patrons.... I could truthfully say the same of the British film industry. American producers are, in my opinion, far ahead of the Germans and British in the art of producing appealing films." Further shortcomings outlined by this individual were that "the actresses who appear in many of the films are not young enough and beautiful enough to satisfy Americans.... [T]he themes [of some of their pictures] are generally gloomy and not of a character which Americans demand."[13]

By early June 1921, the furor over German movies was reportedly rapidly dying out. The S. Rankin Drew Post of the American Legion (New York) suspended action in regard to German films. Its motion condemning them was tabled. At the same time the Hollywood Post was at odds with the Los Angeles Post over the issue. No reason for the waning of interest was given except to cite Samuel Goldwyn's statement that he viewed many German pictures while abroad and he did not think as much as two percent of them would do for the U.S.A. Supposedly that was said to have helped in calming down the situation.[14]

A few weeks later an account reported that many of the buyers of German films—acquired in a hurry in the wake of the initial success of *Passion*—found they no longer looked so good, nor could they be easily marketed. Scorn was heaped on them as some were described as dealing with "freak" stories and having no romance, with nothing but male characters. On the other hand many were condemned for being too sexually explicit and running into problems with U.S. censors. An unidentified U.S. motion picture "authority" grumbled that German producers "make their appeal to the lowest grade of audiences in order to create a general demand for pictures and it is for this reason that the film stories are lurid and sensational." The idea that German films—and all foreign product by implication—were of a very poor quality and offensive was becoming pervasive.[15]

What was perhaps a last-twitch response in this controversy took place in November 1921. For the first time since cinemas had been established in Albany, New York, a feature film was withdrawn from a local house at the demand of the audience, when manager Samuel Suckno of the Albany ordered *The Cabinet of Dr. Caligari* taken off after it had received two screenings on the first day of its booking (it had only been slated to run for two days). When *Caligari* ran for the first time on a Friday afternoon the patrons expressed their disapproval by walking out in the middle of the screening and complaining verbally to Suckno. Later in the afternoon the second screening produced the same result, but was said to have been a more "rambunctious" display than at the first screening.[16]

Early in 1922, an account said that bookings for *Caligari* had been only $78,000 to that point "and the comparative flop of *Passion, Deception, The Golem* and others has been commented on." And the controversy over German films in America was over. It was a strange furor indeed because very few German movies were actually screened for the public. Still, even the idea that a handful of foreign films might capture the public's fancy seemed to be enough to set off a furor. Apparently the U.S. was determined to never again allow foreign films to have any kind of meaningful presence in its cinemas.[17]

In 1925, 250 American movies were imported into Germany while only five German films came to America. Two years later, after the Germans imposed a quota system designed to increase German film presence in America by tying the number of U.S. pictures imported into Germany to the number exported, it was reported that Germany's business in America "which was negligible, has not progressed in the slightest, in spite of various high-sounding contracts made with leading American producing firms."[18]

In 1918, just after the war ended, *Variety* remarked on the dominance of French and Italian films in pre-war America but said it was doubtful that films from either country would command such attention again, although specific reasons were not given. Henri Diamant Berger, director and editor of France's largest film publication, *Le Film*, had recently been sent to New York on a scouting mission by the French government. Berger's task was to see if there was any market in America for French films.[19]

A second mission was undertaken in the summer of 1919 by the French. That time the scout was Rene Silz of the Campagnie Cinematographic Albert Dulac. After sizing up the situation for Paris bankers and the French government, he said that he had come to America to arrange for the distribution of French films, "good pictures, interesting pictures." Asking himself what he had found he explained, "I find that your market is tied up, that I cannot distribute my pictures." As to the solution he felt there was only one thing for him and his backers, with the aid of the French government, to do. "With the aid of our Government we intend to open exchanges throughout America and distribute our pictures ourselves. This I can promise you we will do without fail if we cannot find easy distribution through mediums already established." Silz added the Italians were likewise interested and suggested the two nations might pool their resources in an effort "to break the closed wall of the American market." One U.S. reporter worried that millions of foreign dollars put up privately, and backed by government guarantees, "are going to take issue shortly with the film combination over here."[20]

Those words by Silz may have been brave words and tough words but they led nowhere. In 1927 just five percent of the movies screened in France were French, 80 percent were American. A total of 368 U.S. pictures were released in France that year; only eight French films were imported into the U.S.—and those were not necessarily all released and exhibited. Suddenly, in March 1928, France imposed regulations stating that for each French film a U.S. concern purchased for U.S. distribution and actually released in the U.S., it would be allowed to release four American movies in France. The industry cartel (the Motion Picture Producers and Distributors' Association—MPPDA) lobbied by sending its head, Will Hays, executive Frederick Herron and other employees to France. Hays also got the U.S. Ambassador to France, Myron T. Herrick, to work on the problem.

Often the major U.S. producers would purchase foreign movies to satisfy a particular nation's laws but never intended to—and did not—release or exhibit them for showing in America. Forced distribution was galling enough but the majors could live with it if necessary. It could be viewed simply as a tax. Pay a certain sum of money over and be allowed to import a certain number of films into a country. However, forced releasing and exhibition, as the French were then trying to arrange, was another matter. It enraged the majors.

Herron conceded few French movies were released in the U.S. but claimed it was because the French (and filmmakers in all other countries) did not study the American market: "If Europe asks for American opinion on their stories and their pictures while in the making stage, we will certainly grant it. Up to the present Europe has gone ahead without seeking our advice." All the lobbying worked because the French capitulated in May 1928, and changed the new law. Under the revised statute, the U.S. producers could import 50 percent of the number imported to France in 1927 with no restrictions. Beyond that American firms were granted seven import licenses for each film they produced in France, or seven licenses for each purchase of a French picture—with no obligation to distribute or exhibit them anywhere.[21]

Nothing came from the idea that a joint effort by the French and Italian film industries might tackle the U.S. market. That idea that some type of European combine might be formed surfaced again in 1924. Also, people from different European countries who were ambassadors, consuls and vice-consuls to the U.S.A. had been approached with a view to using their positions to lobby and impress upon the U.S. State Department the necessity of foreign films receiving representation in America. It was understood the State Department had at least lent a sympathetic ear to the requests of the foreign film producers. One rumor that circulated had it that State had approached Will Hays on the issue—that they wanted him to use his influence on the MPPDA membership with the idea that it would undertake as an association the distribution of certain numbers of foreign movies. There were then said to be around 200 foreign movies in the U.S. hoping to find a distributor. Nothing came from any of these ideas.[22]

Britain was another country worried about the "invasion" of American films into its home market while struggling for some degree of reciprocity for its output. American producer Famous Players–Lasky had set up a British branch in 1919 to produce pictures in Britain for the British market. At a meeting of exhibitors, that move was protested strongly. Thomas Buchanan, vice president of the Scottish branch of the Cinematograph Exhibitors' Association of Great Britain and Ireland, complained about the practice of block booking. When British films were shown in America, he added, the names of those British producers were not advertised, whereas U.S. producers were always advertised in the U.K. "Of course they say that British productions are not equal to American," Buchanan continued. "I say that is a lie. We produce some equal to America's best." At that exhibitor meeting, a resolution was passed asking for government support for British films and "appealing to Americans to reciprocate in the display of British pictures in the United States."[23]

Buchanan noted that each U.S. movie screened in Britain sent from 3,000 pounds Sterling to 15,000 pounds Sterling back to America whereas the average return to the home country on the small number of British films screened in America was 800 pounds Sterling. He concluded the U.S. film market was essentially closed to British movies. In 1919 some 90 percent of the product exhibited in British cinemas was American while the proportion of British films screened in the U.S.A. was, reported the *New York Times*, "perhaps one percent." An unnamed correspondent for the *Times* of London visited America in 1920 to assess the situation and to declare that there were "no British films being shown in this country at the present moment." It was an especially unsettling conclusion for the correspondent because there were 11 million daily cinema admissions. Exhibitors in America told him, he related, the British movies were "too slow in action, too insular, and altogether lacking in those qualities which the American audience loves."[24]

In the summer of 1926 a joint committee of representatives from companies in the British film industry met in London. At that session they drafted a proposal that U.S. firms acquire British movies for "bona fide" release and exhibition in America on the basis of the acceptance of not less than one U.K. feature for every 25 U.S. pictures offered for exhibit in Great Britain. A bona fide release, under this proposal, meant that the British films released would receive the same treatment as any other film belonging to the releasing company. Again, this was an attempt to deal with Hollywood's proclivity to buy foreign films for distribution and/or exhibition, pay the fee, but then bury the title with no distribution or exhibition in America.[25]

Surprisingly, an editorial in the *Times* of London issued a scathing condemnation of that reciprocity proposal. That editor argued that American misgivings about the proposal did not arise from any fear that U.K. films, if introduced into the U.S.A., might prove to be dangerous competitors but from the opposite belief that "British films are generally so bad that American exhibiting houses will lose money by showing them." Such a play, worried the editor, "might have the disastrous result of giving encouragement to British organizations which have failed through their own incompetence and were better allowed to die." Film making in the U.K. had fallen into the hands of the wrong men, lamented the *Times*. They were men without taste or culture who were content to imitate the worst that came from America. "It is better that British films should remain at home than British ideas should be seen to be represented abroad by such ambassadors."[26]

Soon thereafter an editorial in the *New York Times* noted the sorry state of the U.K. motion picture industry with U.S. product having virtually driven the English producer from the market. That is, the U.K. market; British films had next to no presence in America. Claiming that many reasons existed for that situation, the editor went on to declare that with "unparalleled money resources, natural advantages and an enormous home market—the American film is bound to dominate." He felt a major problem was with actresses that acted without expression; "whether English directors demand this cultivated emptiness of expression is a question to which the British must find the answer before they can begin making films that even their own public will like."[27]

At the start of 1927, British producers and distributors announced they had a plan and were ready to launch "the first powerful and cogent" effort to establish British pictures in America. In this new effort it was reported that exchanges were to be established in key centers of the U.S. by British producers and distributors from a fund of $2 million raised from those concerns in an effort to popularize their output in America. More money was expected to be spent on each production than in the past. Also, the plan was to concentrate on producing dramas since past efforts to popularize English comedies in America had failed because of the "open face humor."[28]

One strategy used or contemplated by foreign countries in this time period and into the future involved using American personnel or methods in their productions in the hope that would ease their entry into the U.S.A. Back in 1919 the then newly established Italian film trust—the Unione Industria Cinematografico announced it would import American film directors to make features in Italy for the American market.[29]

During a 1919 interview, Edward Godal, managing director of the British and Colonial Kinematograph Company (B&C, a U.K. producer), said he felt certain "America would extend the hand of welcome the moment the films from this country were of a properly high standard." Pursuing that policy B&C had obtained the "best" film staff in Britain "to assist" an American production staff that had been brought to Britain by B&C. Previously they had used the American film star Marie Doro in two of their films. According to one account: "In these three films B. & C. have endeavored to please the public of the world and not, as hitherto, Britain alone." Godal admitted the fight to break into the U.S. was still hard and uphill and that so far their work had been more idealistic than profitable. However, he felt in the long run, once a standard of British production had been established, they expected "profit to join their ideal while universal reciprocity crowned the industry in every land."[30]

A 1922 report declared that a group of English filmmakers had undertaken a long range and determined campaign to get a foothold in the U.S. market by employing American producing values in English studios and by using U.S. screen stars in their films to enhance their sales drive aimed at U.S. exhibitors. Leaders in that drive were Harry and Simeon Rowson, owners of the Ideal studio in London. They were working with Reginald Warde, their U.S. agent located in New York. "Prize" director of the firm was Dennison Clift who had spent several seasons in Hollywood as an assistant to Cecil B. DeMille and who was then producing at Ideal's London studio "using American methods and as far as possible surrounding himself with an American technical staff." Determined to use U.S. stars with the first picture under that plan, the studio began shooting *A Bill of Divorcement* with American film star Constance Binney in the lead. Warde was said to have opened negotiations with many other "important" U.S. film stars to play in Ideal pictures to be produced in London. *Bill* was selected as a vehicle, and the screen rights obtained, only after the play on which it was based had a successful run in New York—the play originated in London. That, plus Binney in the lead, led Ideal to believe the picture was a good bet to be successful "when added to the fact that the picture was to be made according to the best known American methods."[31]

Rowson's campaign, said *Variety*, was a revision of England's former strategy wherein after the war and with the resumption of film production in England, the British "deluged" the market with product; most of it went nowhere. One U.K. agent came to the U.S. with over a dozen films and hired the New York theatre for a week to hold trade screenings in the mornings. Reportedly the trade turned thumbs down on the product and the discouraged agent returned home without making a single U.S. sale— "His product was so far below the American standard it attracted no attention." Ideal's new plan of attack was conceived by Warde a few months after he had imported a group of four Ideal films. Although they had big name authors behind them such as Guy de Maupassant and J. M. Barrie, those movies went nowhere in the U.S. Apparently some, or all of them, were directed by Clift. Still, *Variety* thought the director might be better under Ideal's new strategy because "Clift up to that time had not thoroughly absorbed the American technique and his product had the tone of foreign manufacture."[32]

Near the end of 1924, English film producer and director George Ridgwell came to New York from London. The idea he pitched there was a proposal to make movies in England for the U.S. market "from plans and specifications supplied by the American producers or distributors." One advantage, he said, was that it would be 40 percent cheaper. However, to forestall any possibility that a U.S. major might come over with all U.S. personnel and simply shoot on location to save money, Ridgwell argued any such project had a better chance of success if an Englishman was in charge because U.S. companies and directors "can not become acclimated in England and seem to be out of their element over there in picture making."[33]

English bankers had investigators at work in America at the end of 1925 and into early 1926, surveying the U.S. motion picture industry. About $100,000 had been subscribed to a fund to finance the survey with the investigators' report to determine if the English group would go actively into the making of movies in the U.K. for worldwide distribution. Part of the money was spent by the four investigators to obtain "expert opinions in every line including the likely types of stories for all the world, from American experts in each of the divisions."[34]

Another British expedition to the new world took place in the spring of 1927 when a representative of British National Corporation (U.K. producer) made the rounds in Hollywood trying to persuade some film stars to make movies in Britain. Actors approached with such a proposition included Vilma Banky, Reginald Denny, Ronald Colman, Colleen Moore, and Harold Lloyd. The agent told the actors the films would be shot in the U.K. with American stars and released in the U.S. through First National. However, all rejected the offer as they were on long-term contracts with their U.S. studios. Also approached with such proposals were U.S. film directors, one of whom was Sid Olcott who heaped scorn on the U.K. film industry when he rejected the offer by declaring, "Regardless of the cast I do not believe anything could be turned out over there beyond a fair program picture."[35]

Another strategy employed or contemplated by foreign producers in this period was to distribute their films directly in the U.S. themselves or to buy one or more cinemas in America. Such a strategy would allow the foreign producer to avoid the difficulties involved in placing product with

U.S. firms to distribute or exhibit. Using such a plan, the Swedish Biograph company planned to "invade" the American film market in 1921. It planned to start in areas with a large Scandinavian population, such as Minneapolis, by establishing a circuit of cinemas in such communities and to present in those houses for one night a week a complete Swedish Biograph program. Portland, Oregon was another city picked as an early target for the plan.[36]

Frederick Wynne-Jones, representative in the U.S. for German producer UFA, announced in 1927 that within a year UFA would have a cinema of its own on Broadway. It was to be part of an expansion plan that was expected to include the operation of cinemas in other cities and thus the distribution of UFA films direct from the studio to the American public. A few months later UFA said it would build 60 community theaters in the U.S. that would book only product released through itself. Admitting the venues would be small, with a maximum of 500 seats each, and would provide only a small rental income for UFA, Wynne-Jones said they would give Europe a show window that would be the region's first real break in America. It was hoped that such exposure could be used as a springboard for wider U.S. distribution. First, though, UFA's ambitious plans called for the establishment of five UFA film exchanges, each of those with five to eight branch offices, to cover the U.S. Such a direct approach was necessary, said Wynne-Jones, because UFA believed it was entitled to a better break than it currently received from contracts with two U.S. majors that stipulated that MGM and Paramount would each handle five UFA movies.[37]

Plans by foreigners to buy American cinemas were also attempts to copy a successful Hollywood strategy to penetrate their home countries. By late 1928, the *New York Times* reported that practically all the Hollywood majors then had key theaters, or show windows of their own in London. Designed primarily to be a method of advertisement, they also proved to be profitable. Since the Hollywood cartel controlled the home market through, for one example, block booking, it kept out foreign competition and thus kept the lion's share of the lucrative U.S. film market for itself. That allowed it to spend more lavishly abroad in advertising and acquiring cinemas. In turn that left the native film industry in various countries receiving less of its home country's film revenues. In turn that meant native industries had a harder and harder time even competing at home, let alone making any inroads into the U.S. market. And the cycle continued.[38]

Although the Americans and the Europeans agreed that foreign films had next to no presence in America they took radically different positions as to why that situation existed. The French film publication *Courier*

Cinematographique said in 1920 that if the French movie had not been a success in America it was because of poor advertising.[39]

Leon Gaumont was one of the foremost European producers and cinema owners. For decades he had been the leading French motion picture executive. Explaining in 1926 why the European product could not successfully compete with U.S. ones, he said it took a lot of money to produce films on a scale to match the Americans and that there wasn't that much money in Europe to spend on pictures. Gaumont added that in the U.S. the producers owned chains of theaters "stretching from one end of the country to the other." None of the European producers were in such a favorable position since none owned more than a handful of cinemas, and most controlled none at all.[40]

More succinct was British producer Carlyle Blackwell, who commented, "U.S.A. and Canada are as good as closed to us as markets, because they are both in the hands of U.S. producing trusts."[41]

Oswald Stoll, U.K. producer and cinema owner, was in New York in 1927 trying to place his product. During his stay he gave a talk over radio station WEAF (part of the NBC network) in which he blasted Hollywood for denying foreign films to the American public. He complained that "magnates of your American picture industry, if they will look at the picture at all, will require it to be cut and carved about in an extraordinary manner in order to make it conform to so-called American essentials, until the picture ceases to be recognizable as either British or American and is only fit to be thrown on the scrap heap." Claiming he was not in the U.S. to place his product, he cynically explained that was the case "because selling British pictures in America brings one up against a stone wall." All too often, he felt, the American public was supposed to not want to see a particular foreign movie and they were therefore given no chance to see it. Stoll also argued that it was morally and ethically wrong to deny Americans (especially those who could not travel abroad) the opportunity to see movies that could bring the old world before the new world. They were denied the ability to realize truth by comparisons. "Free exchange of motion pictures is necessary for their own welfare and for the welfare of all countries," Stoll continued. "It would teach the world for the good of mankind that every nation has a living soul, which lives on though individuals perish."[42]

After two weeks in the U.S., Stoll left for London leaving in his wake anger and confusion over his radio attack on Hollywood. It was said, by Variety, to have been "not grasped over here" in many quarters. Speculation circulated that Stoll had become displeased over distributor indifference to his efforts to place U.K. product and that, therefore, his radio talk was nothing more than "sour grapes."[43]

A. Rosenthal, editor of a German trade paper but writing in a British publication in 1927, argued that Hollywood's domination and control of the home market were grounded in the fact that Hollywood was well-organized and substantially capitalized. Writing of this time period, film historians Andrew Higson and Richard Maltby stated, "There can be no illusion about one point. America, for the time being, can [not] be conquered as a market.... The very best European film will be met on the other side by a phalanx of most efficient business undertakings, which—perhaps rightly—claims the American Monroe declaration for films: film America to the film Americans."[44]

When Europeans explained why foreign films had such a minimal presence in the U.S. they almost always spoke of the structure and organization of the industry; when Americans explained the same situation they almost always spoke of the poor quality of the European product. A 1919 article about the U.S. firm Famous Players, which was moving more and more into the U.K. as a distributor and buyer of cinemas, said that the only opposition in the U.K. to Famous Players product was from other American producers because "the average continental production is no more suitable to the English than to the American market."[45]

Famous Players vice president Jesse Lasky, on his return to the U.S. after a 1920 European trip to check out the situation in the motion picture industry, declared the film industry in Europe was very far behind the American producers.[46]

That same year a report in Variety noted that trade papers in London and Paris complained that no British or French picture had a chance in America because the market was closed to them and no exhibitor would give them a screening. However, Variety reported that the consensus of opinion among the U.S. distributors, who had viewed a number of English and French movies then in New York to try and obtain bookings, was that "they could be doctored up to get by in the American market and make some money in low price houses, but none of them compare with average American productions."[47]

A 1922 Variety article observed that the British film trade believed that America was boycotting its films. Admitting there was some truth in that charge the account scornfully explained the boycott had been built in Britain by U.K. film producers who added to it every time they turned out a "dud" and described it as a "great British picture." Those British pictures, said the report, were "badly produced from bad stories, badly played by actors who carry little weight beyond the family circle." Admitting there were a few good U.K. producers the reporter still concluded, "But the majority of their pictures are only fit for British audiences." That is, those were the pictures from the good producers. Then came mediocre U.K. producers and then the bad of varying degrees. Above all things, it was reported, the British producer "detested" a story that was original. "If he produces 'drama' he'll do it trashily as if it were a thing not worth while," concluded the report. "He refuses to acknowledge that most of the big American pictures are sheer drama but with the difference that they are well done."[48]

A letter to the editor of the New York Times from Henry Gilland condemned the foreign films on the ground of quality. Gilland was seconding a letter from E. McCormick who also did not like them and called them inferior. In Gilland's view "these foreigners do not know how—and therefore should not try—to please us."[49]

At a 1926 luncheon, attended by representatives from 18 social, civic, and religious organizations, honoring MPPDA president Will Hays on the fourth anniversary of the establishment of the industry's Public Relations Committee, Hays was praised for cleaning up the film business and for keeping from the screen "books, plays and stories that are not suited for this type of public presentation." John F. Moore, an executive with the Young Men's Christian Association (YMCA) told the assembly of the condition of motion pictures in Europe: "Only when one is in Europe does one realize how far ahead our own films are. Not only from the standpoint of technical excellence, but in their cleanliness and wholesomeness, our own motion pictures are vastly superior. I saw in some of the leading capitals of Europe pictures which would never have been tolerated on Broadway."[50]

Journalist Frank Tilley reported in 1928 that the English paper the Evening Standard complained that every week Variety consistently gave U.K. movies very bad reviews and "every week throws a gallon of vitriol in the face of British films, is pleased to criticize Anthony Asquith's first effort at direction." Tilley then went to great lengths to deny such an accusation, declaring those reviews of British films "err, if anything, on the mild side."[51]

In March 1928, the head of the MPPDA's Foreign Office, Frederick Herron, informed the U.S. State Department that the French would probably defend their recent imposition of a quota system for U.S. movies in France by claiming that the American industry had restricted the distribution of foreign pictures. That was, he said, "not so, never has been so, and never will be so. Foreign pictures have had just as much chance for distribution here as domestic pictures have." Herron told the State Department that the problem lay in the standard of the European product; they did not measure up to the standards of what the public demanded.[52]

So pervasive was the idea that European product was of poor quality, so often was it presented, that even Europeans could be found to endorse that view. When French film actor Louis Monfils complained in Paris about U.S. domination in the business it caused *Variety* to counter with the opinion of an unnamed Frenchman who was in New York on French government business. He was said to have stated that "the definite thing that is keeping French-made pictures out of first class American cinema theaters is that they are inferior in quality." Also, he was said to be familiar with French directors who were active in America and remarked, "I find they agree with my observation that the American film industry is infinitely superior to the French as a work of art." As a final insult this Frenchman was reported to have declared that the French cinema audience "is made up of persons of lower taste and intelligence than the cinema public of America. The French filmmakers turn out a product which shall satisfy that class of patrons."[53]

A 1923 piece in the *New York Times* summarized another article, by an English writer in the U.K., concerning the superiority of U.S. product over British films. Admitted was that the greatest American advantage was money. Amongst other reasons cited was that the U.S. had better actors to draw from. Then the *Times* chipped in with a few items which put the U.S. producer at the top, and which were forgotten by the English writer. One reason was that the English producer "is slow to take a suggestion from the American director." In conclusion the reporter declared, "It is the technical knowledge possessed by most American producers that gives them the superiority over the producers in England, and for that matter in all other countries."[54]

One of the most off-beat explanations came from Dr. Artur Landsberg of Germany who was of the opinion that screen kisses on the lips were universally liked by movie patrons but that courtesy kisses on the hand, accompanied by sweeping gestures, were not appreciated by the film audience outside of Germany and Austria. According to him, "Hand kissing scenes in the grand manner have cost many a German motion picture producer the chance to sell his films abroad."[55]

When U.K. producers B&C took out a full-page advertisement in 1919 to promote Godal's *Twelve-Ten*, with U.S. star Marie Doro in the lead, it touted all the Americans (star, director, cameraman, cutters, property men, and so forth) taken abroad to produce it and others to follow: "Here is American Quality back of big stories selected for the American market in the full knowledge that America's taste is international and unprejudiced if the films are right."[56]

Meanwhile, the Hollywood cartel continued using industry practices that were designed to limit competition and screen time for both foreign films and those from U.S. independent producers. Block booking continued to be one of those practices. In 1918 there were said to be about 14,000 cinemas in America. Of that number it was believed that one company, Paramount-Artcraft, supplied 6,000 of those houses. Paramount signed up exhibitors for five year terms. A decade later Warner Bros. was requiring block booking on their talking pictures. Cinemas were required to contract for the full Warner sound program for the entire season—they could not pick and choose the individual films they wished to screen.[57]

Often enough, exhibitors opposed the foreign movies on their own. An exhibitor group, the American Educational Motion Picture Association, vowed in 1920 to fight the importation of foreign films. "American Films for American Theatres" was adopted as a slogan. The organization struck a committee to generate a list of old U.S. movies that were suitable for revival from time to time as an aid to the exhibitor. According to a report, "They believe that by this method the independent exhibitor will be able to battle the common enemy and still keep America a closed market to foreign-made films."[58]

A 1922 report said that a shortage of feature films was causing difficulties for exhibitors. To address the situation Famous Players reissued seven of its old, already released, items. Famous Players planned to reissue another seven two months down the road. Fox was also in the process of reissuing seven of its old movies. Other studios were said to be considering the idea. The only other solution to the problem was for exhibitors to make use of the large number of foreign films then "lying on the shelves." Wrote a journalist, however, "Even with a shortage of film existing there isn't any desire on the part of the releasing organizations to take over foreign made productions for distribution."[59]

Although foreign producers often tried unsuccessfully to use American stars, other personnel and American methods, America was very successful when it siphoned talent out of any country where it arose—U.S. producers poached talent heavily. They were successful because they were wealthy enough to do it successfully. That gave their films even more worldwide attractiveness, which brought them even more money, which led to more poaching, and so on. For the motion picture industry in the nations from which the Americans poached talent the effect was, of course, devastating. Usually it was the best and the brightest lured out of France, or wherever. No sooner did someone learn his craft and become skilled than American dollars lured him away.

One of the earliest to engage in poaching was Adolph Zukor of Famous Players who brought director Ernst Lubitsch (*Passion*) and actor Pola Negri to the U.S. from Germany in 1921 to "educate" them, and use them in his studio. As an aside, Zukor stated that the occasion on which Famous Players found a foreign film good enough to distribute in America was so rare that "it amounts to less than a fraction of 1 per cent of the entire output of Famous Players."[60]

Lubitsch left for home after only a month or so in America, giving as his reason that he was regarded in the U.S. as an unfriendly person and as an enemy of the American actor. Famous Players had urged him to stay but Equity made statements against him. Also, negative newspaper accounts were mailed to him and he was the recipient of "strange phone calls." However, he would later return.[61]

Variety observed in 1927 that a foreign colony of approximately 400 actors and directors was then engaged, or had been, in turning out American films. About 85 percent of the world's picture output was said to be made in the U.S. "with the majority of the principals of alien birth." Many of those imported players had been in Hollywood for years. Some 200 of them were from the U.K. and British Commonwealth. A very few of them were: Renée Adorée (French actor), Maurice Tourneur (French director), Emil Jannings (German actor), Ernst Lubitsch (German director), Charlie Chaplin, Reginald Denny, Ronald Colman (all British actors), Pola Negri (Polish actor), Greta Garbo (Swedish actor), and Ramon Novarro (Mexican actor).[62]

Noted film historian Paul Rotha commented in 1929 that in Sweden, Denmark, France, Britain, and Germany, the U.S. film producers poached talent. Speaking specifically about Sweden, Rotha wrote: "One by one her best directors and players drifted across to Hollywood, where their work steadily deteriorated." Thus, he concluded, although European countries made every effort to produce films in the face of the Hollywood machine, "these pictures and their makers were doomed to eventual failure, with the inevitable result that the brains were imported into America." Rotha added: "I cannot recall one example of a European director who, on going to Hollywood, made films better or even as good as he did in his own surroundings." Eighteen years later in a later edition of his book, Rotha added a footnote to amend that conclusion: "In view of Lubitsch's career, this point is now debatable in his case."[63]

Yet another strategy used by the U.S. motion picture industry in this period to limit the importation of foreign movies was by lobbying for the imposition of tariffs. John Emerson, president of Actors' Equity Association, announced in June 1921 that an ad valorem tariff on foreign motion pictures would be recommended to Congress by the Ways and Means Committee. "A tariff won't shut up foreign films," said Emerson, "it will simply force foreign producers to compete with us on equal terms."[64]

Within a couple of months the proposal was that a 30 percent ad valorem duty be imposed on each foreign import, ostensibly to bring the cost up to that of a similar work produced in America. That is, say a movie that cost 10,000 pounds Sterling to produce in the U.K. would have cost 50,000 pounds Sterling if it had been made in America. In that case the import duty on the U.K. film would be set at 15,000 pounds Sterling, which would obviously prevent its entry into the U.S. Foreign producers, as was to have been expected, vigorously opposed the tariff. A group of English producers argued the industry must always be an art rather than a trade "and for any country to exclude the artistic works of any other is to deny itself one of the first means of national health." Favoring tariffs were all the film craft unions and most of the small, independent producers and distributors—those with no foreign connections. Opposing the imposition of tariffs were most exhibitors (who believed that more product available would keep prices down) and the major studios and distributors (who made pictures offshore sometimes just because it was cheaper).[65]

Hearings on the issue were held in Washington by the Commerce Department. Among the foreigners who testified there were French producer Louis Mercanton, Alfred Lever of the U.K. Stoll Pictures, and Count di Revel of Unione of Italy (a combination of all producers there). They stated that 85 percent of films exhibited in English, French, and Italian cinemas were American while U.K. films amounted to just one percent of the movies screened in the U.S. In even worse shape was Italy who had one or two big productions "in readiness to send" to America while France had a "few" films then in the U.S. All three told the hearings that if a tariff was imposed, retaliatory duties would be almost certain. Wondering about the proposed tariff, a reporter commented, "The amount of foreign film coming into the country is so small it cannot be a question of the revenue that we would derive for that would hardly pay for the force required to collect it."[66]

A meeting of U.S. industry executives, said to represent 90 percent of those producing and distributing motion pictures, went on record, in August 1921, as against the proposed 30 percent ad valorem duty.[67]

Also coming out in opposition around the same time was Nils Bouveng, production manager of the Swedish Biograph Company—largest of the Scandinavian picture firms. "At present the output of foreign films acceptable to American audiences is only about 1 per cent," he said. "Or, in other words, only about one in every hundred films produced in foreign countries in suitable for showing in America." He wondered what was the point in considering taxing such a small proportion of the market. Although Swedish Biograph then had little or no presence in the U.S., it hoped to in the future.[68]

That ad valorem proposal (scaled back to 20 percent from 30 percent) failed to go anywhere but a new tariff bill was expected to come out of committee shortly and speculation was that it would provide for a specific duty such as one cent a foot on positive films and two cents per foot on negatives. With the resumption of legislative deliberations in the fall of 1921 representatives of the major Hollywood producers had been "quietly at work in Washington." They argued that any ad valorem, or otherwise onerous, duty imposed on foreign films would lead to retaliation and that could cost Hollywood the 25 percent of its total income that it earned offshore. If that happened, warned the cartel, the domestic consumer would have to make up that deficiency through higher prices. Also, the U.S. cartel had found they were able to undersell Italian distributors in Italy, despite a cost difference that on the face of it favored Italian film producers. On the other hand, they commented, "Out of a whole mass of Italian productions there have been less than half a dozen successfully offered in America." Since foreign films amounted to one percent or less of films screened in America, any onerous tariff imposed might indeed reduce or eliminate that presence. However, it was such a tiny sum that it made no difference to Hollywood. But an onerous tariff might set off retaliation against U.S. films in any number of countries—and that could hurt. Congress lowered its sights to aim at a token duty. Hollywood's majors did not need tariffs to keep out foreign films. They had already achieved success in that area through various means.[69]

At hearings on the issue late in 1921, Paul M. Turner, spokesman for Equity, argued that at that moment 54 German produced movies were being exhibited in the U.S. and that four or five of them had combined to gross $2.5 million at the box office. (America then spent $750 million to $1 billion yearly on motion picture admissions.) Turner added that U.S. producers could not compete with the Germans and that pictures that cost from $200,000 to $300,000 to produce in America could be made in Germany for from $10,000 to $12,000. Speaking for the Hollywood cartel against the tariff was Saul F. Rogers, who said that only a "few" foreign films had been successful in America.[70]

Early in 1922, the Senate Finance Committee agreed on imposing a duty on imported films as follows: two cents a foot on negatives exposed but not developed; three cents a foot on negatives exposed and developed; and one cent a foot on positive films—token amounts.[71]

Even Actors' Equity, one of the strongest proponents of a high tariff, had changed its mind on the issue by the end of 1922. At that time organization president John Emerson was just back from a European trip. Before that trip, he said, he had been worried European movies would keep improving and "overrun" the U.S. But after his trip he did not think that was likely with one reason being the Europeans "don't have good stories." An irony was that all of them were aimed directly at America. However, he believed that effort was a waste of time, saying, "They simply cannot understand our tastes, any more than we can understand theirs." Emerson then thought a high tariff on foreign motion pictures was not necessary.[72]

One effective control mechanism utilized by the Hollywood cartel, which allowed it to dispense with such crude and obvious devices as high, onerous tariffs, was the distribution system. Hollywood's major producers also distributed most pictures (their own, foreign items, and U.S. independent product, domestically and offshore) to cinemas that were often owned by them. Alfred Lever, general manager of U.K. producer Stoll Pictures, arrived in America in 1921 with 26 features ready to be released on the U.S. market. Previously Stoll had released in the U.S. through Pathé but the French company had by then disappeared. Lever made no deals during his visits and said the fact "There can be no advances of any nature obtained from American releasing companies at this time comes as a distinct surprise to practically all of the foreign agents who have lately come to the United States to dispose of foreign product." It was customary in distribution deals for some money to be paid in advance. This showed good faith on the part of the distributor and indicated he would indeed distribute the film. Also, it was useful for producers who could use the money on their next production or on a film covered by the contract if filming was not yet complete.[73]

The Danish film *Hamlet* was exhibited in November 1921 at the Lexington Theatre in New York. A featured performer in that movie was Asta Nielsen. The following summer a film buff wrote to a movie columnist with the *New York Times*, wanting to know why more of Nielsen's work was not seen in America. She had been appearing on the European screen for years and was said to be one of the top stars on the Continent. A response to that question came from A. M. Becker of Asta Films, the company that controlled the rights to the Nielsen pictures in the U.S. Becker said *Hamlet* was exhibited at the Lexington Theatre (not on Broadway) because none of the Broadway houses (a more prestigious location) would show it. Asta Films, he added, had "been unable to arrange for a proper distribution of this picture, notwithstanding that the terms on which distributors handle pictures are such as to insure them against any possible loss or risk." Ready then for U.S. exhibition were Nielsen's other great works that included *The Idiot* (based on Dostoevsky's novel) and *Countess Julia* (based on Strindberg's play), in addition to *Hamlet*, but nobody would book them, which meant, said Becker, "These great works are denied the American people, while the most stupid and worthless stuff is dished up to them." A *New York Times* reporter heard that the Nielsen works might be kept from the screens, and commented, "Something is wrong somewhere.... It is well known that the machinery of motion picture exhibition and distribution is not efficient. It often fails to get the best pictures to the people who want to see them."[74]

A follow-up column to the one mentioned above caused the columnist to say that his earlier column about film distribution brought him "an unusual number of communications" from people in the motion picture business and from the general public. "All these communications, without exception," he noted, "add to the accumulated evidence that the machinery of distribution and exhibition does not function as it should."[75]

In yet another follow-up article on the topic, Howard Dietz, advertising manager of Goldwyn Pictures, argued that producers and distributors did not really know what the public wanted, but knew what the public did not want. For example, he said the public did not want a costume drama or a period piece. It all caused the columnist to declare, "Any picture which requires a moderate degree of education and intelligence on the part of spectators is one of the things the picture-going public, or a large part of it, doesn't want."[76]

During the second half of the 1922-1923 film season, the Paramount sales force introduced its new lineup of 39 releases to the trade and the media with the slogan "The new 39 haven't got a single foreign picture in the line-up" at a sales convention in Los Angeles. That was explained to be due to carrying a couple of foreign films in the earlier part of the 1922-1923 season that went on to sustain losses.[77]

Even if a foreign film defied the odds and achieved success in the U.S. it did not mean that other work by the same director would get distribution. For example, in 1925 German director Erich Pommer, despite the recent U.S. success of *Die Niebelungen*, had to pay for a New York press screening of *Der Letzte Mann* after it had been turned down, sight unseen, by all the major American distributors.[78]

When rumors surfaced in 1927 that U.S. firm First National would soon sign a distribution agreement with a German producer, it caused a Berlin publication to comment in general on the few distribution pacts that had been signed in the past by declaring, "[The opening of] the American market for German films by means of agreements has resulted in only modest, partial successes, alongside of brilliant failures." First National then owned 3,000 theaters in the U.S.[79]

In 1926, when foreign films had a minimal presence in America, a tiny,

256-seat cinema opened on lower Fifth Avenue—the Fifth Avenue Playhouse—as an art house for both foreign and domestic productions. It was likely the first art house. The German release *The Cabinet of Dr. Caligari* was its first program.[80]

Statistics for the period showed that few foreign movies made it to America. Figures from the U.S. Department of Commerce showed American exports of positive films to be as follows: 1914, 32,690,000 feet; 1916, 158,752,000 feet; 1917, 128,550,000 feet; 1918, 79,888,000 feet (U.S. entry into war); 1919, 153,237,000 feet; 1920, 175,238,000 feet; and 1921, 111,585,000 feet (first nine months –projected to 140,000,000 feet). Imports were: 1914, 20,057,000 feet; 1918, 2,267,975 feet; 1919, 2,920,000 feet; 1920, 6,233,000 feet; and 1921, 7,375,000 feet (first nine months—projected to 10,000,000 feet). The increase in the export of American films after the war was far greater than the increase in the importation of foreign films. Something in excess of 80 percent of all imports came from four nations. Imports in 1914 came from the following: France, 6,518,000 feet; Great Britain, 6,386,000 feet; Germany, 2,159,281 feet; and Italy, 3,043,000 feet. Imports in 1921 were as follows: France, 2,200,000 feet; Great Britain, 2,000,000 feet; Germany, 2,000,000 feet; and Italy, 600,000 feet. The report also noted: "Only a percentage, by no means all, of the film imported into the United States is ever exhibited. The dreaded 'foreign invasion,' therefore, seems not so dreadful as some would make it appear, especially if it is compared with the American 'invasion,' or occupation of foreign countries."[81]

Commerce indicated that in 1922, 125,337,444 feet of positive film were exported and 6,554,018 feet were imported. One year later the figures were, respectively, 138,656,880 feet and 7,053,232. For fiscal 1925 (July 1, 1924 through June 30, 1925), 210,000,000 feet of positive film were exported, and 5,135,462 feet were imported.[82]

During the 1925-1926 season, it was estimated that some 850 films of feature length were offered in America. The Hollywood MPPDA cartel itself offered close to 400 pictures with about 300 available from U.S. independent producers, at least from those studios the reporter was aware of. He also noted, "The vast majority of prize theaters in America are held by either Famous, Metro or First National." With those unknown independents added "and their output computed, as well as the occasional foreign films imported here by UFA [German] and the few British firms the list of annual features runs well over 850."[83]

According to the Department of Commerce, U.S. film producers realized $75 million in 1926 from foreign sales; $4 million was paid out to foreign producers for U.S. screenings of their movies. An even gloomier report was produced by the Commerce Department for the years 1921 to 1925, in which the agency stated royalties for film rentals received from foreigners by U.S. film companies totaled "at least $300,000,000," while the American royalty payments for foreign films in that period were just $1,000,000. Yearly breakdown for U.S. receipts were as follows: 1921, $40 million; 1922, $50 million, 1923, $60 million; 1924, $70 million; and 1925, $75 million.[84]

During 1928 some 500 movies were to be made in Europe (U.K. 100 to 120, Germany 200–250, France 100, Russia, Sweden, Italy, Spain, and so on, 75 in total). It was acknowledged that some of them were to be made mainly to satisfy some quota requirement and would therefore be shelved, never being intended for exhibition. That same year the combined output of the Hollywood cartel plus all the independent producers large and small was estimated at about 774 features. It meant that perhaps only 300 of those European features would make it to the screen, even in their home countries.[85]

For the years 1918 to 1925, America exported a total of 1,245,496,233 feet of exposed film while over the same period importing 53,559,559 feet, a ratio of 25 to one. In 1926 the U.S. exported 224 million feet of film, and imports totaled 4.4 million feet. Back in 1913 America imported 16 million feet of exposed film, and exported 32 million feet. With American control of distribution and exhibition, almost all of the exposed films were ultimately screened. However, precisely for the same reason, many of the imports to the U.S. never made it to a screen. Of the 125 foreign films that arrived in America in 1922, just six were sold and exhibited. Clarence S. North, in charge of motion picture data with the Commerce Department's Bureau of Foreign and Domestic Commerce, noted in 1926 that most foreign movies arriving in the U.S. were never exhibited before paying customers: "A few foreign pictures—perhaps a dozen—are shown in the United States each year," he said. U.K. film writer William Seabury explained why foreign films were denied access to the U.S. market by stating, "This market can now be profitably reached only through one or more of a group of not more than ten national American distributors of pictures, each of which is busily engaged in marketing its own brand of pictures through its own sales or rental organizations and through theaters owned, controlled or operated by one or more of this group." A roughly equal situation, however, could exist, at least in other cultural industries. U.S. publishers paid foreign writers $1.5 million in royalties in 1925, while foreign publishers paid American writers approximately the same amount.[86]

By 1928, as European agitation over U.S. film dominance of European screens and the lack of European product on American screens increased, Frederick Herron, head of the MPPDA's foreign division, grumbled, "If they would quit burning us up every time they are unable to get a release here for one of their films; if they will follow Germany's stand and send representatives to Hollywood to familiarize themselves with our methods; if they would come out of their shell and take suggestions, why then they would really get down to a basis which would find them a comparatively ready market in this country." France was then the most vocal of the European critics. Herron cited France's leading filmmaker, Jean Sapene, and said, "He told us in so many words: 'If you take my pictures you will have no trouble in France.' Well, we were able to use a few of his pictures, but far less than five per cent of all the pictures made in France in 1927, so the fat is now in the fire." In his final remarks Herron declared, "If Europe asks for American opinion on their stories and their pictures while in the making stage, we will certainly grant it. Up to the present Europe has gone ahead without seeking our advice."[87]

Rotha remarked, in his seminal 1929 work, The Film Till Now, that although much of the European output (from Germany and France) was superior to the Hollywood film, "the vast organizations so liberally equipped financially have presented an insuperable barrier" to their getting U.S. release. To make any real money, those European films needed to be screened in the U.S.; Rotha cautioned, "This at present is almost impossible. A great deal has been said by smooth-tongued publicity men about the Americans wanting British films, but there is little doubt that the Americans are definitely hostile not only to the British but to the Continental industry. They do not want foreign films in America, except as occasional curiosities, and do not intend to have them. Why should they?" When he updated his book later Rotha said, "No significant change in this position can be reported eighteen years later, except for the vastly improved quality of British and foreign films."[88]

As the silent film era ended, foreign films had spent over a decade in the wilderness. They had no real presence on America's cinema screens. Hollywood's cartel had effectively kept them out although to hear them tell it the absence was due to the atrociously poor quality of pretty much any movie produced by other than an American studio. While they might have convinced themselves of the merits of their arguments the Europeans did not buy them for a moment. They grew increasingly frustrated. As for the American public, it was true they never went to foreign films. It was not because they found them wanting, as Hollywood's cartel would have it; the American public rarely had the option of going or not going to foreign films since they were almost never on offer.

3

The Early Sound Era,
1929–1945

[The British] couldn't make a good silent in the past for
America's first runs, and it looks negative, if not worse, on
the talker end.
—*Abel Green*, Variety *editor, 1930*

England lacks stars, trained scenario writers, directors and
adequate story material.
—*Ruth Biery and Eleanor Packer,*
Saturday Evening Post, *1933*

Hollywood thinks British producers cannot get away from
ingrained Britishisms and use worldwide appeal formulas
even if Hollywood teaches them.
—Fortune *magazine, 1945*

The arrival of talking motion pictures caused some initial trepidation
among some in the business who worried about exporting movies to countries where the language spoken was not the same as that in the film. Such
worries proved groundless as subtitling and dubbing quickly developed to
the point of providing a satisfactory remedy, if not always a flawless one.
Practically, that worry applied only to export of U.S. films. Foreign film
producers had next to no presence in the U.S. at the end of the silent era.
It was a condition that continued seamlessly into the sound era.

At the start of 1929 it was announced that French producer Charles Delac would travel to America, representing the entire French film industry, and was empowered to meet with the heads of the major U.S. studios and tell them that U.S. movies would only be able to enter France on the condition U.S. distributors would accept more French films. France's industry hoped to strike a deal similar to one they had just made with the Germans wherein the latter agreed to distribute 33 French pictures in Germany in return for having 100 German movies distributed in France.[1]

American film executives did their best to block the Delac mission and thought they had achieved that objective when it was announced that Delac had fallen ill and the trip was indefinitely postponed. Then the French declared the trip was on again with an equally high profile French film figure, Jean Sapene, substituted for Delac and empowered to give the same ultimatum to Hollywood.[2]

A couple months later, while he was in the U.S., Sapene told the press that unless American film distributors bought foreign-made movies and showed them in the States, the entire European industry would band together to exclude American product. Sapene argued that the current intense lobbying by Europeans for film quotas was attributable to MPPDA cartel head Will Hays. He explained that previous French quota regulations and other restrictive rules were adopted when Hays failed to negotiate with the French. When Hays had been in Paris the previous year he was said to have promised that he would look into the possibilities of distribution of French pictures in the U.S. when he returned home and that he would do something to further a showing of foreign material in the American market. But, Sapene declared, in spite of many urgent queries from France, Hays had ignored the subject since his return home. No matter what the actual situation was, Sapene commented, "All European producers believed that the American industry has a tacit understanding to keep foreign films out of the home market." When Europeans adopted contingent and quota laws, Sapene said, they were only counter measures.[3]

Nothing came of Sapene's visit or his ultimatum. About five years later the French film industry, through Charles Delac, head of the Chambre Syndicate, approached the French government and asked it to "invest" $3330,000 to promote the sale of 25 French pictures in the U.S. Delac wanted the money to be given to a French company for film exports, to be controlled by the Chambre. Sponsors of the scheme made the following estimate of the costs of getting a French film on the market in New York: advance payment to producer, $1,300; shipping, customs, print copies, $650; overhead, $1,300; and dubbing into English, $10,000—a total of $13,250 per film (times 25).[4]

Bernard Natan, film mogul at Pathé-Natan and another power in the Chambre Syndicate, visited the U.S. in the summer of 1934. Just before he sailed, he was asked by the media if he did not consider it curious that he was trying to sell French films to the U.S. at the same time as his company was trying hard to put U.S. movies out of the French market. His reply was that the two situations had nothing to do with each other; "There are too many American films in France," declared Natan. Then he added "French films have never been given sufficient playing time in the U.S."[5]

Back in Paris after his U.S. visit, Natan slammed Hollywood and its practices declaring that overproduction in America made it useless for the French to seek significant outlets there for their product. At his press conference he suggested that perhaps the large French population in the U.S. should organize a series of non-commercial theaters or projection rooms to show French movies. "We'll give them the equipment," Natan added.[6]

Foreign film distributors in the U.S. were said to be concerned, in 1939, about the reported insistence of numerous French producers, who demanded from $45,000 to $50,000 as the price to distribute their features. They pointed to the fact that the original U.S. distributor of *Mayerling* (the top-grossing French movie in the U.S. to that date) only paid around $17,000. Distributors in New York were said to believe that $2,000 to $5,000 was plenty for French features, which was all that was asked as recently as a couple of years earlier.[7] Film historian Tino Balio, surveying the 1930s, wrote that demand for French film "hardly existed" in the American market during the Depression, when only about a dozen pictures a year were imported. Interest picked up later in the decade, but only in Manhattan.[8]

Germany was another country that flirted, unsuccessfully, with quotas and contingent arrangements at the end of the 1920s and into the early 1930s. Under the provisions of Germany's December 1928 decree governing the import of motion pictures, 50 of the 210 import permits (one needed for each imported picture) to be given out during the year 1929-1930 were retained by the Federal Commissioner for Import and Export Permits. They were to be distributed among German firms who showed they had sold German films abroad. Various conditions were attached to try and ensure the offshore sales were true sales. For example, money had to be received by the seller before the deal was regarded as complete, and the movie had to be given "adequate public showing" in the country of the foreign purchaser.[9]

A 1931 account said that German films were the only foreign ones in U.S. showings, with one or two exceptions, and were then the only ones being exhibited. Six were on view in New York that week. During the previous year only one French picture was a box office winner, with the same being true for Italian product. British films had not done well, nor had those in any other language.[10]

That relatively little spurt of interest was enough to catch the attention of journalist Alexander Bakshy who wrote in *The Nation* about "the German invasion." Bakshy argued that five or six years earlier, German films were "the great sensation" in the U.S. but they then declined in quality. That week, he said, of the 21 first-run features being screened in New York, 15 were American and six were German. Yet, he noted, "Probably the entire daily audience of the six little theaters exhibiting the German films does not reach a quarter of the number visiting the Roxy alone." What was significant to Bakshy was not the number of people who went to see the German films "but the emergence of the German work by the side of the American and the apparent eagerness with which it is sought by the so-called little theaters."[11]

Around that same time two of Germany's largest film producers, UFA and Tobis, were reported to be working separately and independently to establish two foreign film cinema chains in America. UFA wanted to establish 10 theaters while Tobis hoped to have at least 17 houses. Behind those moves was the idea that the practice of the moment of restricting foreign films to small houses was not in the interests of foreign producers inasmuch as high ticket prices were necessitated by small capacity venues. That is, they felt it was better to half fill a 1,000- to 1,500-seat house at 50 cents top than it was to run a 300-seat venue at $1 top ticket price.[12]

Cinema operation was begun by UFA in June 1931 when it reopened the Cosmopolitan in New York. Soon thereafter it took over the Carlton in Newark, New Jersey. Although those were the only two UFA–operated houses, the company had exhibition arrangements with about another half a dozen cinemas around the country. However, it was an experiment that never worked, with the Newark outlet said to be a consistent money-loser with all other arrangements coming out at best at a break even point. UFA dissolved its theater operations in America, and liquidated its U.S. branch offices in 1932, as the firm and the German economy went through severe economic problems.[13]

Also in 1932, *Variety* reported there was a considerable drop-off in interest in foreign-language films and that "the novelty vogue that these pictures enjoyed 18 months ago is waning." German films continued to lead that category with Russian product next in box office importance; Spanish movies came third. After that point came French, Yiddish, Italian and Scandinavian pictures, which all ranked about even.[14]

Balio said that during the 1930s only abut 40 cinemas in the U.S.

played foreign films exclusively; another 200 theaters played imports on occasion. In 1931, U.S. exhibition chains Loew's (MGM), Publix (Paramount) and RKO played German movies one day a week in some of their neighborhood houses in metro New York. Three German companies, UFA, Tobis, and Capital, for a time had distribution offices in New York and as a group handled about 70 pictures annually. Their pictures played in German-speaking neighborhoods of New York, Milwaukee, and a few other cities.[15]

Whatever limited success German films enjoyed in the U.S. in the early 1930s began to fade away after the Nazis came to political power. As early as May 1933, a general drop in attendance at German movies in New York was reported. After suffering a 50 percent drop in attendance, the Europa Theatre stopped exhibiting those movies and switched to Russian films. Attendance elsewhere in the city had fallen off from 15 to 30 percent, managers reported. Harold Auten, a booking agent for German pictures in America said, "It would be suicidal to open a German picture in New York now. Where we normally can book a German picture for $5,000 we are now getting $1,000." He added, "I believe the thing will blow over if Hitler withdraws his persecution of the Jews. The Jewish population was responsible for the success of the German pictures in New York and the Jews are now withdrawing their support."[16]

Later that month it was said there were less than six cinemas in the U.S. that were playing German movies then, compared to 100 such houses a year earlier. Three of the six were located in New York, with one of them operated by Tobis. In the previous two weeks, German venues had closed in Chicago, Detroit, Buffalo, Boston, and San Francisco, because of anti–Hitler sentiment. One estimate said that 65 to 70 percent of the audience at all German houses throughout America had always been Jews.[17]

In the summer of 1933, one reporter was moved to comment that "practically nothing" was left of the foreign language film business in the U.S. with only four houses in the nation showing foreign films exclusively, three in New York and one in Boston. He remarked, "It's the lowest ebb ever, even since silent days." He argued that the foreign movie business was always a "piking proposition," until two years earlier when it began building to sizeable proportions. Less than a year earlier it reached its apex, with over 200 cinemas in America using foreign films (on occasion, not all exclusively) and all doing pretty well. Then came Hitler, he said, and with only German product being much of a draw the market dried up. Some exhibitors dropped German movies on their own volition. However, most reportedly tried to hold on. They received protests, angry letters, and so on, and finally dropped German product.[18]

After the Nazis nationalized the German film industry, the Reich offered motion pictures to U.S. exhibitors at no cost up front, just a percentage of receipts (normally a cash advance was part of a distribution or exhibition deal), but only six or so German-language houses accepted the offer.[19]

In order to avoid the stigma against German product, UFA began hiding its identity on a number of films and shipping them around as though produced by someone else. Also, several French-language pictures were brought into the U.S. by UFA. Mostly they were French versions of German films, made by UFA with part French and German casts. No mention of UFA appeared anywhere on the print, but the screen-credited producer was listed as Alliance Cinématographique Europene—the name of UFA's French office. German names had been omitted in the credits. It was estimated there were a maximum of six cinemas in the U.S. that still screened German movies. Even at the 79th Street theater, in the heart of New York's German neighborhood, Yorkville, the UFA trademark was either covered over on poster displays and advertising matter or avoided altogether.[20]

Tobis, Germany's second biggest producer (after UFA), was reportedly set in 1936 to make another attempt to crack the American film market. It had opened offices in New York, again, after earlier closing its U.S. offices and getting out of cinema operation. That earlier attempt to crack open the U.S. distribution and exhibition markets directly had failed around 1932. Officially, in this new effort the company was only interested in selling its product. Unofficially, Tobis staff admitted the first order of business was to "break down anti–Hitler feeling in the U.S." and then to "re-establish the German film in its place of eminence in the American art film market." However, this effort also quickly ended in failure for Tobis.[21]

The country most active in trying to increase its presence in the American market in the 1930s was the United Kingdom. A 1930 report grumbled that nations such as Germany, Russia, the U.K., and others, were scheduling "quantity" releases of their product in America. Leading the way was producer British International (BI—headed by John Maxwell). The firm then controlled the Cohan theater on Broadway, which it had tied up as a show window for the following two years. During that time it contemplated exhibiting 40 U.K.–made features at popular Broadway prices. A further complaint in this account was that the foreigners could produce more cheaply. It was said, for example, that BI paid the U.S. government one cent per foot in tax on all films imported, while American producers were taxed double that for the admission of U.S. product into England. After numerous deals and hook-ups with American partners, all of which failed, BI determined to make its next assault on the U.S. picture market as an independent effort. To that end it leased the Cohan venue and planned to use its own staff to handle all of its U.S. activities. Harold Auten, a BI representative in America, felt that if foreign pictures were to succeed in America, they had to spend their own money and guide their own progress. "In its campaign to invade America, British International will avoid the arty type of theatre," explained Auten. "Past experience has convinced the company that once a picture gets into an arty it is automatically stamped out for houses in other classes." BI hoped its product would be able to break into the big cinema chains through sheer merit.[22]

Yet just ten weeks later the BI experiment was pronounced a failure with the producer then in the process of trying to sublease the Cohan for the remainder of its term. "Even independent exhibitors, however, after looking at some of the all–British product," said a reporter, "agreed with reviewers that England is as far behind in the art of casting and direction now as in the silent days."[23]

About five years later, in 1935, Arthur Dent, general manager of BI, arrived in New York to herald the start of yet another of his firm's assaults on the American film market. Dent's visit was a sort of prelude to the visit of BI president John Maxwell, who was due to follow his executive in two weeks or so. Arriving with his company's biggest pictures, Dent planned to use a Broadway venue where he would preview those movies for the trade and the press with the firm's future U.S. strategy being influenced by the reaction at those previews. At that time BI was not represented in the U.S., although at one time it was said to be the biggest British company operating in the U.S. Its dismal failure at the Cohan was duly noted.[24]

One of the more condescending media accounts came in a lengthy 1933 report in the *Saturday Evening Post* wherein Ruth Biery and Eleanor Packer wrote that the U.K. film industry was getting ready to challenge U.S. world film hegemony. That is, Britain was determined to enter the American market when its pictures "are on a par with the American product." Until then, said the authors, U.K. producers had been prevented from offering "virile competition" to the U.S. producers "by the inferiority of their product." Nevertheless the future promised to be different; the report predicted "They now realize this inferiority and are willing, for the first time, to expend the money necessary to overcome it. They are now turning their energies to learning from Hollywood." In the past, observed the account, the battle between Hollywood and the U.K. had been one-sided because English financiers had "refused" to spend the money necessary to improve the product. To that date the most expensive British movie was said to have cost $250,000, equal to one of the "smaller expenditures" of an American producer.[25]

Still, thought Biery and Packer, the road ahead would be tough because England was missing "stars, trained scenario writers, directors and adequate story material." One London film producer reportedly told the pair that he was searching for an independent studio in Hollywood to purchase and use as a lab, with an attempt made to keep British ownership of that facility a secret. The British owner would then produce cheap American movies with Hollywood experts who found themselves out of work. It was part of the plan that those experts would be "the innocent instructors for English movies planted in various inconspicuous positions to study and learn each angle of successful picture making." After they had tucked "Hollywood's best-guarded secrets into their mental pockets," those people would return home to the U.K. to pass that knowledge on to the English producers.[26]

In the summer of 1934, the Gaumont British Picture Corporation (GB) announced plans for its first organized "film invasion" of America. Jeffery Bernerd, GB general manager, sailed across the Atlantic to begin a "coast to coast distribution of British films throughout the United States." Company managing director C. M. Woolf added that GB planned to establish a chain of distribution centers and to take over key theaters throughout the country to exhibit British pictures. "We're going to make Hollywood sit up and take notice," Woolf predicted. "We will compete for directors and artists and pay as much as—I expect that in some cases we will have to pay even more than—the Americans." Gaumont then produced about 25 movies per year and were hoping at least 10 of that group would have U.S. success.[27]

News-week (as it was then spelled) also reported on Bernerd's arrival in New York as the "vanguard of the British invasion of the American film market." Bernerd planned to have salesmen in every key U.S. city who would show GB films to exhibitors. However, the report said, "[If] the complexities of the block-booking system make this impractical, Gaumont-British will hire or buy theatres of its own." The British firm planned to spend at least $200,000 on each of its pictures targeted at the U.S. Although News-week remarked there were no film import quotas in the U.S. and that the only customs problem was a tax of three cents a foot on exposed and developed negatives, it did not bother to elaborate on the barrier of block booking, mentioned indirectly, which was a much greater stumbling block.[28]

Almost a year after GB's announcement of its plans to tackle the U.S. market, reporter Frank Nugent wondered how they had fared. Michael E. Balcon, production head of the studio, told him box office results were "highly favorable" and the American response was "gratifying" overall.

While an increasing number of Hollywood stars had made pictures abroad for GB, Balcon admitted it was not as many as the English filmmakers would have liked.[29]

Gaumont British was formed in London in 1898 by the Frenchman Leon Gaumont to market films he made in France. In time he added English-made movies to the output with the firm still later becoming all English. At its peak, GB had 31 branches in the U.S., all staffed by Americans. Of the approximately 50 films the firm planned to produce in 1936, 16 were slated for release in the U.S. Most of those 16 were to have Hollywood players heading their casts.[30]

C. M. Woolf, film distributor for the London company British and Dominions (BD), complained in 1937, "We don't get into the U.S. market and I doubt if we ever shall." It was a comment that caused a U.S. film reporter to respond by saying that most trade opinion saw, "not antagonism in the States, but the inability of British producers for the greater part to level up to the entertainment standards demanded by the American public."[31]

Woolf's London remarks were quickly seconded there by two U.K. producers. Isidore Ostrer, a GB producer, said the U.S. would not accept U.K. movies and that unless America provided a better market for British films, GB might cease producing films and limit itself to cinema ownership. He pointed out that U.S. producers netted between $35 million and $50 million annually in the U.K. while British producers got about $1 million in America. Later that day, GB issued a denial saying Ostrer had been misquoted. In its clarification GB said it was merely considering "curtailment of its production costs due to inability to earn sufficient revenue in America at the present time." Independent British producer Julius Hagen admitted he had been misled by visions of a world market and had invested far more per production than he would have done for movies meant only for the U.K. market. He added that he had been doing well while producing British films for the British market but was always being told that if he spent more money on his productions, he would do well in the world market. However, he had found the U.S. market to be "unfriendly" to British movies. One of his features, *Scrooge*, cost $120,000 and grossed $165,000. Hagen said he had estimated a yield of $200,000 from the U.S. on *Scrooge* but had actually received $6,000.[32]

After some four years of operation in the U.S., the GB distribution and exchange operation there was officially liquidated in 1938. New arrangements were made and from then on all GB movies were to be handled in the States by 20th Century–Fox. From the time GB organized its American operation in September 1934 until it was wound up late in 1938, the gross sales totaled approximately $10 million. It was said that it had been evident to the trade for some time that the business of GB in America could not be established on a profit-making basis, and rumors of the demise of its American operation had circulated for a while. "Executives of GB distribution department, as long ago as 1937, intimated that regular, consistent sales of British films had proven unsuccessful as far as obtaining bookings was concerned, and predicted that drastic consequences would result if distribution here were continued with its own booking and sales staffs," said one account.[33]

In 1938, it was time for the U.K. to revise or renew its film quota system for imported product. That caused *Variety* to remark that the U.K. industry found that "British films seldom cross the Atlantic whereas U.S. films have two national markets." British producers were reported handicapped by their inability to command an adequate amount of capital. Only elaborate pictures could succeed at the box office in America, went the thinking, so the British had to spend $250,000 a picture, and at that cost they could not make a profit on it solely from the home market. Yet even after spending that amount of money on a film, the British producers found they still could not get it booked into the U.S. As a result, there were a lot of British film people who wanted to include some kind of film reciprocity clause in the new film quota system.[34]

In the end, reciprocity was not included in the new quota regulations. The original Cinematograph Films Act of 1927 ran for 10 years and was designed to revive a languishing U.K. picture business. Under that legislation it made foreign producers (that is, Hollywood) invest in a number of British-made movies according to how many of their own movies they planned to import into the U.K. Also, the statute made British cinemas program a certain percentage of British films on their screens—to try and ensure that all that enforced production in the U.K. by foreigners (Hollywood) did not get shelved and forgotten. However, that act made no allowance for quality with the result that enforced production earned the epithet "quota quickies." Exhibitors were angry and sometimes screened them when no one was at their venue—to meet the must-screen requirements without running the risk of irritating customers. Under the new 10-year act that became effective in 1938, a foreign producer had to produce, in 1938, 15 films in England for every 100 movies of his own he imported—rising to 30 per 100 over the 10 years of the statute. The new law contained no reciprocity clause and differed from the original act in just one respect: Each of those pictures produced in the U.K. by a foreign producer had to contain at least $37,500 in British studio labor costs. Since that labor cost represented about half of the total cost, it effectively meant that one of these enforced production pictures had to cost at least $75,000. Some extra credit was also available for spending more than that amount on a film, and for distributing those movies outside Britain.[35]

Despite the fact that the new act had no reciprocity clause and was little changed from the old act, *Variety* worried and speculated that in the coming years the number of British films shown in the U.S. would begin conservatively at 50, and go up to 80. Yet according to figures from the Hays office—a part of the MPPDA Hollywood cartel—in the previous 18 months a total of 52 British productions had come through.[36]

U.K. film executive Arthur Dent made a plea at the start of 1939 to have more British films screened in America, in an article he wrote for *Variety*. Noting the vicious circle U.K. producers were caught in, Dent declared, "British films do not get bigger and better because they do not get American distribution; and they do not get American distribution because they do not get bigger and better." Describing one of the reasons he saw for U.S. control, he said, "The key theatres are controlled by the major distributors and mutual booking keeps those theatres well supplied with product." This meant it was next to impossible for British films to do better than to get a few booking dates in America in independent houses; block booking kept most of the key houses out of bounds.[37]

Attempting to employ a Hollywood-style method in their productions continued to be a strategy used by foreign studios. The belief that movies had to be made in a certain way to break into the U.S. market was a belief held by Europeans and by Americans themselves. When a reporter wrote in 1932 that French producers were trying to break into the American market, he explained, "This means that productions intended for such distribution have to be especially made, changing not only the English versions, but also abandoning all local traditions in reference to technique and cost schedules." One thing that was said to mean was that a minimum of $250,000 had to be spent on each foreign film. At the time French movies were usually made at a cost of $40,000 to $50,000.[38]

Another report a year later said that the U.S. market was becoming more open-minded about European pictures because of a shortage in domestic production. Yet the evidence cited was about four European items then being bid on. Still, the Europeans were said to be poaching actors, writers, and directors; those who could help put "American atmosphere and feeling" into foreign productions. Major cinema chains were reported to be showing foreign films. However, the only tangible evidence cited in support of that contention was that the RKO Metropolitan cinema circuit was then screening *Maedchen in Uniform*, a title that had "broken down the chain bookers' general opposition to foreign-mades."[39]

A problem for producers and distributors of foreign films that arose in this period for the first time was whether to subtitle or to dub their movies for the American market. Film historian Tino Balio commented that by the mid–1930s, U.S. pictures were dubbed into practically all languages of the world. It was reported: "Europeans accept them easily and without argument because dubbing has made such exceptional strides technically that flaws are the exception rather than the rule today."[40]

Some international executives felt the time was then right to import dubbed foreign films into America; as late as 1936–1937 virtually all were subtitled. The first successful movie dubbed into English was the then current French release *Cloistered*—made in France, dubbed in New York and screened at art houses. After some success there, the title was given a somewhat wider release including a booking by RKO on its metro New York Circuit. No real test of dubbing had been made in America. Prior to *Cloistered*, several unsuccessful attempts had been made going back to one by UFA in 1932. All those efforts were said to have been of poor technical quality. Also, in at least one case, a British movie was dubbed into American English. To "expertly" dub a feature film in the mid–1930s reportedly cost around $10,000. That represented a significant cost increase for any foreign movie imported into America.[41]

One person who was not a fan of dubbing was actor Charles Boyer. He always inserted a clause in all his film contracts that his movies were not to be dubbed. His Hollywood pictures could not be shown in France dubbed nor could his French films be shown in the U.S. dubbed. Boyer was first brought to Hollywood by MGM to dub French movies, making *Big House* and some others in which he dubbed Wallace Beery's voice. According to one report: "His experience of those days makes him insist that no one must see his pictures with anyone else's voice emanating from the screen."[42]

Around this same time reporter Charles Jahrblum noted the problems involved in subtitling a film—a much cheaper process than dubbing. Those problems included interpreting and condensing with the subtitler not wanting to create too many or too few titles. As well there was the issue of spotting, where to put titles on a film frame so as not to obscure anything. To illustrate the range in the number of subtitles, the Slovak action movie *Jandsik* had just 200 titles while the French satire of the medical profession, *Dr. Knock*, had almost 700. *Escale* (French—*Under His Spell*) had 400 subtitles, which was about average.[43]

Journalist Mike Wear declared that foreign films had their best year in the U.S. in 1937, better than any year since prior to the Depression—although he provided no details of that success. French films were singled out as having improved their position, but Wear admitted their distribution was largely confined to New York cinemas, appearing in no other cities. Most distributors were releasing those French pictures with English subtitles and with the titling done in New York. Experiments in dubbing them into English had not been successful, said the distributors, "besides bringing them into direct competition with American-made films." They said the "Feeling is that it's too early for that."[44]

For the first time, the independent exhibitor who screened foreign films exclusively, or at least some of the time, became important to the foreign producer. While such venues did provide a small foothold for foreign movies in America, they also sometimes limited them to that small "ghetto" market—the art house. A 1931 editorial in the *New York Times* observed there were then about five foreign sound movies playing in New York— two French, two German, and one Italian. "Naturally, these entertainments are housed in the little theatres; differing in this respect from the successful foreign silent films which, with titles in English, have filled some of our biggest houses," explained the editor. Given the number of people in America who were foreign-born, the editor felt they should have a good future.[45]

By the end of 1931, there were estimated to be around 40 cinemas in the U.S. that played foreign films exclusively or part of the time. But not all were operated by Americans: UFA held the leases on five of those venues, Tobis operated eight of them. Mostly the foreign movies were distributed in the U.S. by independent companies; an article explained: "Paramount, Metro [MGM] and other American companies with foreign versions on their hands have practically given up trying to place these in America." Because of that, those movies got very little in the way of bookings from the major cinema chains. Loew's [MGM] used foreign films once a week in about 15 houses in metro New York; Publix (Paramount) used them occasionally for special performances while RKO screened them sometimes in five of its houses in Brooklyn and Queens. Among the cities represented in the list of 40 houses were the following; New York (8 venues), Newark (2), Jersey City (1), Boston (1), Philadelphia (2), Baltimore (1), Cleveland (1), Buffalo (2), Cincinnati (2), Chicago (1), Milwaukee (1), Pittsburgh (2), Portland, Oregon (1), Los Angeles (1), San Francisco (1), San Antonio (1), Houston (1), Galveston (1), Detroit (1), St. Louis (1), and Brooklyn (1).[46]

Toward the end of 1932, there were reported to be over 200 foreign film houses in America, a number that crashed with the coming to power of Hitler to such an extent that in the fall of 1933 there were only six such outlets in the country. With that initial anti-foreign feeling (apparently to all foreign pictures, not just German ones) wearing off, some 15 more opened within a few weeks of each other and 10 more prepared for an imminent reopening. That meant some 30 foreign movie houses were in operation at the end of 1933, or expected to be.[47]

The main American market for exhibiting foreign films has always been New York. In 1936 the 55th Street cinema was about the only art house near Times Square. Both the Filmarte and Belmont there started "first-run foreign policy in 1937 but the latter did not stick with that policy indicating even then," said an account, "that it was difficult to secure enough new draw films from the foreign producers." However, in 1938, in addition to 55th Street and Filmarte, the Normandie, Waldorf, Fifth Avenue, and World tried using first-run foreign. Before the end of that year, the Normandie had reverted back to American pictures while the Fifth Avenue was contemplating a return to its old second-run policy. A shortage of "suitable" first-run foreign had caused 55th Street to run revivals for a time, then to close altogether for a month before resuming first-run foreign.[48]

Nine persons were injured and audiences of 200 people, in each of three venues, were evacuated to the streets in May, 1939, when tear-gas bombs exploded in the Fifth Avenue, the 55th Street and the Thalia cinemas in New York. All the bombs exploded at about the same time—nine PM. All three of those theatres were screening foreign films at the time. Police were investigating a report by the Thalia cashier; she said she had heard a young man who entered the venue just before the bombing remark to a companion about "these damned foreign pictures." However, the authorities believed other causes were more probable. All the houses employed non-union operators and had been picketed some time earlier by Local 306 of the Motion Picture Operators Union, according to police information.[49]

When it came to explaining why foreign films had little U.S. presence in this period, the same sharp division took place as in an earlier time. Americans still raised the specter of poor quality foreign product while the Europeans did not subscribe to that idea, although their reasoning began to drift away from a direct attack on the structure and organization of the United States motion picture industry. One of the more sarcastic articles came from U.K. producer and cinema owner John Maxwell in 1929, in an American publication. "One of the best after-lunch jokes your film magnates tell here [London] is the story of how they want British films ... of how glad they themselves would be to release any British film which measured up," he wrote. "Then they use a measuring apparatus which has a naught at both ends." And being naïve and a "simple and kindly people," he wrote, the British took them at their word: At long last British movies would get a break in the U.S. "And they do, but on the way its spelling changes into 'brake.' Heavily applied," he said. In a mocking tone, Maxwell continued by saying that maybe the British producers had little cause to complain: "Laboring under the difficulties of lack of capital, poor studios, American outbidding for native talent, unrestricted imports and block booking we were not able to make films which looked like anything much but raw stock gone wrong."[50]

A year later the same John Maxwell complained that the American film public did not want British-made pictures. One reason he gave this time was that outside of the U.S. metro areas the British way of speaking was considered "almost a foreign tongue." Seconding that sentiment was Harold Auten, a distributor of U.K. movies in the U.S. In addition, in 1931, an American journalist acknowledged that while Britain had turned out some good films, "Broadway couldn't accept these pictures in large numbers because of the essentially sound local output."[51]

Leo Brecher, an independent U.S. distributor of foreign movies and operator of the Little Carnegie art house, traveled to Europe in 1932 to tell them what they were doing wrong and why the market for foreign films was so poor. Brecher said, "[The] greatest trouble lies in the fact that Europeans are prone to copy Hollywood. Americans don't want to see gangster pictures in German. They can do that just as well or better in Hollywood." He remarked, "What the American audience asks in foreign films is native color and novelty and originality."[52]

German film director Erich Pommer argued the European and American film markets were two separate fields, each demanding its own specialized product. A difference between public taste in those two geographic areas made "the hope for international appeal in the average picture necessarily futile," he explained. He felt pictures that were seeking an international market had to be made in three separate versions, English, French, and German. Also, he declared better movies were needed for both the U.S. and German markets; he added "They can cover both markets only if they are remade again in the country for which they are intended, with a cast familiar to that country." While Pommer looked forward to German pictures for America remade in the U.S., and vice versa, he made no comment on the existing American dominance of virtually all of the world's cinema screens—without going offshore to produce alternate versions.[53]

In a 1943 article in the London *Evening Standard* newspaper, well-known British director and producer Michael Balcon said that British films were virtually nonexistent in the U.S. Among other things, he charged that British movies were being blocked in the U.S. market by "a small group of industrialists who control American theatres." Those remarks caused fellow U.K. producer Alexander Korda to send a letter to the *Times* of London that argued Britons were just creating excuses for themselves and that British pictures, and all others, were assured the success they deserved. Korda had recently become the production chief in London of the U.S.–owned MGM studio there.[54]

Among those on the American side lining up to bad-mouth foreign productions were, once again, *Variety* reviews. In 1929, a controversy swirled around in the London *Daily Express*, conducted by columnist G. A. Atkinson, over the attitude of *Variety* in its criticisms toward foreign pictures in general and the British-made ones in particular. The U.K. press attacked *Variety* for panning U.K. movies exhibited in New York with more than deserved vigor; this tirade commenced some time earlier not only in the British trade press but also in Continental trade publications. When Atkinson wrote a column suggesting *Variety* was prejudiced toward foreign output, it caused the U.S. trade paper to send him a letter in response. In that reply Atkinson was "informed that no British-made picture within memory had made the first runs of America and that until any picture, domestic or foreign, was eligible to appear in the deluxes over here, it could not be listed as a first class picture."[55]

With respect to British producers and their pictures in America, Abel Green, editor of *Variety*, said, "They couldn't make a good silent in the past for America's first runs, and it looks equally negative, if not worse, on the talker end."[56]

Douglas Fairbanks, Jr., was a producer and actor set to make pictures in the U.K. for his own company, in 1936, for American release. Regarding the general problem of the distribution of U.K. films in America he said, "English-made pictures must break down the prejudice of 12 years of bad films with American exhibitors. They must sell the exhibitors to take them back into the theatres." Once those pictures were in the cinemas they would draw an audience, said Fairbanks, because the English realized they could no longer "make national pictures with customs and diversions only comprehensible to the British in them, as they used to do when English films got their bad name with American exhibs." Fairbanks argued the U.K. pictures then being produced were international; he said, "[They] consider the tastes of the American market with true maternal love."[57]

The first Japanese sound picture to reach the U.S. was *Kimiko*, which arrived in New York in 1937. It was reported that for years Japanese producers had wanted to export their films to America but those efforts had "been halted in the main by the inferior quality of the product."[58]

Based on the odd success of a foreign import—in this case *Mayerling*— a reporter stated, "[An] influx of weak European product is glutting the market." He added that many U.S. distributors of the foreign output had come to realize that a country could only be expected to produce one or two hits "in a year or 18 months time." While acknowledging that France and England had combined in the previous two years to produce 15 to 20 good box office pictures, he said, "England has had about 200 and France nearly 150 that no exhibitor in America would book except from hunger." Also noted was the fact that some ambitious French producers had personally come to the U.S. to sell their movies direct (bringing four to eight films with them), run up $5,000 or more in expenses for the trip and not got a single deal. That was bad, thought the reporter, because the European producers went home "squawking" about no chance being given to foreign films.[59]

When European production dried up during World War II, some of the distributors and exhibitors who had handled that product tried to fill the gap by using Spanish-language movies, mostly from Latin America, "but none measured up."[60]

Methods used by the Hollywood cartel to maintain its control and limit foreign film penetration of the home market to a negligible level included many of those started earlier that were by then well entrenched. Abel Green commented that the nationals of many foreign lands complained about Hollywood's "gold" absorbing and depleting the best stage and screen talent from each country, through poaching. Green agreed that Hollywood "raided some of the best talent."[61]

U.S. Department of Commerce employee George Canty, responsible for motion picture data, remarked in 1929 that American film fans liked foreign movies "very much." The reason more of them weren't exhibited was because of their low quality, he said, adding "Good foreign films are not easily obtained." That caused the *New York Times* to issue an editorial that declared: "He did not mention the fact that most exhibitors are compelled to take what the powers at Hollywood decree for them. 'Block booking' and other methods of placing the filmy flora and fauna of California had no place in his remarks."[62]

Writing about the early 1940s, Douglas Ayer said that independent cinema exhibitors who might have been expected to provide outlets for some independent U.S. production were often "forced" by members of the Hollywood cartel to accept onerous contract provisions as a condition for access to their movies. Those ordinary trade practices included block booking, clauses setting minimum cinema admission prices and, remarked Ayer, "clauses committing the exhibitor to a policy of not exhibiting foreign films. An exhibitor refusing to abide by these conditions might be boycotted by his primary source of films, the Hollywood studios."[63]

Another method used by Hollywood to stymie foreign penetration involved doing remakes. When the distribution of foreign product was at an especially low ebb (in 1933 in the wake of Hitler coming to power), some foreign movie agents were reduced to trying to sell their items to Hollywood for remakes. For example, Fox bought the German picture *Her Majesty Commands* for $30,000 outright and remade it in Hollywood as *Adorable*. Fox also bought the French film *The Dressmaker of Luneville* and redid it as *Dressed to Love*. Paramount purchased the German picture *Walzertraum* and remade it as *The Smiling Lieutenant*. In 1938 U.S. producer Walter Wanger had a hit with his *Algiers*, almost a shot-for-shot remake of Julien Duvivier's *Pepe le Moko*. One difference was that in the original Pepe committed suicide while in the American remake he was shot in the back by the police. A year later U.S. producer David O. Selznick, determined to make Ingrid Bergman an American star, imported from Sweden both the actor and her vehicle *Intermezzo*, for a remake.[64]

One unusual strategy adopted by the cartel was to increase the number of features it produced, to make it even less likely an exhibitor would book a foreign product or a U.S. independent picture. Reportedly, in 1935, some 600 movies were used by exhibitors yet only 360 were sold to them by the majors. Those cartel members, said a reporter, "were not inclined to permit the remaining 240 or more features to be supplied by foreign film companies and independents in 1936–1937." Fueling the extra demand from exhibitors was said to be the spread of the double feature program, "unknown" as recently as in 1927. Of the other 240 pictures, about 80 were foreign-made features. The account concluded, "[The] fact that there were 240 features sold exhibitors by competing companies is not what is making the majors increase their output but the extensive distribution accorded them."[65]

Domestic censorship of films in the 1930s first started to be an issue for foreign films then, and would grow worse in the future. Hollywood's MPPDA set up its own Production Code in 1930 to censor movies to be exhibited in America and to forestall any government intervention in the field of censorship. That is, Hollywood felt the lesser evil was to censor itself rather than do nothing and have a government agency step in to impose censorship. In order to have any chance of getting a film screened in a U.S. theater chain, in any important first-run house, that movie had to carry a seal of approval given by the Production Code Administration (PCA). Under this system scripts had to be submitted in advance of shooting to the PCA, as well as the later completed film. Movies without such a seal could still be exhibited but, practically speaking, were limited to art houses and small neighborhood houses. That is, their potential was extremely circumscribed. Subsequent to the establishment of the Hollywood

Production Code, the Roman Catholic Church in the U.S. set up, in 1933, a system of ratings based on their moral values. Ratings by this Legion of Decency ranged from positive endorsement to an outright condemnation. A film saddled with one of those dreaded C (condemned) ratings found itself to be a commercial liability in that most circuits and individual cinemas refused to book such a movie. Although neither censoring body had any legal force they were each very powerful.[66]

One reporter was moved to write in 1937 that love scenes and left-wing politics, contained in some foreign product, were giving art houses an edge in attracting business. Hot love scenes "edited out of all Hollywood productions as a peace gesture to the militant church censors of the U.S.A." were generating word-of-mouth publicity for the small art houses. The political themes from Europe found favor with some newspaper reviewers resulting, wrote the reporter, in "rave notices not artistically justified." Although this account seemed to imply foreign films benefited from the censoring process, in later years it would be shown that the opposite was the case; U.S. censorship was just one more factor that limited foreign penetration.[67]

During that same year, Joseph L. Breen, head of the West Coast PCA (sometimes just called the Hays Code after the MPPDA head Will Hays), spent three weeks in Europe. His principal activity there, in behalf of the MPPDA, was to try to line up film producers in England and France so that they would submit film scripts in advance of shooting to his office. While no detailed results of the trip were given it was reported that some English studios had already started to submit scripts for approval. Such advance submissions were particularly valuable since they could save the later cutting of scenes from a finished movie. In conclusion it was noted, "Breen's missionary campaign on behalf of the Hays organization was made to halt complaints of American producers that foreign-made features hit the market with certain censorable scenes remaining."[68]

The cartel's controlled distribution of movies was another Hollywood method of control. At the start of this period, Germany's largest film producer, UFA, had contracts with both Paramount and Metro (MGM) to distribute its product in America. However, those deals, each for a five-year period, did not turn out to be as beneficial as UFA hoped. Those American companies had the agreements so worded that they could pick and choose at will from UFA's entire output, with the result that only a "bare handful" of UFA pictures got a break in America through those channels. When those pacts expired in 1930, a reporter remarked that "little or no benefit was realized for the German company during the last years of its life." Over the last year of its agreement Paramount did not release a single UFA feature.[69]

When *Variety* said in 1930 that very little foreign product was coming to the U.S., it may have indirectly given the reason in another line in the article: It said, "Unless the foreign specials have something unusual most of the circuit picture experts won't even bother looking at them."[70]

A 1932 article said that foreign producers were "revolutionizing" their dealings with U.S. distributors by not selling their movies on a percentage basis but only doing outright sales. A good average price for complete American rights to a foreign film was put at $20,000 with a down payment, advance, of from $5,000 to $7,000. Nothing about that method was revolutionary; indeed it was a setback. Unsaid by the article was that selling on an outright basis was a sign of weakness on the part of foreign producers. Hollywood's cartel members sold nothing to distributors or exhibitors on an outright sales basis, and had not done so for decades.[71]

Reporting from London in 1933, Ernest Marshall was hopeful the backlash then in evidence against foreign movies would lead to an increase of British films exhibited in America. Speaking of recent contracts entered into by British producers with U.S. distributors, Marshall said that whether or not they would be successful would "probably depend entirely upon the quality of the British productions," which were "to be turned out with a special eye to the American public's taste." Those contracts also, wrote Marshall, "contain a wise proviso that the British-made pictures must be of a kind that will appeal to the American cinemagoer." Acknowledging that some cynics had always regarded such a proviso as a "snag" deliberately placed in the way of a successful British penetration of U.S. territory, Marshall nevertheless felt it was a wise provision since it was based on the "fact" that British producers had "not yet learned the lesson that what may be good fare for an English provincial audience is not necessarily agreeable to foreign tastes."[72]

French producers were questioning the U.S. market in 1939 as a real source of income, with their recent selling excursions to America having convinced them there was little prospect of getting any deals. False hopes had been raised by tentative deals outlined by U.S. distributors visiting France who promised that French movies would play at a first-run house on Broadway. France's trade press also raised false hopes by printing articles that eight cinemas in New York exclusively screened foreign first-run and were available to any good French film. However, by the time the articles appeared in print, six of those houses had either closed or had changed their screening policies to something other than first-run foreign.[73]

While the U.S. distributors were thinking about handling Latin American product during the World War II shortage of foreign production, they considered handling the product "throughout the Spanish-speaking

countries, and elsewhere when warranted," but not in the U.S. itself as they
felt the product was inferior. Illustrating the power of U.S. distributors and
their system was the fact that most Latin American producers did not have
the necessary set-up or organization to distribute outside the country of
origin. Consequently, they would rather make a deal with a U.S. distributor, "even if given lower terms, because of the advantages that go with
organized distribution."[74]

Speaking about the 1930s, Tino Balio commented on the many barriers European films faced as they tried to break into the U.S. market. For
one thing, "they had to wedge their way into the key theater chains—chains
that were controlled by the majors' distributors and were well supplied
with product as a result of reciprocal booking arrangements." As a result,
"few foreign films gained access to the mainstream exhibition market."[75]

Foreign films imported and shown in the U.S. during the period 1932
to 1936 were as follows: 1932, 141 (German 69, British 24, French 13, Italian 4, Spanish 2); 1933, 113 (German 48, British 22, French 10, Italian 6,
Spanish 4); 1934, 147 (German 59, British 33, French 7, Italian 1, Spanish
20); 1935, 190 (German 59, British 33, French 19, Italian 3, Spanish 38);
and 1936, 223 (German 76, British 37, French 14, Italian 19, Spanish 30).
Most of the Spanish films were not dubbed or subtitled. They were aimed
at the Spanish-speaking population of the U.S.A. and screened at ethnic
houses.[76]

If the number of foreign films exhibited yearly seemed to be fairly
large, the money earned was very much smaller since each foreign film
exhibited in the U.S. was on average, compared to a Hollywood release,
exhibited in a much smaller number of houses (having a smaller number
of seats) for a very much shorter period of time. For 1933 the British made
remittances to the U.S. of $26.5 million for screening their films. Against
that the British movies had receipts from abroad—from the entire world—
of $3 million.[77]

Statistics from the U.S. Commerce Department revealed that royalties derived by U.S. producers from the foreign showing of their movies
hit an all-time record in 1936 at $110 million; $85 million was received in
1935. Screenings of foreign pictures in America netted their foreign producers $6 million in 1936, $5 million in 1935.[78]

Hollywood's major producers (the MPPDA cartel of Columbia, MGM,
Paramount, RKO, 20th Century–Fox, United Artists, Universal, and
Warner Bros.) released a total of 336 features in the 1939-1940 year (five
of those were reissues, nine were foreign films); in 1940-1941 they released
324 pictures (seven reissues, eight foreign); in 1941-1942 323 movies were
released (seven reissues, nine foreign).[79]

World War II caused a serious decline in foreign films exhibited in the U.S., albeit from a small starting base. Production was almost entirely shut down in Europe with increased shipping problems bedeviling those that did try to cross the Atlantic. Commenting on that now disappearing U.K.–made share, a trade journalist remarked, "Several scores of English pictures a year were being imported and absorbed into the standard market. Almost invariably of low supporting-dual quality, they have in most cases been exhibited without identification as being made abroad." By the fall of 1939 it was reported that those few foreign items being shown were doing even less business than usual because people reject anything foreign "during periods of international difficulty."[80]

With Europe cut off as a supplier, some importers began to look at new and untapped markets. Reportedly they were surprised to find a lot of features being produced in those untapped markets: India 100, Philippines 40, Japan 120, Argentina 60, Mexico 40, Cuba 24. However, the difficulty was "that too many are not good enough or unsuited for the American market."[81]

Early in 1940 that shortage of foreign movies was called a false alarm, primarily because of the backlog of French pictures then in America but never actually released (some were two years old) and the resumption of filmmaking to some extent in the U.K. Importers were then saying they had enough foreign product on hand to last 12 to 24 months.[82]

Yet just three months later, another report contradicted the above by declaring there was a shortage of foreign product. The evidence was that art houses in New York, which had previously booked foreign movies exclusively, were booking U.S. films, even third-run items. However, six months later still another article insisted there was no shortage, again citing a backlog of two years' worth of foreign films, especially French ones.[83]

Herbert Rosener, the West Coast's major exhibitor and distributor of art films, thought that war news educated the public to places and peoples they never heard of before; he believed this would lead to an increase in foreign movie attendance after the war. Operating cinemas in Hollywood, San Francisco, Seattle, Portland (Oregon), Salt Lake City, Kansas City (Missouri), and Cleveland, he ran what was called the "nearest thing this country has ever had to a foreign film chain." Although he was certain of a good future for foreign pictures, he felt their exhibition would never reach beyond the "intimate exhibition" stage; that is, they would always be stuck in the art house ghetto. After screening thousands of movies from all over the world, Rosener said he had yet to find a single one that "could picture anything anywhere near equal to the American way."[84]

Early in 1941, the Independent Theatre Owners Association drafted a resolution and made representation to the U.S. State Department in Washington against the showing of German and Italian films in America on the grounds they were only propaganda and that those nations did not allow American product to be screened in their own territories or in ones they occupied. Mostly these cinemas had been screening movies that were three- to four-year-old reissues.[85]

When the U.S. formally declared war against Germany in December 1941, all 12 of the cinemas throughout the country using German films before open hostilities began either shut down or changed their screening policies. Of those that stayed open, most turned to programming Hollywood reissues and U.S. independent output. A day after war was declared, agents of the U.S. Treasury Department raided and took over the UFA office in New York, shutting it down. Five of those 12 outlets were located in New York. One closed down but the other four returned to exhibiting German movies by early 1942, after business fell off with their changes in policy. The spectacle of theaters playing movies made in a country with which America was at war caused numerous protests and was called to the attention of the FBI.[86]

During a visit to America in 1945, J. Arthur Rank, Britain's leading film mogul, declared that U.S. GIs in the U.K. were helping to establish British film stars. Players drawing the most response from U.S. servicemen in England were those who would be established most quickly as stars in movies aimed at the worldwide market, especially the American one. Saying all the right things on his visit, Rank told reporters that if British pictures were not successful in the U.S. it was the fault of the British rather than that of the U.S. audience. At a New York dinner in his honor, hosted by MPPDA head Will Hays, leaders of the film industries of both countries stressed the importance of the free flow of movies into all nations of the postwar world, because they were able to "promote international understanding."[87]

Business Week noted that Rank, who was Britain's largest producer and also head of the British Motion Picture Producers Association, tried to promote reciprocity on his visit and took a general "good-neighborly approach" to British and American film relationships. More willing to be blunt than Rank, *Business Week* stated that one of the big problems for British producers in getting their films screened in America was "a lack of enthusiasm on the part of U.S. distributors."[88]

Fortune magazine ran a lengthy six-page article on Rank and his organization in the wake of his visit. Striving to be diplomatic at all times, he had handlers (U.S. film executives) who told him how to behave on his six-week visit. One result was that "Rank adopted himself to the line that the

British pictures had been bad and that he had no doubt whatever that when he made good pictures, as he intended to do, American exhibitors, even those controlled by the big producers, would be glad to show them." *Fortune* stated, "Everybody in Hollywood insists that British pictures have never been excluded from the American market—they have just been poor movies. With this Rank agrees, at least publicly. And he pretended to agree that if his pictures are suitable for the American market, American exhibitors will show them out of self interest." If Rank believed it, there were few in America who agreed because, said the business publication, Hollywood thought British producers could not "get away from ingrained Britishisms and use worldwide-appeal formulas even if Hollywood teaches them."[89]

Another British producer of note who adopted the same approach as Rank was Alexander Korda. In an interview with a London newspaper late in 1945, he said British movies were still having no real success in the U.S. He felt that was because they were still making the same old mistakes: "The onus must be on the maker, not the customer." Also, he felt British producers were not choosing the right subjects or using the right technique.[90]

As this period ended the situation appeared bleak for foreign films in America. World War II had reduced the European film's U.S. screen presence from negligible to something less. Outside of Western Europe no other country had any film presence in America. War ravaged economies in Europe indicated it might be some time before they could rebuild their motion picture industries. In 1944 Hollywood executives agreed that British films were essentially non-existent in the U.S. One studio executive commented, "[Distributors] don't want to buy English pictures made in England, and seldom do." At the same time *Variety* editorialized that it was fed up with British complaints; they had been singing the same old song for decades. The reason U.K. pictures got little distribution in the U.S., said the editor, was simple: "[T]hey're not good enough." Declaring it had no more patience for any more such complaints—since the obvious solution was to make better pictures—the publication demanded that the British "stop complaining."[91]

4

A Rank Attack,
1946–1949

And 99% of British films, no matter how much critics
praise them, do not appeal to average American audiences.
—*Herb Golden, 1947*

Arkansas exhibitors, for instance, ... couldn't possibly be
expected to understand British speech.
—*Anonymous U.S. film executive,*
1948

Stix still nix British pix.
—*Variety, 1947*

This brief period was noteworthy for the start of a resurgence in European filmmaking, beginning with the Italian neo-realist school in the immediate postwar years. Its influence soon branched out to other European nations and lasted for some time. However, it had only a very slight impact on foreign film exhibition in America. In the U.S., the postwar 1940s belonged to a British producer who launched the most organized and best financed attempt to dramatically increase a foreign screen presence in America. What made the J. Arthur Rank organization's attempt different was that it was one of the wealthier film production studios in the world, outside of the U.S. Despite its formidable structure the Rank effort ultimately failed.

In June 1946, Rank was in the process of setting up a U.S. unit to try and sell some of the producer's output of about 50 films that year (18 of which were being handled by two American independent distributors). That unit was headed by Lawrence J. McGinley, who had no sales force under him but personally tried to make direct deals with cinemas in towns of over 150,000 in population for extended runs on selected Rank product. McGinley hoped to make deals similar to that made by United Artists for the Rank movie *Henry V* at a New York cinema: The house was rented on a flat rate basis plus a small percentage of the gross. Also, the terms called for the distributor to pay for the theater personnel and advertising (all of these particulars were opposite to how deals were normally done; this type of deal put all the risk on Rank, little or none on the cinema. When the Hollywood majors distributed, the risk was either shared roughly equally or disproportionately placed on the exhibitor). For each of its "prestige" pictures, Rank hoped a minimum of 60 cinemas could be lined up.[1]

Rank had been trying vigorously to penetrate the U.S. market for about a year at that time and was said to be having some success. Noted by one reporter was that until that time the potential of the Anglo pictures, with only rare exceptions, "were frittered away in the art houses and smaller circuits because of Yank exhibitor indifference." One breakthrough film was *Caesar and Cleopatra* (Rank—United Artists as distributor) which grossed $2 million, an unheard of sum said to have been due at least partly to expensive exploitation. Due to such buildups United Artists was able to obtain up to 47 percent of the box office receipts from exhibitors—"an unprecedented high for a foreign film." The start of the intense build-up campaigns was reported to go back to the release of the *Seventh Veil*, which film executives acknowledged "had to be practically given away in many situations." Officials with Rank said that film was used as a "battering ram" for movies coming up behind it.[2]

Some 20 British movies were screened in America in 1946, with a gross of $8.5 million in rentals from U.S. cinemas, the best year ever. During 1945, only five U.K. pictures played U.S. screens, taking about $2 million. Besides the top grossing *Caesar*, other notable releases, each grossing $1 to $2 million, were *Notorious Gentleman*, *Wicked Lady*, *Seventh Veil* and *Henry V*, all from Rank. Of the 20 British releases, 13 were produced by Rank.[3]

Near the end of 1946, U.K. producer Alexander Korda wrote a long article condemning Hollywood and the idea often promoted by the cartel that the screen must be free (of quota restrictions, tariffs, and so forth). Korda cited American film columnist Bosley Crowther who argued the screen was not fully open to U.K. pictures. Crowther said that whether

Caesar and Cleopatra (U.K., 1945, Vivien Leigh). One of the many U.K. films made by the J. Arthur Rank organization and released in the U.S. in the immediate post-war years as Rank tried to dent the American market.

British films would ever have a free and generous showing on the American screen did not depend only on their quality or on the favor they would find with the American public if they actually made it to viewers. Crowther warned, "The American screen is too tightly organized to offer such a freedom for any number of British films and, frankly speaking, the Hollywood film industry is not generous enough to offer a really liberal opportunity for British films in America." Crowther also criticized "a Hollywood which talks of the freedom of the screen, tells of reciprocity, of exchange of talent, but does precious little about it."[4]

Indicating that the few 1946 articles abut the breakthrough of British films (especially Rank's) in America and their surging popularity were greatly exaggerated or premature were the events at the very end of 1947. Stafford Cripps (British Board of Trade president) threatened to impose further restrictions on U.S. films in the U.K.; his conditions were: "[T]hey improve in quality and ... English pictures receive more U.S. playing time."

That threat came on the heels of the British Film Producers' Association recommendation for more stringent quotas. Journalist Herb Golden said that U.S. film executives, "after taking a conciliatory attitude toward the British industry for months," were greatly annoyed by those comments in London. Those film executives "readily admitted" the justifiability of some of the British complaints and had been taking steps to improve the situation, "such as urging exhibs to give a better break to British product." They resented, however, what they saw as misinterpretations of their actions by government leaders in London and a patent lack of understanding—willful or not—of the competitive situation in America. Some U.S. industry leaders attributed that threatening U.K. behavior to a number of more global factors: "[T]he British are using big talk to compensate for an inferiority complex as they readjust themselves to the possibility of becoming a 'secondary' nation." Following the remarks by Cripps, U.S. producer Samuel Goldwyn said, "If British producers would stay away from Parliament and concentrate on making good pictures, they'd be better off."[5]

Golden reported that especially irksome to America was the unwillingness of the British to understand the operation of free enterprise in the States as it applied to films. Pointed out was that no one was more international in outlook than a U.S. exhibitor "if he can make money at it." But no exhibitor would screen a movie that did not attract an audience, said Golden, adding, "And 99% of British films, no matter how much U.S. critics praise them, do not appeal to average American audiences. It all goes back to the same old thing—make good pictures and they'll find plenty of playing time." Also, the Americans were angered by an idea the British had "that what goes into U.S. houses can be controlled from the top, or by any other criterion than boxoffice." U.S. film executives were also infuriated by statements such as the one Cripps made in which he declared that Hollywood earned in Britain "at least 10 to 20 times the amount earned by British films in America," despite the fact that the States had at least four times as many filmgoers as found in the U.K. Golden seemed to feel he refuted that by noting that in 1946 the U.S. took about $80 million out of Britain while the reverse flow was $8.5 million, "less than 10%."[6]

Back from a six-week European trip, in April 1947, Universal's foreign chief Joseph Seidelman warned that the U.S. film industry faced a crisis in Britain and possible curtailment of remittances, unless it did something about improving the position of U.K. pictures in the States. Conditions were so serious that the Bank of England ordered the J. Arthur Rank organization to report to it weekly on its foreign receipts, especially those from the U.S., Seidelman said. He declared the U.S. firms had it within their power to forestall serious action by allocating increased playing time in American cinemas to generate more dollars for the U.K. According to Golden some 5,000 to 6,000 cinemas in the U.S. had never screened a single British film.[7]

A New York press conference in 1947 was attended by many U.S. film executives, including MPPDA head Eric Johnston (Johnston took over as head of the MPPDA in 1945. That same year it was renamed the Motion Picture Association of America—MPAA). There, J. Arthur Rank diplomatically stuck to the idea that slow but constant progress in establishing British movies in the U.S. market was taking place. Getting testy at one point, Rank lashed out and said, "We have got to have much more playing time. That starts with the affiliated circuits [cinemas owned by the cartel members], and when we have started with them, we can go down the line to the subsequent runs." One in attendance was Universal executive vice president Matty Fox, who said Universal had set a target of 50 cinemas for the foreign product it handled but was then stymied in meeting that goal because exhibitors "made a lot of money in the past five years and were asking exorbitant prices for their theatres."[8]

A few days later Nate Blumberg, president of Universal, commented on the progress of British pictures in American cinemas. Admitting, "It's far from good," he went on to declare, "Exhibitors must be made to realize that their welfare and the welfare of the American film industry depends a good deal on their giving British films a fair break here."[9]

All the pressure applied by the Rank organization seemed to pay off in 1947, when a guarantee of $10 million in U.S. theater bookings was given by the five major circuits to J. Arthur Rank, plus another anticipated $2 million from the independent exhibitors. One reporter felt the agreement served to accentuate "the continuing lack of public and exhibitor acceptance of foreign films." A *Variety* correspondent observed, "Most sections of the country—in fact, virtually every section except the metropolitan centers along both coasts—are continuing to exhibit the same time-old allergy to foreign films which were evidenced before the war." In general, said the account, foreign product had made its only real penetration in such areas as New York, Los Angeles, San Francisco and Boston that had cosmopolitan populations: "The Midwest and South continue to be as much citadels of isolationism in their picture tastes as in their politics."[10]

That Rank pact with the majors for $10–$12 million in theater bookings meant each of the five major exhibitor chains (Paramount, 20th Century–Fox, Loew's [MGM], Warner Bros., and RKO) would average $2 million each, although the larger chains (the first two listed) might do a little more while the other three might do a little less. One thing that may have influenced the arrangement of the pact was that Paramount, Fox and

RKO product was used in the U.K. mainly by two large cinema chains, Rank's Odeon and Gaumont British. Warner said it would cooperate itself because it was in the best interests of the film industry and the approximately $75 million the U.S. majors took out of the U.K. each year. Rank reiterated that the exercise was not just about money but rather about getting playing time in "important American cinemas."[11]

Around that time figures released in the U.K. Parliament by Chancellor of the Exchequer Hugh Dalton revealed the U.S. motion picture industry had taken out of the U.K. an average of $68 million annually over the previous three years. That figure differed from the American film trade's generally accepted $75 million number.[12]

Very near the end of 1947, it was revealed that the Rank deal that was hoped to yield some $10 million per year to the U.K. producer had fallen far short of that goal at the end of its first year—$4 million was estimated to be the actual take. In explaining the shortfall, a journalist said the prevailing feeling was that there was a "decline in quality" in the movies after a "fast start" and subsequent failure of British films to make any headway in small towns and in neighborhood, independent houses. Since distribution fees plus advertising and print costs ate up about half of the U.S. rentals, Rank officials thought the $4 million figure was a "fairly generous estimate."[13]

In a media interview early in 1948, J. Arthur Rank implied the U.S. distributors had not worked hard enough to sell his movies in America. He stood by his opinion that his company's films were among the finest in the world and that the U.S. would do well with them if they were screened.[14]

British pictures continued to do poorly. Eric Johnston said, in July 1948, that his previous estimate of $7 million as the figure British films would do in the U.S. that year had to be revised. He said there might be no net earnings whatever. Johnston also said that foreign earnings of U.S. movies in 1946 were $120 million.[15]

The battle became more intense when the British started selling their movies to U.S. television. This was in part due to the frustration of not being able to break into cinemas in what they deemed to be a satisfactory way. On the other hand, selling to television enraged the MPAA cartel members as they all had a gentleman's agreement that they would not sell to the new medium; that is, they would not help out a competitor and a threat to their existence, as was the somewhat exaggerated view of the challenger at the time. U.K. producer Alexander Korda sold 24 movies to New York television station WPIX for video broadcasting. It was a move that irritated American independent exhibitors. Ed Lachman, president of a

New Jersey exhibitor organization, declared the move wouldn't "cement relations between American exhibitors and English film distributors." Lachman said American theater owners had formerly indicated a willingness to go along with the general industry plan to give more playing time to British movies but Korda's action put a different light on the situation because it assisted in undermining U.S. cinema owners by building up television competition.[16]

Supporting Rank's attack against American film companies for purportedly closing their doors to British pictures, Korda threatened further reprisals through television against U.S. theaters. Korda said that all British producers would sell to television outlets in the U.S. if American cinemas continued their refusal to give playing time to Anglo films. "Both Rank and I will turn our film over to television if we cannot get theatre bookings," Korda declared. "We will see how the American picture industry likes that." Agreeing he would not get much money from television sales compared to the theatrical potential, Korda argued video sales would give British producers some money since they "were virtually getting nothing." The films Korda had licensed to television were old ones that had all had a theatrical release (in America); he began threatening to license new (never screened in U.S. cinemas) ones. "The activity of a small group of fanatics is not what is keeping British product from American screens," explained Korda. "The real Sons of Liberty are the presidents of the American [major] companies."[17]

Later in 1948, J. Arthur Rank asserted there could be no peace or real understanding between the British film industry and Hollywood until British pictures received "reasonable playing time in the United States." Eric Johnston happened to be in London about a week later. In response to Rank's comments, Johnston met with reporters and strenuously denied that American exhibitors were combining to limit the screen time of U.K. movies in the States.[18]

For the fiscal year ending on June 1, 1949, British gross film earnings in the U.S. were about $2.5 million. After taking out expenses, about half of that sum was available for remittance to England.[19]

Rank, which produced half of all British films, found itself in deep financial trouble in 1949. Over the course of several months the company sold some of its studios and laid off 1,800 workers, 35 percent of its staff. Some observers argued the producer had grown too quickly, moving from 25 films a year to a production schedule of 60 pictures. Rank planned to scale back to make only 12 movies in 1950. Thus, the aggressive attempt to crack open the American market also had to be drastically reduced.[20]

French producer Sacha Gordine, in the U.S. for a visit in 1947, doubted that French filmmakers planned to join the British in an invasion of the U.S. picture market. He declared the French industry was suffering from a severe shortage of equipment and a lack of capital and was in no position financially to make a pitch for American cinema outlets. Gordine pointed out the British push was led by J. Arthur Rank, "a very rich man"; with movies made in the same language, it was also easier to find a market in America than it was for French producers whose U.S. exhibition was restricted to a limited number of art houses. Ilya Lopert, a U.S. distributor of French movies, refuted claims from overseas producers that their movies were getting the brush-off in the States. Lopert declared, "Since foreign films are still limited in their mass appeal, it's necessary that they operate under low overhead."[21]

Later that year, importer Noel Meadow argued that more French films were then being screened in the U.S. and were more popular, compared to the 1930s. Meadow argued that until 1933, French and German movies were about equal in popularity but the German-made product died out after the Nazis came to power. However, the audience for French films remained confined to those who spoke the language and, to a lesser extent, those who were discontented with Hollywood fare. "They combined to form an audience of insignificant size," said Meadow. In those days there were said to be just 10 houses that showed French product (either exclusively or some of the time—in New York, Chicago, San Francisco, and Los Angeles). But in 1947, said Meadow, there were 25 outlets in New York and close to 90 in total in the country.[22]

Well-known film critic Bosley Crowther reviewed a few French pictures in a 1948 column and was disappointed with them all. He yearned nostalgically for what he called the lost golden age of French films, which he dated to the period from the mid to the late 1930s.[23]

The first foreign film in America to break the $1 million in gross receipts mark was the Italian film *Open City*, which reached that figure in 1946. Previous high was the approximately $225,000 garnered by the French-made *Mayerling* a few years before the war. *Open City* achieved that record while playing only at art houses. That movie was brought to the U.S. by Rod Geiger, who reportedly paid just $3,000 for the U.S. rights, "a usual figure," according to one account.[24]

Illustrating the problem foreign films had in America was the fact that no one seemed to know just how many venues—art houses—there were to potentially accommodate them. Sometimes the numbers used were quite dissimilar. According to Oliver A. Unger, vice president in charge of sales for Distinguished Films (a distributor of foreign product), 1944 marked a low point for foreign films with just eight outlets in the nation. But in the

Open City (Italy, 1946, Maria Michi). **First foreign film released in America to break the $1 million in gross receipts mark.**

spring of 1947, Unger said, such product could be found in 200 houses (not all exclusively screening foreign-made items).[25]

When Americans explained in this period why the foreign fare was not making much headway, they tended to be more tactful than in earlier periods. In the wake of lower than expected U.S. earnings for Rank product, all the heads of the Hollywood cartel-member producers vehemently denied there was any discrimination against British films. In response to requests from Rank, they gave suggestions on how the Anglo imports could be improved for the U.S. market. A primary point made, said a reporter, was that the British films were "still not intelligible enough for Yank audiences. Several company prexies declared that it took them 25–30 minutes of a British pic before they could understand what was being said." One studio president reportedly said, "We can understand perfectly what Winston Churchill says, but not your actors. They don't talk at all like Churchill." Another company president asserted that the dialog in British pictures must be entirely unintelligible to "Arkansas exhibitors, for instance, who couldn't possibly be expected to understand British speech." Two other suggestions were given to Rank. One was that British movie stars still needed further buildup with the American public. Second suggestion was that U.K. producers "should lay off the longhair themes aimed at attracting intellectuals and play for the great mass of filmgoers."[26]

A month later in 1948 another report commented on the box office decline of foreign movies. Experts were said to have declared that experience had demonstrated that unless the foreign picture had "a strong sex hook on which to hang some razzle-dazzle exploitation or some other extraneous angle which makes it typical and atypical," then it would not do well at the box office.[27]

A 1949 article said that the critical praise that foreign productions had received was ended. "The local shouts of praise which most American critics have been sounding for the past five years for almost any foreign film— in contrast to the Hollywood variety—have died away to a whisper," went the story. Still, the reporter argued that some critics were still writing as though first-rate foreign product was still coming through and accused them of "living in the past." Current foreign fare just wasn't very high in quality.[28]

Hollywood's censorship added to the problems of foreign movies trying to get screening time in America. It was another method by which the cartel exercised an unofficial control over that product. Joseph Breen, the head of the MPAA's censoring arm, the Production Code, returned home from the U.K. after 10 days of meeting with British film producers and "endeavoring to set them straight about the Hollywood industry's Production Code." He was invited to England by the British Film Producers Association. While he claimed to have been "cordially" received by the London film people, he did admit the British press "was not quite as friendly as the producers."[29]

Less than a year later, any effects of the Breen visit seemed to have worn off because it was reported that British movies were having a "hard time" at the Breen Production Code office. Mentioned in the report were seven British movies that were held up because changes were demanded by the Breen office before the films could receive a seal. Winning that seal was the only way a film (U.S. or foreign) had a chance to get at least theoretical access to the bulk of America's cinemas—albeit a very, very slim chance for foreign product.[30]

A 1947 letter to the editor of the *New York Times* from William C. Powell was about cuts made to three British films screened at that time in New York. Cuts which, he said, were unnecessary and destroyed some of the films' credibility and continuity. Apparently he had first seen those movies in the U.K. Powell was warning readers to keep that in mind when seeing British films. At the end of that letter the editor added a note that read: "Scenes are frequently cut out to shorten the running time of a picture or to quicken its pace."[31]

As always, it was Hollywood's control of the distribution system that was most important. Abel Green, editor of *Variety*, reported a worry in 1946 that if more British film screenings did not happen in the U.S. the foreign market might inflict retaliatory measures. "It's for that reason every local film-maker concedes that the Yank exhibitor must open his datings to foreign product, particularly British, because of the language affinity," Green wrote. He was being ingenuous here as the Hollywood majors were the distributors and owners of many of the cinema chains themselves. The problem was rooted in the MPAA cartel, not the exhibitors per se.[32]

Later that year critic Bosley Crowther argued in favor of more screen time for British movies in the U.S. After describing a number of them, such as *Henry V* and *Caesar and Cleopatra*, as good quality, he noted that even those ones did not get the full type of booking the American screen could provide. "The American movie-going public has a right to see pictures of this sort—literate and beautifully acted," Crowther concluded.[33]

When Rank made its big push to expand in America, it had a few distribution deals with U.S. distributors, both independent and part of the majors. Mostly, however, it tried to do its own distribution. Deals with American firms were always for a very limited number of films and allowed the distributor to pick and chose from Rank output, even to the point of handling no items. Rank's deal with Universal (to distribute its product) made it mandatory for the U.K. producer to spend a minimum of $1 million on any movie that Universal was to distribute in the U.S.—an amount much higher than Rank usually spent on a film.[34]

Arthur Jarratt, an associate of Korda's and managing director of British Lion Films, returned to London after a visit to the U.S. in 1946. Back home he said Hollywood's moguls had been singing the praises of British movies but the "plain truth" was that the films themselves were not getting anything near the proper distribution in the States. Jarratt declared the major cinema chains were not booking the pictures all over America as they did their own productions. Urging the employment of more stars known to Americans as a necessary move, Jarratt added a reminder that Hollywood was "feeding the complacent American nation escapist pictures" while U.K. movies went "all out for realism."[35]

Allegations, such as those Jarratt raised, that British films played small houses for small money while being shunned by the major theater chains were commonly voiced; they were hotly denied by U.S. film executives. Universal executive vice president Matty Fox claimed, contrary to common belief, "A British picture is no harder or easier to book than its American equivalent. Moreover, we get the same rental terms. We, therefore, deny that there's any discrimination."[36]

In 1947, 20th Century–Fox announced it had made a distribution deal to release in the U.S. all production turned out by Alexander Korda over the coming four years—expected to total 14 films. Fox president Spyros Skouras said it was the most important releasing contract the firm had ever made. Skouras added that the restrictive laws that the British government was threatening to impose against the importation of U.S. pictures into the U.K. "did not and would not affect in any way operation of his agreement with Korda."[37]

For the year 1948, industry executives on both sides of the Atlantic agreed that remittances to Britain from U.S. screenings were no more than $5–$6 million. Distribution costs, and other expenses, meant that remittances home were at most 50 percent of the U.K. film receipts (the distributor/producer share of the box office take—itself roughly 50 percent). Rank's expensive *Caesar and Cleopatra* took $2 million in rentals but the estimate was that only $500,000 of that amount reached England after distribution fees, print costs and $500,000 in advertising expenses were deducted. A reporter observed that the five biggest major Hollywood producers, all of which owned a lot of cinemas, were of the opinion that every time a U.K. picture was booked into one of their chains it meant that a Hollywood film had to be bypassed. "Certainly, the theatre-owning companies are not going to sidetrack their own product to inferior houses and dates for a fractional cut in increased British monies," he argued. "If the affiliates don't go big for British films, it's a cinch that the indie exhib isn't going to extend himself for the imports."[38]

In a switch from its previous practice, Universal, from July 1948 onward, planned to aim its advertising and publicity campaigns on all Rank pictures it released in the States strictly at a few key cities, leaving smaller centers to generate interest through word-of-mouth. That decision was reached after Universal publicity chief Maurice Bergman met with Rank executives in London. Arguing they all realized the best market for U.K. films lay in the big cities, Bergman said, "[Universal] will spend less money in plugging the Rank product but hopes to get better results by spending in a more selective way." The new system, he said, did not mean that Rank product was to be slotted into art houses. Because a market was there, declared Bergman, Universal would "no longer try to conceal the fact that a picture was made in England."[39]

Other changes were imposed by Universal. Instead of a mandatory minimum of 12 Rank movies being peddled on a purely commercial basis during 1948–1949, as previously agreed, Universal set up three brackets for its share of Rank's product. Reportedly, that was over the opposition of Rank. Universal reserved for itself the right to reject any Rank movie if it did not feel the item would do acceptable business. As for those that it accepted, the company had the sole discretion to determine whether the picture would go into general release or into one of two different special handling units—aimed mostly at art houses. Final decision on how a British import would be handled rested with William A. Scully, Universal's distribution vice president, with no input or veto right held by Rank.[40]

Jack Warner explained the distribution system in 1949, as it applied to the majors. Although he did not directly mention foreign films in America, his discussion of the system made it clear there was little room for outsiders. Looking at the gross receipts of a Betty Grable movie and *The Treasure of the Sierra Madre*, Warner announced that "art was out." He said, "In America a picture must be distributed before it is made. Without a guarantee of distribution at first-run houses (virtually indispensable for a wide release afterward) no agent will let his top star sign a contract, no bank will lend money, no picture will be made. The exceptions are negligible in number, if not in quality." Both producers and the moviegoing public, Warner added, were used to cinema runs of about four weeks at most in the "metro palaces" that functioned as showcases, after which came simultaneous exhibition at perhaps 20 neighborhood houses (in the same city) for three days or a week, and then shorter runs in towns and villages. When this account was written, of all the movies playing in New York and Boston, only one picture in each city had been playing for over three weeks. In Los Angeles there were none that had been screening for over two weeks. Under such a system, Warner continued, there was no time for a film to build an audience. However, Warner admitted that considerable experience in England, and some in America, indicated that even if a picture dropped below the profit mark in its fifth or six week, it could recover on the strength of word-of-mouth publicity to run half a year. Be that as it may, Warner emphasized that the American system, geared to rapid change, could not "wait for this to happen." The majors (and many independent producers) were committed to the manufacture of average pictures for average runs. "The releasing system is complex and firmly rooted, and each organization would have to set up a separate, in part competitive, unit to handle the kind of picture that requires long runs," said Warner, "at single theaters, without immediate distribution to the chains."[41]

Distribution provided headaches for foreign producers, and so did the exhibitors. According to Robert B. Wilby, head of the Atlanta-based Wilby-Kincy cinema circuit, J. Arthur Rank was making a serious mistake in trying to "pressure" U.S. exhibitors into playing his films. Wilby said the only way Rank could hope to get American distribution for his movies was to make pictures with international appeal. He based his claims of pressure on what he heard on a recent trip to London, at a dinner for film executives from both sides of the Atlantic, when Rank complained about a lack of British penetration in the States. Paramount owned 50 percent of the Wilby-Kincy circuit. As for the tactic of shaming U.S. exhibitors into playing English pictures Wilby sneered, "It's the one thing you can't do to an exhibitor—shame him."[42]

A 1947 account explained that Metro International's (MGM) program of importing "top" foreign pictures for general Metro release in the U.S. was "running into many difficulties, chief among which [was] the antipathy of most exhibs, in the key cities as well as small towns, against playing foreign product." Metro initiated the strategy as a way of cementing relations with foreign producers, by proving to them that a U.S. market actually existed for their product. Another hope Metro held was that its strategy would forestall any further attempts by foreign nations to impose legislative restrictions on the import of U.S. pictures. According to a reporter, "Most exhibs are averse to booking the films on the grounds the only place for them is in the art houses." Metro had, at that point, released only three foreign movies with exhibition limited almost completely to art houses, "and not that many of those."[43]

When Paramount president Barney Balaban stressed the need for exhibitors to screen more British product, at a meeting of exhibitors, several of them reportedly told him they would rather play a good American B film than a top British film anytime.[44]

Nevertheless Balaban declared that Paramount's theatre circuits and those of its partners would give more playing time in the future to British films, although he stressed the fact that Paramount could not dictate policy to its partners. Robert Benjamin, president of Rank's U.S. organization emerged from a meeting with Balaban also convinced that Paramount would increase its bookings. Robert Wilby, one of Paramount's southern partners, apparently had a change of heart and pledged support on behalf of the exhibitors after Balaban's speech. Independent circuit operators were less than enthusiastic. According to Harry Brandt, president of Brandt cinemas, there was "no kind of market now for the run-of-the-mill British picture." Any British film had to be "very good" or its star well-known enough to rate heavy playing time, Brandt observed. A journalist concluded his report by saying, "[The] best bet for the Britishers, it's believed, is a greater number of American names in the pictures, so that U.S. audiences may become accustomed gradually to the British stars who appear with the U.S. stars."[45]

Even the world political situation worked against U.K. pictures in American houses. In 1948, a radical wing of the Zionist movement launched a boycott in America against British films. Said to be a successful campaign the boycott drive was sponsored by a group called the Sons of Liberty. Tactics of the boycott included sporadic picketing of exhibitors. As far as the two major circuits in Gotham were concerned the boycott was 100 percent effective since RKO "was compelled to pull" Korda's *An Ideal Husband*, distributed by Fox, while Loew's (MGM) had "not played a British film for many months." Independent cinemas had also reportedly pulled or postponed U.K. movies. Milton Eisenberg, research director of the Sons of Liberty, said the boycott would continue until the U.K. halted "their instigation of the Arabs in Palestine." Also, Eisenberg claimed five major metropolitan circuits, which he refused to name, had agreed to cooperate.[46]

One circuit owner won over to the group's point of view was Harry Brandt, who declared he would not book a British picture into any of the 140 theaters he controlled until Great Britain dropped its "pro–Arab actions." Said Brandt, "Any exhibitor wants to play what the patrons want and there is no question now that the patrons are definitely set against British films." Brandt explained he had been approached by three or four organizations to drop British bookings and that "the refusal of the public to patronize Anglo pix was proof of the strong resistance."[47]

In 1946, releases by the eight majors and three others totaled 405 features (273 for the majors and 132 for three minors). Fox released 35 films (of which four were reissues—R); RKO 39 (of which two were Westerns—W); Paramount 24 (two R); Universal 47 (one W, one R, eight British—B); Columbia 51 (14 W); MGM 32 (one R); United Artists 20 (two W, one R, two B); Warner Bros. 25 (two R); Republic 50 (16 W); Monogram 45 (14 W, one R); and PRC 37 (13 W). Thus, the Hollywood cartel members distributed only 10 foreign films that year, all British.[48]

Release figures in 1948 for 14 studios indicated 412 features were released that year, plus 68 westerns, plus 26 British pictures. Fox handled four of the latter and Universal distributed 12 of them.[49]

In this period it was reported that the average good foreign movie would gross about $75,000 for its distributor, which meant some $30,000 for the foreign producer and $45,000 to the U.S. distributor for its costs and profits. On most foreign films, the distributor's take was mainly determined on the first-run in New York and that of 15 other first-run art houses across the nation. After two years of touring, an average foreign film got 60 percent of its revenue from New York, 40 percent from all the rest of the U.S.A. If the foreign movie was particularly sexual then 25 percent of the total revenue came from New York, and 75 percent from the rest of

America. On Hollywood product, New York generally supplied around 10 percent of the movie's domestic gross.[50]

An average French or Italian film, distributors estimated, figured to take $20,000 to $40,000 net profit in the U.S., with more in the $20,000 to $25,000 range than near the higher number. It was an average that was dragged down by the low grosser. Many of those movies seldom recovered their print costs (including the cost of duping negatives, titles, duty, and so on) that ran from $2,500 to $3,000. A low grosser went into small-capacity New York art houses where the average picture of this classification seldom stayed longer than two weeks. That meant the distributor's share would be $400 to $500, and his newspaper advertising bill often took the bulk of that amount. Key cities outside of New York, such as Chicago, Boston, Los Angeles and Philadelphia, were left for the distributor to try and obtain an additional $1,500 to $2,000, which would allow the distributor to break even. The very few really successful foreign films released each year managed to net about $200,000 or slightly higher.[51]

As this period ended, the motion picture industries in Western Europe were in the midst of a strong revival and resurgence as they reconstructed after the war. However, those foreign films made next to no headway in America. The major push made by the British, especially Rank, to increase penetration was largely unsuccessful and the cost of that campaign was one of the reasons the Rank studio ran into financial difficulties. Still, the MPAA cartel paid lip-service to the issue, and engaged in window-dressing efforts. In 1949 the MPAA set up a committee to advise foreign producers on how to get the maximum income from the States. Also, they planned to offer advise on how the foreigners could get the best distribution deal, and so forth. Said MPAA president Eric Johnston, "If we want to do business in foreign countries we must make sure that trade is a two-way street."[52]

5

The Golden Age, 1950–1959

Yanks pick stories for world appeal, British don't, and lose, but squawk.
—Variety, *1955*

Why don't the creative men and women on the other side of the oceans try producing in an idiom our people favor.
—*S. H. Fabian, U.S. cinema owner,* 1959

French resent American [censorship] code; taking $10,000,000 globally but almost nothing from U.S.A.
—Variety, *1955*

Years later, when observers looked back on the period of the 1950s through the mid–1960s, many would declare it had been a golden age for foreign films, both for their artistic and creative accomplishment and for how they fared in America, a period when they had reached the apex of their popularity. Yet at the time the situation for offshore movies in the States, in media accounts, seemed little changed from what it had always been—bleak. There was perhaps a slight increase in the prevalence of such films in America during that period but it came on top of a baseline presence that was so negligible that even a large percentage increase would have barely been noticeable. While the period featured an tiny improvement in the position of foreign pictures, it was all very relative and hardly constituted a golden age in any objective or absolute measure, with respect to how those items made out in the U.S.A.

As the 1950s began, a triumphant and very smug article in *Variety* commented that the U.S., worried back in 1946–1947 that it was facing a world-wide battle for supremacy in foreign markets, was then in a position to relax since all those threats, particularly Rank's, had evaporated in the previous three years. "The American industry's position, as a result, is more secure than ever as the world's undisputed champion maker and purveyor of films," it reported. Hollywood had been especially worried by J. Arthur Rank because he was rich and "obviously fully-supported" by his government, but "in less than three years he discovered money to be no substitute for Hollywood's production know-how or ... skill in distribution and exploitation." Back then Hollywood was even fearful of losing a large chunk of the domestic gross in America to the offshore producers. That also had not happened, the account gloated. British films had "very limited" acceptance while the French and Italian movies were "insignificant in the total grosses they draw."[1]

In the assaults made by various countries on the U.S. cinema screens, Britain was again the most active, including a weakened and financially diminished Rank. The firm's managing director, John Davis, declared in 1953 that American exhibitors were blocking the expansion of British films in the U.S. market. Davis's remarks came on the heels of similar criticism from London film critic Reg Whitley. Exhibitors declared they would gladly screen more British product if they thought an audience would come, but claimed, "British releases are of limited appeal, and some hold none at all, at least for run-of-the-mill houses over here." Condescendingly those cinema owners added that, nonetheless, U.K. pictures had made great strides in America since the war despite their "slow pacing, unknown stars and strange accents."[2]

Just a few weeks after he criticized the exhibitors for not giving U.K. pictures enough playing time Davis lashed out at Universal, Rank's U.S. distributor, for not doing enough to increase Rank's business and receipts in the States. As a comparison Davis noted that the Rank films doing good, even record-breaking business in Australia were not doing very much business in America. Executives at Universal replied to the criticism by stating that Davis "simply refuses to emotionally face the facts of the American market."[3]

Six months later Davis complained again, stating the earnings of British movies in America were "more than disappointing." Because of U.S. film domination it was found, Davis explained, that to open up screens to British movies, investments in overseas cinemas were necessary. After that strategy had been followed, Rank product had done well in Commonwealth countries such as New Zealand, Australia, South Africa, and Canada. With regard to the failure of U.K. product in the States, Davis said Rank had been told by Hollywood "that the subject matter was not acceptable to the American people and they were told that the accents of British artists were not understood." Particularly galling to Davis about that explanation was the extent to which Hollywood used those same British actors in their films. "When the film is produced in an American studio, although the artists tell me they have had no special voice training, there appears to be no difficulty in finding public acceptability for the films in the American market," asserted Davis. Also, he found it difficult to believe the film tastes of the American people were so different from those in other nations which turned out to see both British and U.S. pictures.[4]

Substantiating his claim that British movies did not get a fair return in America, Davis revealed the following data. Domestic gross receipts for *Genevieve* in the U.K. were $1,050,000 while its U.S. gross was $400,000 ($220,000 of that amount was actually remitted to Rank in the U.K.). Domestic gross for *The Cruel Sea* was $840,000; in the U.S. it was $600,000 ($338,000). *The Pool of London* had a domestic gross of $392,000; $40,000 in America ($20,000) while *The Promoter* (starring Alex Guinness) took $476,000 in the U.K. and $400,000 ($200,000) in the States. *Outpost in Malaya* (Claudette Colbert had been cast as a lead in the film deliberately to increase the vehicle's appeal in America) had a U.K. gross of $509,000 but only took $90,000 in the U.S. Davis estimated that a good return for a top British movie in the U.S. should be approximately twice its gross from the U.K.—due to a much larger filmgoing public in America—but that no Rank film had ever reached that level, or even come close.[5]

By the mid–1950s, Rank was struggling to handle its films in America by itself, without the "help" of Hollywood at either the distribution or exhibition level. Through its subsidiary, Rank Film Distributors of America, it operated some 10 offices throughout the States. It also had a lease on the Sutton Theatre in New York and had an arrangement to receive half of the screen time at the World Theatre in Philadelphia. The British Treasury had made $2 million available to Rank for the new unit, if needed. Also made clear was that no further money would be forthcoming from the British Treasury.[6]

British Lion Films also used its own distribution arm to try and get onto the American screen. Arthur Jarratt, British Lion managing director, commented that once a U.K. producer started trying to copy Hollywood, one was left with neither a good British nor a good American film. Yet he also said he thought Britain then was not producing movies with international appeal. Trying to establish British films in America, he thought, would necessarily be a slow job. "It consists of a combination of publicity and salesmanship," Jarratt explained. "We must try and get the exhibitors to play maybe just a couple of pictures at the start."[7]

The head of the British Lion distributor arm, Lion International Films, was Victor Hoare. Arriving in New York late in 1955, he took a shamelessly obsequious position as he spoke erroneously about the situation, perhaps hoping it would be more effective than a list of complaints or threats. Hoare said U.S. exhibitors were "very receptive" to British movies and perfectly willing to evaluate them on the basis of merit alone. "I've talked to quite a few people and I can find no prejudice against the British films as such," he said.[8]

Once again British politicians got involved in the issue. During a 1954 visit to New York, British MP and film union spokesman Tom O'Brien stressed the need for a commercial film reciprocity agreement on a voluntary basis to expand the screen time of British movies in U.S. cinemas. He said he had come to the conclusion that an insufficient number of good British pictures were being exhibited in America: "They're available, but they are not being plugged hard enough." O'Brien argued there were plenty of people who would be happy to see U.K. product, provided they were given the chance, but "they aren't given the opportunity." The only practical solution he saw—although he said he did not favor a legislative one—was a commercial agreement between the U.S. cinema circuits and the British producers, providing for the chains to book a certain number of U.K. features every year.[9]

A couple of years later, in 1956, Hollywood was accused in the British House of Commons of having pushed the British motion picture industry into a small corner of its own domestic market—where it held only 30 percent of screen time. Americans were also accused of "nationalistic" biases against British pictures in the U.S. market. Conservative MP John Hall suggested that the reason such a film as *The Cruel Sea* failed in the U.S. was because it showed the role the British Navy played in winning World War II. "While we are happy to watch films showing Americans winning the war," he said, "there is a much stronger nationalistic feeling in America." Other handicaps attributed to U.K. pictures in America, by the *New York Times*, were the use of "heavy" English accents, lack of humor that Americans understood, lack of action and poor sound.[10]

British MP Stephen Swingler complained in Parliament about the apparent "unfair discrimination against British films" in America. "I do not think we get 'fair do's' in the American market," he added. "I think

Carry On Nurse (U.K., 1959, Kenneth Connor and Kenneth Williams).
One of the titles in the long-running British Carry On comedy series.

we should be a little more sticky and aggressive." American film executives
reportedly dismissed the charges from the MPs as "utterly ridiculous." The
U.S. Supreme Court ordered divorcement at the end of the 1940s: Declared
a monopoly, the Hollywood majors that owned cinemas were ordered to
divest themselves of those venues, among other provisions of the decision.
It was noted that American film executives found it difficult to make it clear
to industries and governments abroad that after the decision, Hollywood
could "no longer force" a movie onto the circuits.[11]

Still smarting from the U.K. MP attacks, U.S. film industry personnel remained firmly convinced that the U.K. did not understand the way
the U.S. motion picture industry worked and that it had fixed but wrong
ideas. "Europeans with their minds accustomed to strong government control or collaboration in business decisions," explained a reporter, "simply
fail to understand that the American film industry is private.... Joint action
is always difficult and frequently impossible to organize." Among the "major
illusions" Europeans labored under were that a Hollywood major taking

on a foreign film to distribute could automatically channel it into the big cinema chains and, if volume bookings could be achieved in the States, the receipts would take care of themselves. One U.S. film executive said, "They haven't realized yet that, in the U.S., the exhibitor is king when it comes to foreign films."[12]

Continuing the debate on whether or not U.K. pictures got fair treatment, a summary of trade opinion in London declared it was no answer to say that many British features were unsuitable for America and therefore did not get booked into U.S. cinemas; they gave the simple reason that many American films were equally unsuitable for British audiences and yet they received play dates in U.K. houses. One comment from London stated, "The Yanks ask us to believe that almost all British features are unacceptable to the U.S. market other than features starring Alec Guinness, who is as British as they come." Another consensus comment from the London trade said, if U.K. movies had been trying to crack the American market with only minor results for something like 40 years, "It is just possible that the American film industry, distributor and exhibitor alike, want it that way and all their arguments are no more than double-talk."[13]

With all the charges of prejudice being hurled by the Europeans, especially the British, worry increased in Hollywood that foreign nations might take even more compensatory action at a legislative level. An unnamed executive with a Hollywood major—he was in charge of handling foreign product for the studio—acknowledged that the U.S. industry's stake in countering the prejudice charge was made difficult because "in some respects, it has a basis in fact." He said he preferred to call it "resistance" rather than prejudice. Expanding on the theme, he said the resistance was a reluctance to make the effort to appreciate something that might be new or different: "It would be completely foolish to pretend that even a good foreign film has the same enjoyment and box office potential in this country as an ordinary good American picture." A problem with that reasoning was that it seemed to put most of the blame on the audience even though much of the time the audience did not get a choice as the foreign item did not get booked at all.[14]

British producer Herbert Wilcox agreed that resistance against British films did exist among American audiences. He deplored the fact that the American film industry did not take the view that at least 10 percent of what it earned in Britain should go back to that country by way of U.K. movie earnings in America. Wanting a two-way street, Wilcox described the Hollywood majors as "unintelligent" in allowing the trade to have become so one-sided. "If Metro [MGM] makes a lot of money in Britain, and derives dollar revenue from our country," he explained, "why shouldn't it then turn around and make a real effort to sell British pictures in its own market?"[15]

Five of Britain's film trade unions, in a 1958 memorandum to the British Board of Trade, put forward a proposal that U.S. film activity in Britain be restricted in ratio to the release and earnings of U.K. pictures in America. Film executives in the States dismissed the idea as "surprisingly unrealistic."[16]

A dispute later that year perhaps indirectly shed some light on Hollywood's real view of U.K. features. British producers asked American producers making films in Britain to affix to those pictures an identifying title that read "This is a British-American co-production." Americans took the view, said a reporter for *Variety*, that such a prominent identification was likely to hurt the chances of the item in the States. The British petitioners wanted both to have their work identified and to stop the U.S. practice of sending co-productions (made mostly to satisfy U.K. quota regulations) into some countries as British pictures and into others under the American flag only. "Past experience has shown that films identified as British tend to do less than British pix which can be exhibited without that label," explained the reporter.[17]

Visiting New York in 1950, Alfredo Guarini, vice president of Enic, an Italian film organization that controlled the Cinecitta studios in Rome as well as a chain of 160 cinemas throughout Italy, remarked that the problem of broadening the U.S. market for Italian and French movies was a tough one. While some European executives believed the way to get a financial boost in the U.S. was to win extensive circuit bookings, Guarini thought it was more practical to concentrate on producing films of artistic merit such as *Bicycle Thief* and *Shoe Shine*, which he said had no difficulty in drawing patrons to U.S. art houses.[18]

Life magazine did a large, seven-page spread in 1952 on the "invasion" of Italian movies declaring a mixture of sex and naturalism was the trademark of the postwar Italian film. "Skillfully exploited, it has made the Italian industry the nearest thing to a rival of Hollywood existing today," ran the account, in a highly exaggerated manner. The Italian industry was said to have shot past those from England and France in the previous year to take second place behind America. One of the catalysts for the article was the fact that a week earlier a group of leading Italian stars and directors had come to New York for a Salute to Italian Films Week, presenting a selection of the best Italian releases.[19]

Under an existing deal between the MPAA and the Italian motion picture industry, 12.5 percent of Hollywood's earning from its films screened in Italy went to maintain the Italian Films Export (IFE) organization, a

The Lavender Hill Mob (U.K., 1951, Alec Guinness on the left). Guinness was one of the few foreign actors to achieve a star presence in the U.S.

group that distributed and promoted Italian movies around the world, including in the U.S. When that pact expired in 1953, a deal was put in place that reduced the support level of the IFE to 10 percent. A clause, which had not existed in the old agreement, specifically barred the use of those IFE funds from being used for the subsidized distribution of Italian pictures in the States. Major impetus for that clause came from the newly formed Independent Motion Picture Distributors Association of America (IMPDA). It was those independent distributors who wanted the IFE blocked from distributing, with U.S. funds, and limited to promoting.[20]

Some 14 months later a new deal was struck between the parties in which all the money to the IFE was dropped. American negotiators pointed out to the Italians that due to a variety of circumstances, supposedly including Federal Trade Commission pressure, the MPAA was no longer in a position to grant those funds. By way of contrast, a recently signed French film agreement provided for an outright payment of $400,000, with conditions attached, to the French motion picture industry. The new Italian deal was described as a "big moral victory" for Hollywood.[21]

Eitel Monaco, president of Anica, the Italian producer and distributor organization, declared on a 1954 visit to New York that the Italian motion picture industry was pinning its hopes for the future in the U.S. market on dubbing and an increased number of Italian-American coproductions using Hollywood stars. Italian producers' net take in the world market had increased from $3 million in 1950 to $9 million in 1953 but in the States the Italian industry realized only $800,000 to $900,000 in 1953 (part of the $9 million).[22]

In another country with a major film industry, France, a film costing 100,000,000 francs ($300,000) had to get 40 percent of its receipts from the foreign market to get its money back; one costing 60,000,000 francs could amortize itself with French-speaking countries such as Belgium, Luxembourg, Switzerland, and Francophone Canada. Films in the 25,000,000 franc range could get their money back in the home market. The need for

Manèges (*The Cheat*) (France, 1949, Bernard Blier and Simone Signoret).

a foreign market led to the founding of Unifrance Film in 1949 to hype French movies abroad. Supported financially by both the government and the film industry, Unifrance created special weeks of French pictures abroad, was in charge of all international film festivals, and created publicity campaigns in an effort to make countries French-film conscious.[23]

Following the pattern of the Italian film agreement, the Hollywood cartel (through the Motion Picture Export Association—a subsidiary of the MPAA) entered into a new deal with the French industry in 1953 that provided the latter with a payment of $400,000 over a two-year period. France intended to use the money to set up an office in New York with the specific purpose of launching and promoting French imports, especially in the areas outside New York. Under the terms of the agreement, it was specified that the French activity would be restricted to publicity and promotion and that the money was not to be used for distribution purposes.[24]

When Unifrance president Georges Lourau announced the French would use the $400,000 to set up a New York office, he said that French producers were "disappointed" over the showing of their films in the U.S. because they did not "understand American audiences." Lourau explained, "They fail to comprehend that, because French audiences like something in a film, it is not automatically liked by American audiences."[25]

A haughty 1954 article in *Variety* started off by stating: "The individualistically-minded French producers cannot see the point of undertaking an industry-wide effort to put French features in the U.S. and instead prefer going their separate ways." Apparently that was a slap at the French for using Unifrance to promote their work rather than contracting with the Hollywood cartel members. By this time, however, Lourau had ruled out the possibility of establishing a French industry office in New York. Instead, Unifrance was setting up new or expanded offices in Madrid and London. Of the U.S. he said, "We just don't have enough money to do a job here." Lourau was one French producer who believed that the French should continue making their movies primarily for their own domestic audiences and not with a view to their potential in the American market. Forty percent of the French film industry's revenue came from abroad (50 percent from the U.K.) and of that 40 percent, only 10 percent at a maximum was derived from the States. He felt there was little the French could do to increase their U.S. take. Representing Lourau in the U.S. was John G. McCarthy, who felt that a problem for foreign producers was that the U.S. was "self-contained." Unlike exhibitors in other countries, U.S. cinema owners could get along without imports, he thought; "So the best we can do is just nibble around the edges of the market and hope to get as much of it as possible," he concluded.[26]

Yet six months later Jacques Flaud, director of the Centre National du Cinema Francais, the coordinating body of the French film industry, announced plans for the opening of a French Cinema Center in New York in the fall of 1955. It was to serve as a public relations liaison between the French and American film industries. Flaud said that foreign receipts from French films in 1954 totaled $11 million, with just $140,000 of that coming from America. Latin America yielded $1.5 million of the total, Israel $300,000.[27]

Flaud expressed the view in 1956 that French releases weren't being handled properly in the U.S. outside a handful of key cities and that French producers would be better off dealing with the Hollywood majors for distribution, or at least with independent distributors "of substance." Those independent distributors argued, of course, that the French would be better off with them since they could devote more attention to an individual film, and so forth. "There literally exists no grass-roots' market for the French product unless it is dubbed," those independent distributors said, adding, "The average French feature is far better off playing a limited number of art houses than losing money in extended circulation." Commenting on the subject was Al Lichtman, distribution director for 20th Century–Fox, who said it paid his company to take on foreign releases, provided they could be dubbed. "Otherwise," he said, "it's a waste of time for us." A reporter concluded, "Americans hold the French and other foreign producers underestimate the lack of interest in foreign film that characterizes American audiences generally."[28]

In response Flaud repeated a few weeks later his view that American independent distributors did not have the means of giving full exploitation to French pictures due to their lack of full, nationwide distribution facilities. A main argument against them, he said, was that they could not even give art house films the 500 bookings around the States "which should constitute the minimum circulation for French features."[29]

Seconding Flaud's opinion was Henry Deutschmeister, head of Paris-based producer Franco-London Films, who credited New York independent distributors with aid to the cause but added, "They just can't get us widened playdates in the States. Only the majors can help us." Deutschmeister had just completed *Marie Antoinette* (Michelle Morgan and Richard Todd) by shooting it twice (once in French, once in English) with some different bits. For example, the accusation that Antoinette had committed incest with her son was present in the French version but absent in the English one. In conclusion Deutschmeister remarked, "If the French, who loathed it at first, could acquire a taste for Coca-Cola, sometimes to the exclusion of wine, then there are no limits to changing national taste and the United States could learn to like French films."[30]

Germany was another country trying to break into the U.S.A. with its movies. According to Henry Lester (an American living in Germany who represented the Germany producer Carlton Films), the German film industry, while enviously watching what "success" had been achieved in the States by Italian and French features, failed to grasp the idea that "Italo and French films have a certain 'snob' appeal among American audiences, [but] German imports do not." He added that a label reading "Made in Germany" may have had that type of appeal when it came to toys or scientific instruments, "but not on pictures." Yet there was a feeling in the German motion picture industry, explained Lester, that the lack of success of German features in the U.S. had "been due primarily to poor handling." Disagreeing with that idea, Lester said he felt that lack of success was due to the fact the German features had not yet found a distinct style of their own: "They're just making haphazard things that often attempt to copy Hollywood." Another reason he offered was "the very definite resentment of things German which lingers in the U.S. as an aftermath of the war period."[31]

Carlton Film head Guenther Stapenhorst felt the problem was that the picture content was dictated by German distributors who held the purse strings through advances to producers. "The distributors say: 'Make safe pictures. Make them for German audiences,'" explained Stapenhorst; "They aren't interested in international appeal. They are interested only in the business at hand, that is the domestic market. Under those circumstances it's very difficult to change one's approach." Having a different opinion on where the problem lay, German distributor Herbert O. Horn (head of NF distributors) remarked the real problem was to be found in the film budget. German producers could not afford to make features that cost more than $350,000, he said, adding, "How can such a production expect to compete abroad with a $1,000,000 French or Italian production?" According to Stapenhorst, a German movie got about 80 percent of its cost back in Germany and German-speaking nations but the average feature showed a 20 percent loss because the foreign market was "almost negligible." Coproductions with Hollywood were suggested by Stapenhorst as one possible solution to the problem of getting a foot in the door, but he admitted the solution was impractical for the German producers: "We can't afford to pay those high star salaries."[32]

Wolf Schwarz was the chief executive of German producer Bavaria-Filmunst. "There is no reason whatever why the American companies should not take one German picture a year and give a $100,000 guarantee," he argued; "It's simply a question of good will. They must start taking a risk once in a while." Observing that Germans were used to dubbed movies and that it had taken time to get used to them, he saw no reason the U.S. should not be likewise. "The American firms won't do anything with dubbed pictures. It practically amounts to a boycott," he lamented. Claiming that he was pro–U.S., he related that in Germany he was being attacked for that position: "Increasingly, I find myself in an isolated position because of the American attitude. The U.S. companies will do nothing for us. They talk a lot, but no action!" According to Schwarz, Hollywood took out of the German film market something like 60 million marks a year ($15 million). "Is there any reason why we shouldn't get back at least 6,000,000 marks ($1,500,000) from the U.S?" he wondered. Schwarz said he was eager to sit down with MPAA head Eric Johnston to go over various aspects of film industry relations "and to make him understand that some signs are needed that the American industry is willing to do more than just make empty gestures."[33]

Horst von Hartlieb, head of West Germany's Distributors Association, traveled to America in 1956 to study motion picture industry conditions and the chances for the German film. He felt the German film industry, with government support and money, needed to move quickly to establish a film promotional agency in the States and that German producers had to think more in terms of both domestic and export appeal in choosing their film subjects. "The agency and acceptable films go hand-in-hand," he declared; "One is useless without the other." After talking to many film people in the U.S., von Hartlieb said, "I came to the absolute conclusion that there are no deliberate restrictions whatever against us— the foreign producers—in the American market. No one wants to stop us." However, he added, "There is a resistance against foreign pictures, but it isn't directed against any one nation." A journalist noted that few German features had played in America outside of their own language houses (the ethnic market where films played without dubbing or subtitles in English) in New York and elsewhere since the war. "One of the reasons has been the quality of the German product, which has been pitched quite deliberately to the unique screen tastes of the German public," he wrote.[34]

Another German film executive to visit the U.S. in this period was Gyula Trebitsch, production chief of Real Film of Hamburg. By the time of his 1957 visit, Germany's film industry produced around 110 features a year. Trebitsch remarked that those German movies had to "re-educate themselves to American tastes" if they wanted a chance to "recapture the large audiences in the United States enjoyed by German films three decades ago."[35]

By the end of the 1950s, German movies were still not having much success in the States. Some 20 German features were sold to the U.S. in

1958 (out of 114 produced) but less than one-third of those achieved a gross producer/distributor share of the box office take of $50,000 or more. All this came before the 35 percent distributor's fee was paid and other expenses deducted; said a reporter, "There has been little or nothing in the kitty to return to the producer."[36]

Attempts to introduce U.S. movies to Russia always failed when Russia insisted that any agreement had to include reciprocity. Americans insisted that the type of reciprocity demanded by the Russians was not feasible under the U.S. system.[37]

Then, in 1958, MPAA cartel head Johnston signed a Soviet-American film deal in Moscow that called for the Soviets to buy 10 Hollywood features and for the cartel members to handle a total of seven Russian movies in return. Under the agreement U.S. distribution of those Russian features called for the "widest possible" disbursement and for publicity for the titles. Reportedly the entire U.S. film industry was unhappy with the deal—unhappy with reciprocity per se, unhappy at the 7:10 ratio, and so forth. Hollywood worried that a number of precedents had been set. "If the Russians could get a reciprocity deal, the other Communist countries won't want to be caught napping," grumbled one anonymous U.S. film executive; "They'll all want the same concession." The precedent was said to be even worse for the friendly non–Communist nations who had long wanted reciprocity but were told by the cartel that such proposals were impossible since they were outside the power of Hollywood. Johnston and the MPAA had only signed the deal with the Russians because they were under pressure—both the U.S. State Department and the White House asked for the pact to be signed.[38]

According to a 1957 article, India became, at that time, the latest foreign country to "badly misunderstand" America film economics. That remark was in response to editorial comment in an Indian trade publication, *Cine Advance*, with regard to Indian moves to limit U.S. movie imports and to raise the existing tariff. Mentioned by the editor was the argument that the situation would have been different if American film interests cared to import a fair number of Indian movies. Such a two-way traffic would have balanced, or nearly balanced, the foreign exchange position of the film trade between the two nations and would have made a cut in the import of American films unnecessary. "But America has raised a virtual stone wall against Indian films," said the editor. Trying to dismiss those allegations the American reporter argued, "What is consistently misunderstood abroad, and so frequently held against the film companies, is the fact that—in the U.S.—audiences follow their own inclinations and can't be told what to see or not to see." Ignored by that argument was the distribution control exercised by Hollywood, de facto block booking of U.S. movies, massive and expensive advertising campaigns, the fact that many foreign films received no screen time at all, and so forth. India produced some 300 movies a year yet only a handful had ever been released in America. Jack Hoffberg, whose firm had released three Indian movies, said it was difficult "to get more than a couple of dates for them." When one of them did play, explained Hoffberg, it showed "a very limited staying power, proving that audiences just weren't very interested." One film executive declared, "To ask a major company to distribute an Indian film would be insanity"—they were just too "weird."[39]

A strategy to Americanize their films deliberately, to copy Hollywood, remained a tactic used from time to time by foreign producers. At the start of the 1950s, some foreign producers turned out films simultaneously shot in two languages with the same multi-lingual cast in both versions. German filmmaker Henry Deutschmeister said he felt a more practical method, when possible, was to make films in English and then dub them into the language of the home market. It was just good business sense, felt Deutschmeister, to cause European producers to put more emphasis on getting an English version of a movie—aimed at the U.S. market—"which can produce so much more money for even a run-of-the-mill film in English than for the best of the subtitled jobs." Deutschmeister believed it was better to dub in the home language since it was cheaper than to shoot a full second-language version; he also explained, "Dubbed pix are well-accepted outside the U.S. ... Yank audiences, on the other hand, unused to the procedure, generally won't accept it." French producers Jacques Bar and Robert Dorfmann also produced movies in two languages. They claimed it only cost 30 percent more since the same sets, costumes, and so on, were used. One reason advanced for using this tactic was a reported diminishing interest in subtitled films, which themselves were limited to art houses.[40]

Several years later Max Ophuls directed Lola Montes in three languages (French, English and German) and Jean Renoir had started Elliena et les Hommes to be made in French and English with an international cast led by Ingrid Bergman and Mel Ferrer. Cy Howard did the English script and made changes from the original French script to "have it more in keeping with the U.S. tastes." Commenting on this strategy, a journalist declared, "It is felt that only in this way can they get into the general market instead of being kept permanently in arty theatres."[41]

Attempts to Americanize U.K. pictures drew the wrath of domestic actors in 1950; through their organization Equity, they protested to the Labour Department that American players were permitted to take British roles in British-made productions. Their action followed the screening of

The Night and the City, starring Richard Widmark and Gene Tierney, which drew unfavorable comments from most of London's film critics. One of them described the movie as "about as British as Sing Sing." Equity urged that the entry into the U.K. of foreign stars, "particularly American," be limited. In clarification, Equity said it already had made it clear that it would not object to Americans playing American roles in British pictures. They warned, however, "We could not accept the existing position in which the Ministry rubber-stamps applications for American stars to play British parts in films which attempt to portray the British way of life."[42]

A year later a media account wrote about the popularity of British movies on U.S. television stations, without supplying any supporting data. In reality very few U.K. movies showed up on television at that time. Nevertheless the report used the popularity idea, bogus as it was, to declare it had completely revived the thinking of English producers regarding the U.S. market. They were said to be refusing to make any concessions to the potential U.S. cinema audiences in their production planning. Led by Rank and Korda, those producers had reportedly come to the conclusion that their best hope for profits lay in aiming strictly for the British home market and in selling their less expensive items directly to American television distributors. They had come to believe that slanting production for the U.S. market "as they started to do in the early postwar years," created "nothing but deficits on both sides of the Atlantic." They explained, "It detracts from the value for the home territory and it still fails to dent the American theatre market." Aiming a film at the American market also "greatly" increased its cost.[43]

As television cut into the motion picture audience, one of Hollywood's responses was to cut back drastically the contract players list. That led to a certain amount of talent exodus to Europe where producers were ready to put Hollywood names into their features. One of the main reasons for doing that was to enhance their box office chances in the States.[44]

Apologists for the situation wherein foreign films were barely visible on U.S. cinema screens often argued it was because the foreigners did not produce what Americans wanted to see. Yet when those Europeans did try from time to time to Americanize their product they were condemned for it. Journalist Fred Hift said that 1953 had been a bad year for imports and one reason that foreign movies were bad was because they had their eye on the U.S. mass market. Long-time importer and distributor Noel Meadow said, "They're now trying to emulate the American ways of exploiting their imports"—that is, by adding more sex appeal. "They'd do better forgetting all about the U.S. Who wants a replica of a Hollywood picture in French or Italian?" asked Meadow. Some good European movies did not get screen time

Lola Montes (France, 1955, Peter Ustinov on the left and Martine Carol). Director Max Ophuls produced this feature in three languages, one of which was English, in the hope that such "Americanization" would give the movie better prospects in the U.S.

at all in the States. Six months earlier, *The Wages of Fear* had won best film honors at the Venice film festival but it had not been exhibited in the U.S. to that point. Blame for that was placed on the film's European producers who were said to have an "exaggerated" idea of what it was worth, in relation to the amount of money they wanted for U.S. distribution rights.[45]

J. K. Stafford Poole, president of the Scottish section of the British Cinematograph Exhibitors' Association, told an annual meeting of exhibitors that if British producers could supply the right type of films for the American market, there would be a strong demand to see them. He thought that perhaps two versions should be made of each movie, one for the "purists" at home in the U.K. and one for the world. Calling for more "glamour and oomph" in U.K. movies, he said, "If we are to crash the world market, we simply must have some femininity that occasionally inspires the wolf in the males and sighing admiration in the females." People Poole had in mind were the Italian actors Silvana Mangano and Gina Lollobrigida.[46]

Leonard Goldenson, president of American Broadcasting–Paramount Theatres, said he planned to stimulate overseas production of films suitable for the American market. He told a company stockholders' meeting in 1954 that he would go to West Germany that summer "with the intention of influencing the employment of American writers and directors by German filmmakers." As well, he planned to visit J. Arthur Rank in London to recommend to the producer that he slant his product more for the U.S. by using more U.S. personnel. Goldenson recalled that earlier he urged Italian producers to do the same thing.[47]

Another attempt to emulate American ways was in the use of promotion by the foreigners. European producers realized that the U.S. was "as star-conscious as ever" and that it was difficult to sell films with no marquee names. Thus, some of them launched their own star tours in America. A French group that arrived in 1957 included Micheline Presle, Jean Marais, Francoise Arnoul, and Gerard Philipe. From the roster of the British, Kenneth More was in the U.S.A. for the same purpose, given publicity treatment by the Rank organization. Doing the same were Italy's Giulietta Masina, her husband Federico Fellini and German-Swiss star Maria Schell. Still, such treatment did not always work. One example was Italy's Gina Lollobrigida, who received a big buildup, lots of American magazine covers and stories, yet several of her subsequent pictures failed to register at the box office. In many cases, wrote Fred Hift, the U.S. press, magazines, and so on did not jump at the chance to profile all of those foreign stars. Also, some of those players were said to be resistant to a U.S. buildup.[48]

Around the same time journalist Robert Landry wrote that with respect to the "problem" of foreign movies, there was nothing wrong with British, Italian, French and "even Swedish" product "which couldn't be cured by money." What he meant was money to be spent in promoting those movies, most of which he felt arrived in the U.S. quietly. Landry wrote, "Americans don't know the stars, don't know the titles, are confused as between titling and dubbing." It was an ignorance found not just in the general public, he said, but also among America's cinema owners and theater bookers. Explaining the primary weakness that held back foreign pictures, Landry said, "They simply don't promote.... Their product is unsold in the land of sell." Instead of promotion they relied totally on favorable reviews from the film critics and word-of-mouth from the "moviegoing elite."[49]

Throughout this period Hollywood feared for the future of its own product offshore since it seemed to always face governmental threats of legislation or other measures to increase the presence of their own features in America. Executives in America viewed such attempts and threats with rising alarm because they feared they would intensify the already widespread belief that there was a conspiracy in the U.S. to prevent foreign imports from getting any broad circulation there. Such fears were needlessly exaggerated, of course, as the threats turned out to be idle and any regulations imposed proved to be ineffective in increasing foreign presence in the States.[50]

Dubbed films had been accepted all over the world long before the 1950s arrived, except in the States. The rest of the world did not have much of a choice since Hollywood distributed most movies in most countries, and dubbed pictures were what Hollywood usually sent. Americans, however, were different. Foreign producers and American distributors of offshore product, therefore, continued to be confused about whether or not their product should be dubbed. Italian producer Alfredo Guarini was skeptical of the value of dubbing as a means of developing U.S. audiences. That technique, he said, might be suitable for a "commercial" feature but it would spoil the "subtle situations" of an artistic film. However, he did admit that in Italy dubbing was the rule for practically all imported movies.[51]

Proponents of dubbing held the technique would tap new audiences that until then had been untouched, thus leading to a much larger potential gross take. Those opposed to dubbing believed a foreign movie would lose a great deal of the "sensitivity and peculiar qualities" that helped to identify it as a continental feature if it was dubbed. Some seemed to think that the dubbing of imports would more or less automatically lead to a broader market. That idea hinged on the hope that Hollywood would sharply reduce its crop of B features—the second half of the double-bill—and dubbed foreign product would move right in. That imports would fill such a gap, though, was just wishful thinking; exhibitors played Hollywood product "good or bad." Relentless competition from television did indeed cause a sharp reduction in Hollywood output and the elimination of B movies. Exhibitors, though, did not fill that gap—they eliminated it. The double-bill gradually disappeared.[52]

In the mid–1950s, it cost $10,000 to $20,000 to dub a film, a considerable additional cost for a foreign item that got very limited exposure. But the temptation to dub was always there since it remained a widely held belief amongst foreigners that a dubbed item had a chance to play regular release houses (beyond the art house) that would never open their doors to subtitled movies. Peter Riethof, president of American Dubbing, said 1954 saw a substantial increase in dubbed items. "Whereas a good foreign film can earn money only in the art theatres, an English-speaking version can be shown everywhere," he claimed. In his opinion, dubbing was not new in the U.S., it had been done for a long time but in the past the quality of dubbing and the corresponding box office returns were not good enough to merit any expansion in the practice. Due to technical advances and a couple of recent successes, Riethof argued the cost of dubbing could be justified because of higher receipts. "Our audience expects a dubbed film to be for all practical purposes indistinguishable from an original version," said Riethof.[53]

Other dubbed successes in the 1950s, *La Strada* and *And God Created Woman*, revived interest in the technique on the part of several countries, especially Germany, which had not had a hit in America since before World War II. In fact, one account described German films in the States as being "virtually non-existent." Here the quality of dubbing was said to technically leave much to be desired; one report said, "There's little question that distributors aren't eager to tell the public that they're handling a dubbed import." *La Strada* cost $25,000 to dub in the States. Seymour Poe, vice president of the Italian film agency IFE, said he "wouldn't dream of dubbing a movie in New York because of the cost when Italians could do a very good job in Rome for $8,000 to $10,000." After its success in a dubbed version *La Strada* was brought back for extra art house dates in subtitles, its original release format. Another advantage of dubbing was that the technique gave the movie a chance at a television sale, at least in theory. It was generally accepted that a subtitled movie had no chance of being sold to, on seen on, television.[54]

Subtitle writing in this period took anywhere from one to six weeks with all the freelancers and firms in the business based in New York. A total of 750 to 1,200 separate subtitles were produced on average for each film. That represented anywhere from 50 to 85 percent of the original dialogue. The cost of subtitling was around $60 a reel with a 10-reel feature (100 minutes) being average. Additionally, charges for the task of spotting (determining where on a frame a title should be placed) were another $20 or so per reel. In *Shoe Shine*, a character said, "Just say those things in court and not even Christ will be able to prevent your brother from getting five years!" The subtitle said: "Tell that in court and your brother's a goner!"[55]

Noted film writer Bosley Crowther set off a long debate on dubbing when he wrote a newspaper column against the practice in September 1958. Commenting first on its recent surge in popularity (mainly on the back of a couple Brigitte Bardot movies), he argued that most people in the motion picture industry thought the practice was acceptable, with the only snag being its cost. If dubbed, however, the picture had a chance of being sold to the big cinema chains instead of being confined to the art houses. "If the dialogue isn't in English, the peasants won't buy it, the wise guys say," declared Crowther. But he argued there was no denying the fact that a sound-track dubbed into English "vastly changes" a foreign picture. In the first place, he continued, it tainted the "natural flavor" of the location in which it was set and of which the original language was an "important communicator." The film lost, for example, its "Frenchness." A second and equally damaging problem, he said, was that the dubbing frequently caused changes in the visible personalities. With an inappropriate American voice, Brigitte Bardot, for example, was no longer Brigitte Bardot. With respect to dubbing Crowther concluded: "If this practice becomes common, it can ruin the character of foreign-language films."[56]

The audience for foreign movies, as small as it was, was seen as different from the mainstream audience. Richard Griffith was assistant to the director of New York's Museum of Modern Art Film Library. Writing at the beginning of 1951, he told of a golden age of the European film that started right after World War II and was "largely over" after only a few years. One of the few foreign films of recent years to be liked by the American public, he said, was *The Third Man*, although the U.S. trade was said to have attributed its box office success to the popularity of the theme song. All the rest of the films—British, French, Italian, and so forth—"found few audiences outside New York," Griffith added. He remarked, "And here their audience—at least their vocal audience—has been composed of the intelligentsia." He saw metropolitan intellectuals as the only articulate audience for foreign films, and regarded them as "the sole yardstick European film-makers can use in aiming at the American market." Griffith could think of only three postwar foreign-language films that reached beyond the intelligentsia to the American public at large—*Open City*, *Paisan*, and *Bicycle Thief* (all of which were Italian productions).[57]

A profile of art house patrons was produced in a report sent out in 1954 to American Broadcasting–Paramount Theatres affiliates by company vice president Edward L. Hyman. According to the report, the typical art venue patron did not fit into any single category: "In some cases he is a college graduate, but in many cases he is not. In the main, he is a person who is easily bored with not only hackneyed fare of any sort, but who thoroughly relishes new theatrical experiences." Hyman added that a point to remember was that the art house and foreign film patron usually was a former avid movie-goer who had given up the habit because "of disillusionment with run-of-the-mill product and because of certain discomforts and inconveniences sometimes attendant on movie going."[58]

When the U.S. motion picture industry was asked to comment on the negligible presence offshore pictures had in theatres, they often offered the thought, as they had in earlier periods, that the foreign product was simply no good. Although it was a patently false, even silly, idea, Hollywood never seemed to tire of advancing it. A 1950 article in *Variety* stated that 80 percent of the foreign-language films being imported into the States "should never have left Europe." As a result some of the art houses had been "forced" to mix regular American movies into their programs just to keep their houses open. Ilya Lopert, head of the importing firm Lopert Films, remarked that before World War II only about 12 foreign films a year played in the States—the rest weren't good enough. Lopert reiterated his contention that it was impossible to "make a business" of foreign film distribution in the U.S.A.[59]

Two years later a report said that foreign movies had found it to be tough going in the States "largely because of their limited story scope." Another account declared the lack of foreign-language films with broad audience appeal for America was underscored by the fact that the Hollywood major RKO, which two years earlier had announced its intention of taking on "good" offshore product for American distribution, had come up with only a single movie—*Rashomon* (Japan). RKO general sales manager Charles Boasberg said, "We are looking for films with a wide market appeal rather than art-house product."[60]

Importer and distributor of foreign movies Noel Meadow stated in 1953, "American distributors are meeting increasingly serious resistance to two-dimensional films largely in black-and-white, with dialog spoken in a foreign tongue." Compared to 1947, said Meadow, the quality of those offshore films was "off sharply." In 1947 a distributor found it hard to miss with even a so-so product. Meadow once had from 300 to 400 foreign movie outlets in the U.S., but he said the number had dwindled to perhaps 45. There was no lack of supply, admitted Meadow, who observed there were then 50 on the shelf, but because of their "generally poor quality," distributors would not take them for free. Foreign-language pictures

Paisan (Italy, 1946). One of the few post-war foreign films that reached a fairly wide U.S. audience.

had proved to have virtually no television value at all, he said, because the English titles came out too small and "the average TV audience just doesn't measure up to the traditional taste or intellectual level of the foreign film devotee." In his attack on offshore product Meadow damned product from virtually all the offshore foreign-language nations—France, Italy, Germany, and the Scandinavian lands.[61]

Another 1953 account stated there was unanimity among importers on the question of the quality of foreign movies: "It just isn't the same as it was in the prewar days, they say." Veteran importer Joseph Burstyn complained, "The old world doesn't make good pictures any more." It was a decline he attributed to a lack of ideas, while others saw it as the "result of European producers trying too hard to make films suitable for the American market."[62]

Also, as in the past, foreigners could be found who joined with Hollywood in condemning their own output. Ivan Foxwell, a British producer, said in a 1955 visit to New York that in his opinion there was no bar to British pictures in America. He felt there were three reasons to explain why the British output did not do well. One reason was the lack of marquee names known in the States. Secondly, he said, "Our subjects are too local in character and frequently too subtle in treatment." Thirdly, the British "rarely get a crack at the truly international stories, big plays and novels." If British films did not do well in the United States, "it was mostly because they were not the kind of pictures they want to see here," Foxwell said. "Even our well-made films frequently don't have international appeal. And for that we really don't have anyone to blame but ourselves," he concluded.[63]

Tom O'Brien, general secretary of Britain's National Association of Theatrical and Kine Employees, remarked in 1956 that the British motion picture industry was to blame for its poor U.S. reception. "Good films, wherever they are produced, have a ready market anywhere," he believed. While O'Brien found the idea of producing British movies portraying the British way of life to be commendable, he concluded that movie-goers in all countries "were not very much concerned in paying to see the British way of life."[64]

More direct methods of controlling and limiting a foreign screen presence included the U.S. star system. As that system collapsed to some extent in the 1950s, independent American producers, faced with a limited array of top names, had taken to producing movies that depended more heavily on storyline than name casts. Supposedly a development such as that was helpful to imports since the U.S. public would be conditioned gradually to accept films lacking the attraction of big names. (Of course, it did not work out that way.) "Star consciousness of the American public has always been a sizable handicap for the foreign film whose personalities are barely established in the U.S. mind," commented one reporter.[65]

One of the oddest reasons given for a weak foreign presence came from Edward Kingsley, head of Kingsley International Pictures (distributor of foreign and specialized movies). According to Kingsley, the U.S.A. was a "title conscious" country, and the only way a foreign import could break out of the art house ghetto and into general release was through "a snappy name switch." Candidly admitting that the imports had only the rarest of chances of obtaining a first-run general release, Kingsley maintained that exhibitors and film bookers bought their second features (for the bottom half of a double-bill) by title values. For the second feature market, he said, they liked movies with commercial titles that could be paired with an American first-run item. "With the right title, many foreign films—particularly British—can earn their way into general release," he argued. England and

The Third Man (U.K., 1949, director Carol Reed on the set, at left).

other countries were not concerned about titles, believed Kingsley, since they had a "pre-sold" market for their product in their home nations. "Since most of these pictures have no star value they have no chance of becoming sleepers here unless the titles have some appeal to American audiences," he added. As examples of title changes designed to attract bigger audiences in the States, Kingsley cited *Scotch on the Rocks* (from the original *Laxdale Hall*), *Murder at Monday* (*Home at Seven*), *Young Scarface* (*Brighton Rock*), *The Young and the Damned* (*Los Olivdardos—The Lost Ones*), and *The Horse's Mouth* (*The Oracle*).

The current pattern for imports, he felt, was to receive first-run bookings in art houses and second feature status in commercial houses if they gained "acceptability via an attractive title." All imported films were "reborn" in New York. "Each picture starts from scratch when it gets here. The promotion and advertising must be planned for the American market," he explained. "If it doesn't get off to a good start in New York, it doesn't have a chance any place. You might as well burn the film." Only with a good "commercial title" could an import expect to have a chance to obtain second feature bookings. Another problem, Kingsley said, was that European producers had an "inflated" idea of the appropriate asking price for U.S. distribution rights for their movies: "Their price expectations are up in the clouds."[66]

Talent poaching continued to be a practice used by Hollywood, with negative effects for film industries in the nations that were raided. Arthur Jarratt, managing director of the producer British Lion, complained in the mid–1950s that, when British Lion was trying to establish its stable of stars, each rising star was "snatched" away by Hollywood. Jarratt did not go along with the argument that in some mysterious way it was all for the best for the U.K. industry. "Once one of our stars goes to [Hollywood], their price goes up so that no one at home can afford him again," he explained. "And then, too, there's a question just when the star will find his way back to Britain. His being in American films doesn't help us in any way."[67]

Harry Brandt was the American owner of a large cinema circuit who thought that poaching in reverse was a mistake. He argued that foreign producers could get farther in the U.S. market by selling their own personalities, rather than American actors. Brandt was confident that the U.S. public would "buy" them at the box office, adding, "The foreign producers are in a good position to create new stars for the U.S."[68]

Director and producer Stanley Donen said, in 1958, that if you were a producer and wanted to use an unknown for a part, you were apt to pick a foreign player with a name in Germany, France or Britain instead of somebody whom absolutely nobody knew. "It makes sense, and it's some sort of insurance right from the start," explained Donen.[69]

Hollywood's MPAA cartel dealt with outcries from foreign producers—and occasionally foreign politicians—by pretending to deal with the situation. The MPAA formed a new arm, the Advisory Unit for Foreign Films, late in 1949. It was designed and implemented to create the illusion that the situation of low foreign film penetration would be dealt with. Also, it was hoped that such a public show might help in preventing or limiting any legislative responses contemplated by foreign nations. Renato Gualino, president of the Italian Film Producers Association—and one who served on the Advisory Unit—arrived in New York in 1950 to confer with MPAA head Eric Johnston and with B. Bernard Kreisler, who headed the MPAA's consultative service for foreign producers who were looking to improve the American market for their product. Delegates from five other countries were due to arrive over the course of 1950 for similar consultations.[70]

Also in 1950, U.S. independent foreign film distributors decided it was time to organize themselves. Reporter Thomas Pryor remarked that the fact that the decision to organize came shortly after the MPAA formed its Advisory Unit "was not just simply a coincidence." Officially the attitude of the independents was to cooperate wholeheartedly with the MPAA in any activity that would be beneficial to foreign producers and the exhibition of their movies in America. Unofficially, though, the independents were worried. While the Advisory Unit was welcomed by some as an indication that foreign product might stand a better chance of increased bookings, some saw the specter of the majors trying to move in and influence or dominate the course of foreign pictures in the States. Also, the independents were annoyed that the MPAA went ahead with its plans without consulting them or asking them to assist in the formation of the new unit. Basically the new independents' organization planned to do the same types of things the Advisory Unit had in mind: to provide information about marketing foreign movies in the U.S., to better relations with foreign producers, and to sponsor a public relations program to interest more Americans in foreign films. Said one independent distributor: "The M.P.A.A. could make a big contribution toward international good-will if it could influence the circuits to give even one day a year, say July 14, to the exhibition of outstanding French films and, similarly, to designate Columbus Day as a day when the best Italian films would be shown generally throughout the country."[71]

Three top French film executives, Georges Courau, J. P. Fogerais, and Robert Cravenne, arrived in the U.S., also in 1950, as delegates of the French motion picture industry to the MPAA's Advisory Unit. They expressed the hope that a larger audience could be found for French films in America although they claimed to recognize the problem of non-acceptance by the general American public of foreign films of any kind. On their schedule were meetings with Johnston and the majors' presidents to assess their chances of getting more bookings with large cinema circuits. They said they knew too little about the Production Code (Hollywood's censorship mechanism) to give an opinion on whether they would adhere to it as an aid to increasing their playdate numbers. They emphasized that French movies would continue to present the French way of life with no concessions to U.S. audience tastes, but admitted that "on certain minor points it might be better to follow the code in production than be forced to scissor their product in order to get it past American bluenoses."[72]

The three Frenchmen returned home after an American visit that lasted four weeks. During that time they also met with Production Code Administrator Joseph Breen. Reportedly some advice was given, and taken, by the French during their stay. Apparently they were ready to devote more effort to promoting movies, to explore the use of more dubbing, and to perhaps sponsor a French film festival in New York. Also, French producers were advised to try to sell new categories of French pictures here, such as musical comedies, which, said a reporter, had "seldom found a market before in the U.S." When the French returned home, they seconded the thoughts of Italian delegate Renato Gualino when they declared, "With few exceptions, most French pictures do not have the general appeal necessary for mass audiences in the U.S." Such pessimism caused a reporter to conclude that despite the hopes of foreign producers for more screenings they were "apparently convinced" of the unlikelihood that this would happen anytime soon.[73]

By the beginning of 1953, both the MPAA's Advisory Unit and the independent distributors' International Motion Picture Organization were reported to "have more or less disintegrated." The latter group was said to be in existence but "inoperative," while the Advisory Unit was described as "more or less defunct." However, an account late in 1956 said the Advisory Unit had been handing out procedural advice to offshore producers for several years and had arranged trade screenings of foreign films for interested parties.[74]

Censorship problems plagued and limited foreign films in the 1950s to a much greater extent than ever before. American censorship attacked at many levels: within the industry itself (the Hollywood cartel's self-imposed Production Code); privately from outside the industry and government (the Roman Catholic Legion of Decency); from state and local governments (some of whom imposed their own censorship, at least for a time); and from the federal government (through the Customs Service). Hugh M. Flick, the New York State censor, suggested in 1954 that American importers of foreign movies should work out a set of standards that should then be communicated to producers abroad for their guidance in "adjusting their thinking to the moral standard realities of the American market." Regarding the foreign pictures he reviewed, Flick remarked, "It isn't what they give us, but the degree to which they go in presenting it." He found it regrettable that the public had gotten the impression that most French films had "smutty, sex-ridden themes" and he thought that "a voluntary restriction, particularly on the part of the producers, would go a long way in dispelling that idea." Flick was considered, said a reporter, to be "by far the most liberal and conscientious of the state censors" at that time. Only rarely had his office banned a picture that had been passed by the Production Code in Hollywood. There were even a few features, such as *The Moon Is Blue* (U.S., 1953), which did not get a Code seal but were passed by his reviewers without difficulty. Of the foreign films that arrived in New York, Flick said, 80 percent did not have a Production Code seal and most did not even try to obtain one. Flick argued that instead of fighting "enlightened censorship," the motion picture industry "should cooperate with it" because the alternative could be worse.[75]

Of the 1,190 foreign and domestic features and shorts licensed by the New York State censor between December 1, 1953, and November 30, 1954, a total of 550 of them—47 percent—did not carry a Production Code seal. Of the 698 American features and shorts, 615 had the seal, 83 did not. Of the 492 foreign films approved by the censor that year, only 25—five percent—carried the Code seal.[76]

Dave Williams, sales representative for Italian Films Export, reported in 1954 that in Tennessee the Memphis censor Lloyd T. Binford had banned three Italian films sight unseen. No reasons were given and the movies were never exhibited there. However, things began to change at the state level. In Pennsylvania, the State Board of Motion Picture Censors was declared unconstitutional in 1956 by the Supreme Court.[77]

As part of the paranoia of the early 1950s McCarthy era, all foreign films imported into the U.S. had to undergo a "security check" under the McCarran Act. Questionable movies would be delayed at customs for clearance into New York or at other ports of entry pending investigation. Overseas distributors had to sign statements that their films contained no threat to the American way of life. Distributors in London were said to be complying with the regulation. Every film entering America had to be accompanied by the following statement and signed by someone who had knowledge of the facts: "Film described above contains no obscene or immoral matter, nor any matter advocating or urging treason or insurrection against the United States or any forcible resistance to any law of the U.S., nor any threat to take life or inflict bodily harm upon any person in the U.S."[78]

Carl Dymling, president of Sweden's Svensk Filmindustri, complained in New York in 1958 that the authority of the U.S. Customs department to ban films was "incredible" and would be totally unacceptable in Europe where government generally played a much more active role than it did in the States. Dymling added that his company once had two pictures held up by Customs for several months. On that occasion, he asked the MPEA (Motion Picture Export Association—an agency of the MPAA that dealt with foreign matters) for help but that group got nowhere.[79]

Just six months later, French producer Jacques Bar declared in New York that French film producers should unite and take action against the "arbitrary censorship" of the U.S. Customs. He reported his feature La Loi had been held up by Customs for several weeks. At first Customs said seven reels of the picture were objectionable. Later that was reduced to just two scenes in a single reel. Bar agreed to the cuts and the movie was released from its hold. It was one of several imports to run into trouble with Customs censorship. Other movies sat on hold there, unreleased. Importers charged the Customs censorship, under Irving Fishman, Deputy Collector of Customs, went beyond the limits of the law, which provided that only "lewd and obscene" material could be kept out of the country. When word got out that a film had trouble with Customs, it made it more difficult for the producer to sell that item since it was automatically assumed the picture had been cut to ribbons. That gave distributors an edge in negotiating a deal. Some foreign producers were reported to be shooting "protection scenes" for the U.S. market, in anticipation of problems with Customs.[80]

Most censorship problems for offshore producers came from the MPAA's Production Code and from the Legion of Decency. The Production Code refused to grant seals to Italy's *Bicycle Thief* and France's *Devil in the Flesh*. Both movies won critical raves and did good business in America. Mexico's *Los Olividados* played a few New York art houses but made little impact. It did not apply for a Production Code seal and, wrote a journalist, it would not have got one if it had. To avoid production of that type of film in the future, the Mexican government (involved in funding) was insisting on vehicles that measured up more closely to the Legion of Decency rules in the hopes that would "make for a stronger U.S. boxoffice." Without a Production Code seal a film would not be booked into any cinemas circuits, large or otherwise. Effectively the only outlet it had was limited to art houses. While the Production Code censorship was purely voluntary, all of Hollywood's majors (and most of the independent producers) and all the exhibitors who counted rigidly adhered to the institution.[81]

So frustrated by the whole system was William Shelton, vice president of Times Film (a U.S. distributor of foreign product) that he said the Production Code Administration should create a special classification for imported movies—"adult" was the one he suggested.[82]

Much resentment was said to exist in the mid–1950s among European producers over what they considered to be an increasing censorship problem in America. Europeans were particularly "scornful" about U.S. Customs censorship, which could vary by port of entry. Producers abroad told visiting Americans that U.S. censorship was discriminatory against foreign product in that it appeared to apply different standards to their pictures from those applied to U.S. productions. A foreign film faced three hurdles: U.S. Customs first, then the Production Code, and third, the Legion of Decency. Art houses played product without a Production Code seal or the Legion okay, but there were only a couple hundred such venues in America. No mainstream cinema played a film without a Production Code seal and only a small number of those would screen something without a pass from the Legion. At this time seven states had their own censor boards. Lack of a Production Code seal and the Legion's approval seriously crippled a movie's chances at the box office.[83]

Agitation over the Production Code by European producers continued to grow as they remained convinced that Hollywood's censorship machinery operated "easy" on U.S. producers and "tough" on foreign and was therefore not impartial. Europeans threatened to enact a retaliatory code, a code-for-code strategy. Foreign producer Paul Graetz argued, with others, that foreign films should not have to undergo Code scrutiny or else that a special rating should be created for them. No legal challenge had ever been made against the Production Code, although by the mid–1950s cracks were beginning to appear. One blow came when the Production Code refused to grant a seal to *The Moon Is Blue*. That film went on to play a great many dates (at theaters that normally required a seal) without it. Following that was RKO's *The French Line* (U.S., 1954), which resulted in the MPAA fining RKO for releasing a movie without its seal. RKO never did pay that fine as it was destined for bankruptcy a few years later. As Europeans spent more money on each of their productions, they were more likely to consider submitting the item to the Production Code since they were even more desirous of increasing their potential U.S. take.[84]

Jean Goldwurm, an American distributor of foreign product, drew up a memo in 1954 declaring the MPAA, in conjunction with the large cinema circuits, had succeeded in imposing its code not just on its own members, but also on independent U.S. producers and even distributors of offshore items. Goldwurm called the MPAA's policy "definitely an act of discrimination against foreign films."[85]

Any European idea that the Production Code was harder on its product than it was on domestic output seemed to be borne out by example. Universal declared it would not distribute the British film *The Young Lovers* (later *Chance Meeting*) in the U.S. because the movie could not get a Code seal. Objectionable was the ending in which the heroine was pregnant but there was no marriage ceremony (Universal did distribute that Rank picture in South America). Yet in Fox's *Untamed*, the story ended with Susan Hayward with a son by Tyrone Power but also no marriage ceremony. *Untamed* received a Code seal. As a reporter noted, "Major companies won't take on a foreign film unless it's got Legion and Code okay."[86]

According to Jacques Flaud, director general of France's Centre National de la Cinématographie (on the occasion of the first visit to the

U.S. by the French government's top film executive), French producers could not understand why, as a condition of possible success in the U.S., they should be expected to permanently submit their scripts in advance to a foreign censor, Hollywood's Production Code. (Submission of the script to the PCA before shooting was said to be in the interest of the Hollywood producers since it was cheaper to change a script compared to changing a finished film. Once the movie was shot it was resubmitted to the PCA, to make sure the PCA demands had been followed.) Flaud said he felt strongly that Code and general censorship standards applied to foreign movies, which weren't made under the provisions of the Code in the first place, were unfair. While in America he was scheduled to meet with Production Code Administrator Geoffrey Shurlock in Hollywood, to present the French case for separate and more sympathetic treatment of imports. "It is important that this American self-censorship, as applied to foreign films, should not be allowed to cut us off from the American audience," he stressed. "There is no reason why our pictures should be treated the same way, and from the same point-of-view, as the Hollywood films." Flaud added that French producers could not accept the idea that their films just would not sell in the U.S. French films were expected that year to bring in about $10 million in foreign earnings (25 to 30 percent of their total, down from 40 percent in prewar years). Asked what America's contribution was to that $10 million, he replied, "Close to zero." Remarking that in Europe censors only looked at the finished product, Flaud declared, "How can a national industry accept the idea of submitting its films to a foreign censor in advance of their making?"[87]

Columbia went on record at the start of 1956 stating that it would not handle any imports to the U.S. unless they could get a Code seal. This was a Hollywood major that had set up a special unit to distribute foreign movies. During 1955, the number of Production Code seals granted (for features only) for domestic films from MPAA cartel members was 210 (as compared to 187 in 1954, 272 in 1950, and 229 in 1947); seals granted for domestic films made by non–MPAA members that year numbered 31 (45, 107, 141). Seals granted for foreign films in 1955, handled by MPAA members, went up to 45 (41, 22, 16); those for foreign films handled by non–MPAA members fell to 19 (30, 28, 18).[88]

When he was visiting Europe in 1956, MPAA head Eric Johnston was questioned wherever he went about the Production Code and whether he thought the U.S. did all it could to facilitate entry into America of foreign-made features. Strongly defending the Production Code, Johnston declared, "The Code was vital to the film industry's own public relations in America." He added, "Foreign producers who ignore or defy the Code needlessly

hamper their own economic advantage in crashing the Yankee markets."
As an aside Johnston said he was personally opposed to any flat taboos in
the Code, such as the one surrounding narcotics subjects. He was not with
the MPAA when the Code was drafted. Not practical in his mind was a
separate Code rating for foreign movies, such as "adult." He also said it was
"impractical" to revise the Code to make certain allowances for imports.
"Why can't they make pictures that conform to the Code? That would eliminate a lot of the trouble," Johnston said. "One of the reasons why our pictures are so popular everywhere is that they are good for family audiences."[89]

Still, foreign film producers continued to ignore the Production Code,
failing to submit their movies for the Code seal. Figures from the New York
censor for the year ending April 1, 1957, showed a total of 477 features
from overseas were submitted to its office. Only 22 (four percent) carried
a Code seal; the remaining 455 did not. With regard to American films,
332 were submitted, and only 45 (14 percent) lacked a Code seal. That New
York censor asked for a single elimination (from one picture) from the 287
domestic films that carried a seal, and cuts in five movies (11 percent) from
the movies that did not have the okay. On the foreign side no eliminations
were asked from the 22 features with a seal, but cuts were requested from
30 pictures (seven percent) of the 455 imports without Code approval. A
reporter observed that, with the exception of the British, most foreign producers failed to even submit their products to the Code office.[90]

William Shelton, of the distributor Times Films, sometimes sent films
to the Production Code for a seal. After a denial in one case he wrote a
letter of appeal to Production Code Administrator Geoffrey Shurlock: "As
matters stand now, with the Code seal denied most imports ... devotees of
these pictures are all but relegated to a kind of plush 'art house ghetto.'"
He still wanted the Production Code machinery to establish and implement a special classification for foreign movies.[91]

Late in the 1950s importers again grumbled that the Code was harder
on imports than it was on domestic product and that a special category
needed to be set up for foreign films. One problem was that independent
distributors were disappearing, swallowed by the majors. For example, Lopert Films merged into United Artists and Kingsley International was
acquired by Columbia. As long as those majors were members of the
MPAA, the majors were contractually under obligation not to release films
without a Code seal. It meant a reduced number of distributors potentially
available to handle overseas product. Columbia had gotten around the
problem by setting up a separate subsidiary under Edward Kingsley to handle non-seal bearing foreign items. It was a setup that the MPAA had not
challenged, to that point.[92]

The U.S. Supreme Court decided in 1952 in favor of the Italian movie *The Miracle* after attempts were made to prevent its screening in America. Independent distributor Joseph Burstyn alone fought the case to the highest level of the court system. Thus, foreign importers could continue to import pictures without fear they would be banned on "sacrilegious grounds." Reporter Henry Brill thought the decision on *The Miracle* would not effect Hollywood at all. "The American movie industry is controlled entirely by New York financial interests," he explained. "Hollywood has adopted, therefore, as everyone should know by now, voluntary self-censorship and is resolved to make movies which will offend no single pressure group and will be money-makers if nothing else."

That decision led to a new campaign to get Italian producers to adopt and adhere to a production code of their own, a campaign by the Roman Catholic Legion of Decency. Two U.S. priests arrived in Rome in the summer of that year. One was the Very Reverend Monsignor John McClafferty, who had headed the Legion of Decency until 1948 and remained a dominating influence in it. Accompanying him was Father Joseph Mahoney. Those two were guided around Rome by John Perdicari, Italian correspondent for *Film Daily*, an important U.S. trade paper. One meeting the three had was with Eitel Monaco, head of the National Association of Italian Film Producers and of Italian Films Export. At that session McClafferty proposed to Monaco that the Italian industry, in order to avoid "past errors," should either have an American "adviser" permanently stationed in Italy to warn Italian producers against "infringements of the American moral code," or send an Italian to the States for orientation who, on his return, would act in such a capacity. "We feel that by approaching the producer before a film is actually made we can point out to him certain things which are unacceptable to Americans," McClafferty explained to Monaco. He believed that no question of censorship was involved. "We have certain moral codes in America which differ from those of, say Japan or Italy," he stressed. "These moral codes must be defended and enforced."[93]

When *La Ronde* arrived in Chicago none of the city's newspapers would at first accept ads for the motion picture, which did not have the Legion okay. Later, several of the papers changed their minds but one of the most important newspapers, the *Chicago Tribune*, did not relent. Importers cited Catholic pressure for that situation.[94]

The Legion of Decency classified motion pictures into several categories: Class AI, morally unobjectionable for general patronage; Class AII, morally unobjectionable for adults; Class B, morally objectionable in part for all; and Class C, the dreaded "Condemned" category—a film given this rating by the Legion had difficulty getting booked. A journalist observed

in late 1954 that of the 73 movies then in the Legion's condemned category, only two were being handled by U.S. major distributors (that is, cartel members): *The French Line* (RKO) and *The Moon Is Blue* (United Artists).
Neither of them had received a Code seal. No other releases from the Hollywood majors lacked a Code seal. "The vast majority of the condemned
pix are of foreign origin," said the reporter. That almost complete absence
of Hollywood features in the Legion's C class showed "the extent to which
the moral standards of the Legion" were similar to those of the Code. Concluded the account: "It further reflects the distribs' reluctance to take on
films that lack Legion approval at some level."[95]

As foreign producers tried harder to extend their presence on American screens, they had to pay more attention to both the Production Code
and the Legion of Decency ratings. Being passed by those two bodies was
the only way an import had even a theoretical chance of being booked into
at least some mainstream cinemas. A 1955 account declared, "While it's
generally acknowledged that a Legion nix today is less of a [box office] barrier than it was some years back, it's also true that it can still represent a
formidable obstacle in many parts of the country when it comes to booking in commercial houses." Also noted was that since the Production Code
tended to weed out most of the material that the Legion might find objectionable, the C rating "applied for the most part only to foreign imports."
In conclusion the report stated, "[The] Industry generally feels that the
Legion is much harder on imports than it is on American product, partly
because it's on the lookout for trouble. Same is said of the Code."[96]

During the visit to America by France's Jacques Flaud (from a Catholic
nation), he said the attitude of the Legion appeared to be that American
films were sufficient for the market and that nothing good could come
from abroad. French producers had been considerably puzzled, he added,
when, on several occasions, movies that had received Catholic prizes in
France and the rest of Europe had run into trouble with the Catholic
reviewing group in the States.[97]

Catholic protests against the playing of C-rated films by the Queen
Anne theatre in Bogota, New Jersey (Bergen County), occurred in October 1955. Parishioners of Catholic churches were told from the pulpits that
the Queen Anne was "off limits" for them. Exhibitor David Frankl, who
had reopened the venue the previous April after it had been dark for five
years, said the protest was based on three C-rated movies out of a total of
43 he had screened. Frankl stressed that, unless he could show foreign
imports, he could not remain open. When he first reopened, he pro-
grammed American fare but was not successful. "Since we switched to foreign pictures, we are getting a good patronage from all over the county,"

he said. "People like to have a place where they can see foreign films without having to go into New York." His venue was the only Bergen County house to show imports on a regular basis. Trouble started with a visit to Frankl by a delegation of three men from St. Joseph parish. They expressed concern and very soon thereafter Mrs. Lester Searfoss, president of the St. Joseph's School PTA, got together a petition to the borough council, criticizing the exhibition of the three Cs. Following that was a second petition. Other PTA organizations said they would also start investigating. Next came denunciations from church pulpits. Bogota was described as about half Catholic but with a considerably lower percentage in the rest of the county. When the controversy first arose, borough attorney Irving Evers admitted he had searched the books for a statute under which censorship might be imposed. However, in the end the borough council rejected all notions of censorship, merely urging the house to stick to "clean" films. Covering the story a reporter concluded, "Impression gotten is that the objections in Bogota actually go beyond 'C' tagged pix and extend to all foreign films."[98]

One 1956 story had it that the Legion of Decency ratings also had an effect on art house cinemas—venues that traditionally did not care about Legion okays or Code seals. A number of such outlets which had always played imports without regard to review status were said to be refusing to play pictures condemned by the Legion. Jack Ellis, distributor of *Three Forbidden Stories*, disclosed he could not get the film shown in Baltimore, St. Paul, Providence, or Washington, D.C., because the Legion gave it a C. The only parts of America not concerned about the Legion were the south and the southwest, according to Ellis. Such key cities as New York, Chicago, and Los Angeles were open to playdates but the exhibitors still would have preferred it if no C was attached to the movie. Outcomes such as that were hard on distributors like Ellis because they generally struck deals to handle imports prior to inspection by the Legion. If an item was later rated C, the distributor sustained a financial setback. A conclusion drawn in this account was: "The Legion has become more powerful than the Production Code has long been recognized. No major circuit will give screen time to a 'C' entry, whereas *Man with the Golden Arm* played all the top chains." That film was okayed by the Legion but rejected for a Code seal because it dealt with narcotics (a blanket ban on the topic existed under the Production Code).[99]

A statement was issued by Bishop William A. Scully of Albany, New York, chairman of the Episcopal Committee on Motion Pictures, Radio and Television, the committee that set the National Legion of Decency policy. In it Scully said that radio and television programs in general did not pose a problem of moral judgment for members of the Roman Catholic faith but motion pictures, especially those shown in drive-ins and art houses had to be kept under continued surveillance by the Legion. Scully's statement was a reminder to Catholics that on the following Sunday they would be asked to renew their pledge of loyalty to the Legion. That loyalty pledge had been said annually in Catholic churches for some 20 years. Many foreign films exhibited in the U.S. constituted a danger to American moral life, said Scully, adding, "The problem of such foreign films is growing daily because their exhibition is no longer limited to a few art houses in the major cities; with each passing day foreign films are making a deeper penetration into theatres all around the country." Scully remarked that American bishops had, from time to time "commended the motion picture industry for their organ of self-regulation, the Production Code."[100]

One 1958 French import did more than any other offshore product to ease restrictions on the playing of C-rated films—but did not eliminate the bar completely. That was *And God Created Woman*, starring the towel-draped Brigitte Bardot. Some of the major circuits refused to book the C-rated movie but others did book it. Easing of restrictions, or flaunting of the rating, was said to be most noticeable in areas with no strong Catholic influence. In Austin, Texas, an import usually played just one cinema in that city of 110,000—an art house near the University of Texas campus. However, *God* played four different theaters in Austin.[101]

Ironically, the Americans had been refusing in the mid–1950s to submit their films to Japan's counterpart of Hollywood's Production Code. Their reasoning, said an account, was "that Nippon film men, who administer their own set of standards, might bar important U.S. pictures from Japan and permit entry, via their seal of endorsement, for only product that would not be too competitive with native features." Like the Production Code, the Japanese Code of Ethics was voluntary. It was all quite embarrassing because foreign producers took substantially the same position that the Americans were taking in Japan. Hollywood, of course, insisted there was no such market roadblock for the foreigners such as they were faced with in Japan.[102]

As the 1950s ended, independent distributors of foreign films were upset over Eric Johnston's insinuations that the real root of the current censorship problem lay with the imports rather than with the American product. Said one importer, "We're being used as scapegoats. Johnston knows perfectly well that the current agitation is about purely American films and not about the foreign releases, which still are fairly limited." They saw it as an obvious attempt to shift the blame to a smaller group with a comparatively weak voice and away from the majors. Increasingly a prob-

And God Created Woman (France, 1956, Brigitte Bardot and Curt Jürgens). The dubbing of foreign films for American audiences—rarely done—became a little more popular after the arrival of Brigitte Bardot movies.

lem was whether or not the Code should continue to classify films since its seal was more and more seen as untrustworthy and irrelevant, unable to keep periodic agitation over the perceived lack of morality in the movies from arising from time to time.[103]

Distribution of foreign films in the U.S. continued to be the major stumbling block for that product. The majors barely bothered to handle them. Figures from the MPAA revealed how many films were given a Code seal and released in the U.S. by the eight majors (plus Allied Artists and Republic, from 1935 to 1939). In the foreign production group were movies produced or co-produced by the Hollywood studios and foreign films acquired for U.S. distribution by the MPAA-member companies. That is, the number of movies that were truly foreign films were less than the stated total: In the year 1935 (334 domestic productions, 9 foreign productions); 1936 (337, 0); 1937 (339, 0); 1938 (322, 5); 1939 (366, 0); 1940 (325, 0);

1941 (406, 5); 1942 (369, 12); 1943 (256, 10); 1944 (284, 6); 1945 (230, 14); 1946 (254, 16); 1947 (229, 16); 1948 (229, 25); 1949 (252, 21); 1950 (272, 22); and 1951 (282, 32).[104]

Rashomon (Japan) was hailed as a big box office hit when, at the start of 1953, it had grossed an estimated $200,000 in the U.S.—a lot of money for a foreign release. Contrasted with that were the earnings from domestic rentals of U.S. pictures. All-time lead grosser was *Gone with the Wind*, with $26 million from its initial release and three reissues to that point. Movies released the previous year, 1952, included *The Greatest Show on Earth*, grossing $12.8 million (second all-time); *Quo Vadis* with $10.5 million (third); *Ivanhoe* with $7 million (12th); *Snows of Kilimanjaro* with $6.5 million (14th); *Sailor Beware* with $4.3 million (62nd); *African Queen* with $4 million (81st); and *Jumping Jacks* with $4 million (87th). On the all-time list were 95 films with domestic (U.S.A. and Canada) rentals of $4 million or more.[105]

Grumbles from distributors over their costs were common. Foreign producers expected too much money for the output and many of those distributors felt, in 1955, that a guarantee of $15,000 to $20,000 was the most that should be asked. Besides price the distributors blamed a host of factors for the disappointing level of foreign screen penetration, including the "low quality" of the European movies, which itself arose from misguided efforts to "tailor" movies to a U.S. audience. As well, Americans rejected subtitled films but did not accept dubbed efforts, and they blamed exhibitors for not booking the offshore product often enough.[106]

Arthur Davis, an importer of foreign movies, complained about the increased cost of importing color movies, as foreigners turned to them more and more. In the past he had imported the negatives and had about 10 or so black-and-white prints made at a cost of about $250 each; he said, "The subtitles are no problem, and whatever the take, it certainly covered print costs and allowed for a profit." With color films, he said, the cost of prints had gone up to around $850. When subtitling costs and import duties were added, a print could cost as much as $1,400.[107]

Universal's eastern advertising manager, and a "specialist" in plugging British imports, J. Livingston, said the advertising budget and approach for selling British movies "must take into account the limitations of the audience." In the beginning, Universal had made the "mistake" of giving British films the same advertising treatment as other important Hollywood features with national appeal, he explained. They found out they were overspending and that their efforts were wrong. In view of that experience, Universal then spent a maximum of $35,000 to promote and exploit its British releases, compared to the $200,000 it might spend to promote an

American film. All of its British films were launched in New York at art houses.[108]

Sometimes the majors picked up foreign films for distribution in other parts of the world; said a reporter, "Rarely do these companies undertake the release of such films in the United States, feeling that their releasing orgs are not geared for the handling of product which generally falls into the art house slot." On occasion, if "practical," those features were turned over to independent distributors in America who were experienced in imports but the pictures were often "never exhibited in the U.S." Warner Bros. was then handling a pair of French movies for which they held western hemisphere rights, but they were only releasing them in Latin America. MGM had two French features it was distributing in Latin America and the Near East. Fox was handling about 15 foreign items in various parts of the world while Columbia, RKO, Paramount and Universal also were handling foreign output the same way. In all cases the majors were not distributing those movies in America.[109]

Columbia Pictures set up a special department (a subsidiary company) in 1955 to distribute what it said would be a "limited number" of foreign films in the U.S. Behind the formation of that unit, said the studio, was the realization "that certain foreign films need special handling and are apt to die when pressed through the regular release mill." Indications were that the new company would not handle any product that had a C-rating bestowed upon it by the Legion. The few movies it had selected to be first handled by the new division were described by a reporter as the kind that "aren't likely to run into censorial trouble." Columbia's move had been in the works for a year and was said to be evidence that exhibitor reluctance to screen foreign pictures was being overcome. Yet this new unit was targeting only the specialized market, that is, the art houses. Columbia's art film section planned to handle primarily subtitled product and selected U.K. items. Thus, Columbia became virtually the only Hollywood major to have an active subsidiary devoted to handling foreign films. Universal had such a unit but it was then "fairly inactive," since Rank had taken its films elsewhere. RKO reportedly had been "half heartedly" trying to do something with imports and Fox had a few "in the regular lineup."[110]

In a 1955 article on whether a foreign producer was better off with his movies distributed in America by one of the majors or by an independent, a journalist commented, "The majors' attitude in taking on foreign films isn't always motivated by a pure desire to see such pix succeed in the U.S." Often it was a matter of pleasing those producers abroad and their governments, since some of the Hollywood majors may have had an ever harder time abroad unless they had some of the native pictures available for distribution in the U.S., at least theoretically. An advertising and publicity executive with one of the majors discussed the handling of a British film. He asked the British representative how much the latter thought the item would gross in the U.S.—the reply was $300,000. "And for $300,000 we are supposed to put into a picture the same time and effort that would go into selling a potential $3,000,000 or $5,000,000 grosser," complained the U.S. executive. "It just doesn't figure."[111]

Another account stated the main stumbling blocks for foreign film penetration in the U.S. had been "the numerical lack of films suitable for American audiences and the exhibs' reluctance to go out on a limb with imports." Distributors, however, had two categories of offshore product— British and dubbed items—that could be sold "without clear identification of their foreign label." As might be expected, offshore producers were not always happy with the blurring of their labels. For example, J. Arthur Rank was reported to have been furious with Universal when the latter dropped the Rank insignia and markings on some of its British releases in South America.[112]

Fred Hift authored an opinion column of rationalizations and false hopes with regard to offshore product, in the mid–1950s. Observing that Hollywood's foreign earnings were $215 million in 1955, he acknowledged that the quid-pro-quo argument made by foreigners was valid "to an extent"; he added, "As a result, Hollywood has gone quite far in making concessions." Cited as examples by Hift were millions of dollars spent abroad by Hollywood to produce movies there, giving local employment; the MPAA's set-up "long ago" of a special section to advise foreigners, and a U.S. "loan" to Italy as a subsidy, a debt that was later cancelled. (It was a payment to the Italian industry that was negotiated as a part of an Italian and American motion picture industry agreement. The money was not a loan to be repaid.) Cinema divorcement, when the majors had been ordered by the court to sell their theatres, thought Hift, "put a crimp into any intensive efforts to 'press' foreign films into the theatres." Hollywood's majors, who were most exposed to foreign urgings for a better break for their movies in America were, therefore, not in a position to do much of a job when it came to exhibition, explained Hift. He added, "Most of them are not really geared to adequately distribute imports.... As a matter of past experience, the vast majority of productions made abroad don't qualify for the Code okay and thus are 'out of bounds' for MPAA members [to distribute]."[113]

Overseas producers were said to be intensifying their efforts to increase their share of the U.S. market in 1956 at a time when it was widely held there was a product shortage in America. Yet the foreign share did not increase, a situation that left the offshore producers confused. Fred Hift returned to explain the situation: "Unlike their European counterparts, Americans have never lacked in native film fare. They were raised on it and they developed a taste for its subjects, its pace, its moralistic values, etc." What was widely misunderstood in Europe, Hift continued, but readily recognized by those who came to the States "in search of helpful information," was that the resistance to imported movies by the mass audience was not based on chauvinism or on negative feelings against any specific countries. "Rather it is a reflection of a spirit in a huge country, with a single language but whose public tends to be regional in its outlook and its attitudes," he explained. Hift said that within the past year U.S. exhibitors had told foreigners of their increased willingness to accept offshore pictures but this "added considerably to the confusion since the lip-service is a long way from the facts." One film executive had declared that several thousand U.S. houses would close in the coming few years (from the effects of television) and "the vast majority" would do this "without giving foreign films even a try." Again Hift wondered about the best way to distribute foreign pictures in America—directly by the foreigners through a new distribution channel they created, or through an existing channel. While Hift did not answer his own question, he pointed to the failure of one such channel, the Italian Films Export (IFE), which he described as "an ambitiously conceived project, which has floundered mostly because Italy stopped turning out a volume of interested pix." American observers, he concluded, "tend to feel that quality is an overriding consideration."[114]

The MPAA, through its foreign arm, the MPEA, had long wanted the Europeans to set up their own distribution organization so they could see how "hard" that market was; the hope was that the Europeans could no longer complain that the lack of their presence on U.S. screens was a fault of U.S. distributors—Hollywood. Europeans might still blame American cinemas owners but the MPEA was said to believe it could convince the Europeans that its members no longer controlled the circuits, and so Hollywood would again be exonerated. It was a situation that constantly worried the MPAA because it so dominated cinema screens around the world—fear of retaliation of some kind.[115]

Foreign film producers complained that they rarely got an honest financial accounting from the independent distributors in New York and that was one of the reasons they asked for such "high" guarantees. Most independent distributors, of course, denied the allegation. They pointed out, without detail, that compared to the financial set-up between Hollywood distributors and U.S. independent producers, the overseas producer got "by far the better break."[116]

Dan Frankel ran a one-man firm that imported and distributed foreign films. One problem he faced was that in Manhattan there were 11 cinemas with a regular policy of screening first-run foreign films. Four of them, however, were owned by a man who also controlled booking at 120 other, regular cinemas. Also, he distributed foreign so his items got preference. That left seven venues, but one was controlled by Rank. Of the six remaining, two were owned by another man who also distributed foreign product, as was one other by a different person. Thus, said Frankel, for him there were only three cinemas that could be approached with any hope of success—and 30 other distributors competing there.[117]

Once again Hift returned, in 1958, to explain the situation, remarking that although the flow of foreign films into America had risen to "flood tide," distribution methods had not substantially changed. "With the logical exception of the British, most imports still are confined to strictly limited circulation," he remarked. Even though a dubbed import had a better chance of obtaining a wider playoff in America, it still usually failed "in the second-feature category." Speaking of the release of foreign-language films by the Hollywood majors, he said, "The feeling is still widespread that the big companies aren't geared for specialized handling," adding, "However, producers abroad continue to dream of 'major' distribution." Columbia was then said to be the only major that could even remotely be called active in the field—a few other majors were then handling something like one foreign film each, the others had none. "The vast majority of imports get little more than token circulation in the States," admitted Hift. There were only about 300 houses in the States then that regularly booked foreign films. It was a situation complicated by the fact that many of those houses were owned by distributors who tended to showcase their own films in those outlets. Bizarrely, Hift then turned around to state: "foreign films are beginning to give Hollywood a run for its money in the domestic market." Contradicting himself, the reporter then said there were 700 to 800 art houses in the U.S., of which about 400 would play foreign movies. Exhibition in New York still accounted for 50 percent or more of an import's total U.S. income.[118]

About 40 companies distributed foreign films in the U.S. in 1959, most of them small; a handful of them (the biggest ones) were either affiliated with a major or owned their own venues. Just a year earlier, Rank had shut down its American distribution unit because of the expense. So small were most of those 40 firms that they had few or no branch offices, relying on sub-distributors. United Artists and the independent it had recently swallowed, Lopert, jointly owned the Plaza Theatre in New York, while Columbia and its newly merged independent, Kingsley, had a working agreement with the Paris Theatre in New York. Most of those 40 companies complained about the lack of profit in the business. Richard Brandt, president of Trans-Lux Distributing, remarked, "At Trans-Lux we've had two hits in four years. The rest of the films were no good. I wouldn't call that a particularly encouraging average."[119]

The East German film production and distribution company, DEFA, reported that four DEFA features had been sold to the U.S., two to Excelsior distributors and two to Brandon Films, in the late 1950s. However, by 1959, it was reported it had not been possible to obtain screen time for any of them to that date.[120]

Importer and distributor Noel Meadow discussed the importance of the New York run of at least eight weeks—this remained an absolute prerequisite for a foreign film's acceptance in other cities. Also important were at least fair press reviews in New York to go along with a decent run. Then the movie could go on to get bookings in others cities such as Chicago, Philadelphia, Detroit, Boston and Los Angeles. Meadow argued, "The absolute rule [up to around 1951] has been that any foreign film is whipped to a standstill by a bad press in New York—especially in the *Times, Herald Tribune,* or *Post,* which foreign film fans read." But it was a jinx he felt *Orpheus* (Jean Cocteau, France) beat, though most of the daily papers' critics panned it, because the movie impressed *Newsweek, Time,* the *New Yorker,* and some other "slicks"; the picture caught on quickly. It might have been the exception to the rule, thought Meadow. He cautioned, "But that rule remains valid—the daily press reaction is of first importance.... In foreign films, a flop drops with a very loud crash. There's no chance of sneaking a few hundred bookings for it as the bottom half of a Hollywood dilly."[121]

Distributors, especially the Hollywood majors, were prone to exonerate themselves and to blame the exhibitors for the difficulties foreign product faced in America. There was some truth in the allegations. Reportedly there was a decline in New York of cinemas devoted to foreign product in the early 1950s, a decrease caused by a paucity of good foreign movies. Art house operators were switching to English-language items (U.S. or British) rather than foreign-language pictures, assuming they could draw a larger audience that way, even if they had a minor quality Hollywood or U.K. film. Reportedly there were then only three art houses in New York that would play foreign-language movies, "except if actually forced to by the lack of other product." At one time art houses were nicknamed "sureseaters," because a potential patron was sure of getting a seat no matter when he turned up, at a time when sellouts in regular cinemas were far from uncommon.[122]

Jack Ellis, an importer of foreign fare, was annoyed by what he described as the "continued aloofness" of many exhibitors to foreign product despite the alleged scarcity of Hollywood films. He found it "rankling, to say the least, to receive a deaf ear by so many exhibitors when you start to talk about foreign product, whether it be English, French or Italian." In many cases, he thought, it meant they had once played a foreign movie that had flopped and they vowed to never play another foreign item. Ellis found exhibitors would not even look at the financial figures for offshore product that had a proven track record.[123]

At a 1954 meeting of United Paramount Theatres (UPT) affiliates, Edward L. Hyman, UPT vice president, proposed the gradual introduction of foreign movies on a regular basis in houses not normally given to booking imports. That plan was said to be the first move on the part of a major circuit to push imports in areas where, up to then, foreign-language features had stood little chance. Apparently the plan was tied in to the trip taken to Europe only a couple of months earlier by Paramount executive Leonard Goldenson when he told European producers the U.S. was wide open to European films "suitable to American audience tastes." Hyman noted the "bitter criticism" abroad over the reluctance of commercial houses to play European pictures and that in view of that "it might be wise for exhibitors in [the U.S.] to consider ways and means of popularizing the foreign film." By introducing an "art policy," warned Hyman, operators would in most cases be "seeking to establish an audience where there has been none before." He warned, "You must therefore proceed with patience and foresight." It was better to introduce the plan gradually. For cinemas that had not previously screened foreign fare, he suggested that "one night a week or at most two nights would be sufficient as a starter." Less important was the number of times offshore product was played per week; more important was the regularity. Hyman called those cinema owners pioneers, bringing a new entertainment form to many people and cautioned that it took time for people to develop new tastes. Some other theater circuits, notably Walter Reade Theatres, had introduced foreign fare on a limited basis, "but never in the sticks." Those circuits mostly followed the pattern outlined by Hyman, with foreign movies shown on certain nights.[124]

Oklahoma City's Plaza Theatre (part of the Cooper Foundation chain) used something like the Hyman plan when it booked a series of eight foreign features to find out if there was enough box office support for offshore product. In an effort to publicize its move, the Plaza contacted the language and art departments of the nearby Oklahoma University. Eight admissions were offered for $4; regular ticket price at the Plaza was 80 cents.[125]

When Alexander Korda's British movie *The Constant Husband* was slated for an NBC-TV premier in the fall of 1955, it became the first movie to be broadcast on a network in primetime. Independent distributors expressed some surprise at NBC's choice. "It's the kind of British film that we've been trying to sell for years, and frankly with limited success," said one, continuing, "Here the theatres have been saying that the 'broad public' won't take this type of fare. Now NBC comes along and right away it becomes a 'spectacular' to be seen by millions. It's a little ironic." Another said if the feature had been offered first to cinema exhibitors they "would have complained about the profusion of dialog." A reporter said British features had gained ground in America over the past few years, but added, "They're nevertheless still confined for the most part to the keys [major cities] and get a poor playoff in some areas, particularly the south." Korda had sold the film to television because he could not get it screened in American theaters.[126]

A week later it was smugly observed that more foreign producers were "accepting their limitations in the U.S. theatrical market" and were focusing attention on television as a potential source of income. Germans especially moved their efforts to television since they had even less cinema success than other foreign lands. Some of the networks, specifically NBC, had told German producers they would be glad to consider buying some of their features—but stipulated they had to see the dubbed product first. This meant that the Europeans would have to take a financial risk and dub their pictures before NBC would even look at them. If they could dub a feature for $8,000 to $10,000 (in their own country) and came up with an acceptable job, they thought they could sell the item to television for $15,000 to $25,000 (a good dub job in America cost around $15,000). Also, the film could then be more easily sold, thought the Germans, to theatres in Britain and other English-speaking countries. In the end television provided next to no market for foreign features. Most of those pictures were not dubbed and television then would not touch subtitled movies—the text became too small on television. Hollywood initially boycotted its new rival by refusing to sell movies at all to television, in order not to aid its competitor. It was a resolve that collapsed relatively quickly and television was rapidly saturated with movies—virtually all American. Television never intended to broadcast many foreign films. When it showed a few at the beginning and pretended to court foreigners, it was just trying to pressure the majors into dealing with it.[127]

The main cinema operators trade group, Theatre Owners of America (TOA), conducted a 1955 survey of American exhibitors who operated a total of 3,000 houses. It was a survey sent to 212 exhibitors, with 138—60 percent—responding, which looked at attitudes toward British features. No prejudice per se against U.K. films among exhibitors was found by the survey; it did find that they could not improve their showing at the U.S.

box office until they were made "more entertaining for the mass of American theatre-goers" and British stars became better known to U.S. patrons, and until they used better exploitation at the national level.[128]

The TOA poll allowed for exhibitor respondents to make recommendations on what the British industry should do to gain a bigger share of the market. Suggestions ranged from personal tours of U.S. cities by British players, to a single sales organization for U.K. pictures, to elimination of "heavy" accents, to a greater effort to determine the preferences of the American audience. One of the conclusions in the TOA report said, "The aim of British producers should be to reach the patrons of the regular houses, and to make pictures more in keeping with Hollywood's approach. They must find out what the American public wants." Specifically, the report recommended (1) a greater use of color and new processes; (2) a greater use of American scripts; (3) employment in England of American authors and American directors; (4) greater use of American techniques; (5) analysis of why certain British players did or did not do well at the U.S. box office; and (6) the loan of British stars to Hollywood to act in U.S.-made movies. Most of the exhibitor comments made the point that the British method of making films just did not correspond with what the American audience wanted and expected. One cinema owner said that in his circuit being identified as British was "the kiss of death." Another remarked, "Some English pictures are good, but most lack American directorial technique. They seem to waste footage on long drawn-out scenes which seem to have little bearing on the story and American audiences become impatient and bored." Summarizing TOA's report, *Variety* declared, only partly tongue-in-cheek, "If Britain made its pictures in Hollywood and employed American talent and methods—from script to exploitation— British films would stand an excellent chance with American exhibitors."[129]

Another exhibitor comment asserted, "If a committee of American theatre men would look at English pictures before they were distributed in this country, picking out those which meet the American public's requests, I believe the English pictures would have a better chance for general distribution here." One wanted British producers to make more down-to-earth movies that would be more acceptable to Americans because British films were "inclined to be arty, generally too slow, too long, and too dragged out." Still another gave the following advice: "First, avoid heavy unintelligible accents. Second, quit regarding realism as the acme of entertainment." From a different cinema operator came this: "I think British producers should eliminate a great deal of the dialogue and have more action in their pictures. Also, by and large, their male leads and supporting players are too effeminate in appearance and action for the American audience."[130]

Response to TOA's survey came from various independent distributors of foreign fare. "There's only one thing worse than a bad foreign film, and that's one 'tailored' to please American audiences," one commented. Edward L. Kingsley of Kingsley International stated, "It's an unnatural thing for a foreign producer to try and slant his product to an audience which he barely knows and to a market from which his returns in the past have been quite small." Kingsley added that, in light of past experience, there was nothing to indicate that the advice of U.S. exhibitors was valid or that foreign movies slanted toward the supposed taste of the American market had been particularly successful. British pictures appealed precisely because they were different. Morris Helprin, Alexander Korda's representative in the States, said accents were really not a problem. He commented, "They don't seem to object to a Ronald Colman, a Laurence Olivier or a Richard Burton. If Jean Simmons can be fine in *Guys and Dolls*, why should she suddenly be hard to understand in a British picture?" In Helprin's opinion the people who were primarily responsible for keeping the audience from acquiring a taste for the good U.K. features were the exhibitors. They were setting up the barriers and gave "neither the public nor the British producers a real chance."[131]

When E. D. Martin, TOA chairman of the board, came back to the States in the summer of 1956 after an extended visit to Europe (as an exhibitor representative at the Cannes Film Festival), he said that unless the European producers changed their methods and designed movies specifically "for the taste of the average American," there was little chance of their products getting a widespread market in the States. Stressing he had "nothing against" the foreign movies that were "wonderfully made," he went on to say he was certain that general American audiences would find it "difficult to appreciate the quality and artistic value of the pictures."[132]

Later that year, a series of formal screenings of a group of selected foreign movies was run for delegates attending the TOA annual convention in New York City. Those screenings were not open to the public, being strictly for the trade. With regard to that strategy, film writer Bosley Crowther described TOA as "an organization of movie merchants who have heretofore generally shunned the output of foreign producers as alien to the average American customer's taste."[133]

When Fred Hift did a lengthy article in 1957 on American exhibitors' resistance to offshore product he concluded that British movies had the best chance but all foreign product was "handicapped." He argued those features were still "a long, long way from finding acceptance outside the big cities in the United States," being limited to a core of some 250 art houses and a small number of commercial houses that on occasion had experimented successfully with imports. Sampling exhibitor sentiment, Hift said many commented, "Our people don't know those foreign stars and they can't be bothered reading subtitles. They've never heard of those pictures. If you put 'em on, they just die at the boxoffice." There was a consensus that offshore fare had made no headway in the commercial market and that imports did okay in university towns. Several of the cinema men also believed that dubbing was not a salvation for the product—people would not attend a foreign film just because it had an English soundtrack.[134]

One of those Hift spoke to was Arthur K. Howard of Affiliated Theatres in Boston (with 90 New England venues), who said, "We've tried foreign films, but they just don't sell tickets. From time to time we try them, but almost always without success." Glenn Ashmun of the Ashmun Theatres at Caro, Michigan, reported that interest in foreign pictures in his area was "virtually zero." A spokesman for the Oklahoma-based Video Theatres (150 houses) said only four to six towns in his circuit had any potential for imports. "We've tried all sorts of tricks, from special campaigns to the 'festival' type of event," he said. "We've tried to literally force foreign films on the public in some situations. But it's no good in the long run. They won't buy it as a steady diet and there aren't really enough foreign pictures of quality around." Hift also found that many cinema men "opined that the use of American stars would be of great help in putting over foreign films. And several mentioned that the casting of foreign stars in American pictures definitely was smoothing the way for future imports in which they might appear." Exhibitors in conversation with the reporter, though, were eager to end the impression that they stood as a "wall" between imports and the U.S. audience. They also agreed it was probably difficult for foreign producers to accept the situation when American movies were fully and widely accepted by foreign audiences whereas imports in the States couldn't "get to first base with the vast majority of Americans."[135]

Time magazine announced in 1957 that some 20 new European movies were showing on U.S. screens, and "not only in art houses." The magazine went on to enthuse, "Hundreds of independent theater owners have decided that U.S. moviegoers will gladly jump the language barrier if they are promised plenty of sex on the other side." All this happened because of the notoriety gained by the Brigitte Bardot French film *And God Created Woman*.[136]

Rank Film Distributors of America got involved in 1958 in a dispute with the 108-venue Schine circuit. After the latter allegedly refused to book two different Rank movies and also refused to hold talks with Rank officials, the U.K. firm went ahead and made arrangement to open one of those films in a high school auditorium in Ogdensburg, New York, in opposition to a Schine cinema. Ogdensburg was a closed town, which meant that all houses there were controlled by Schine. Reportedly Schine had agreed to take the movie, but only for three of its houses. Rank wanted it played on the whole circuit. The picture was screened by Rank for four days in the auditorium, with the item also receiving the usual amount of advertising and publicity.[137]

As television helped to drastically reduce motion picture attendance, periodic crises broke out in the industry as the cash flow to Hollywood shrank. From time to time there were serious worries over a product shortage, real or imagined. During one of these crises, exhibitor S. H. Fabian chaired the Committee on Ways and Means to Increase Motion Picture Production, which produced a 1958 report for the American Congress of Exhibitors. With regard to imports, the report stated that foreign producers "should only be too willing to aim their product toward our standards, tastes and policies to get a fair share of the revenue." Also pointed out was that a movie that was aimed successfully at the American market was usually successful in the world market and got worldwide distribution. "Foreign producers should be impressed with this fact and an attempt made to have them make more pictures aimed at the American market," added the report. Independent distributors of foreign product greeted the report's suggestions with "anger and astonishment." Many dismissed the report as "nonsense."[138]

Despite exhibitor talk about a shortage of product, the need for more product, the need for imports to be given a chance, and so on, reporter Fred Hift observed in 1959 that they were still not "giving the imports a real chance on any extensive scale." He said it was still true then that an exhibitor would usually choose a reissue western over a new French film.[139]

S. H. Fabian, president of a large cinema chain, remarked that same year that there were then some 650 foreign films available in the U.S. "and not a blockbuster in the lot." Agreeing that Hollywood no longer supplied an adequate number of features he lamented that foreign production had not "adjusted itself" to fill in that gap. American-made features totaled 238 in 1958, down from 400 in 1951. For Fabian a truism was that a movie that succeeded in the States was "a money picture throughout the world." He explained, "If you aim at Italy, for instance—it's sheer luck if you ring the bell in the American market. But if you aim at the American customer and you hit the bull's eye—you also have the world market right on target." According to his analysis of U.S. movies made abroad and successfully exhibited at home, there were certain basic ingredients that should not be "difficult" for European producers to duplicate: They used an American star or two and the producer or director was American. Fabian concluded his article by wondering, "Why don't the creative men and women on the other side of the oceans try producing in an idiom our people favor?"[140]

Formal barriers against the entry of foreign films into America, such as through tariffs, duties, quotas, and so on, remained non-existent or negligible. That was in the best interest of the Hollywood cartel. As employment in the U.S. industry declined in the 1950s, mostly from the effects of television on attendance, there was a periodic call to impose such restrictions on offshore product with the idea in mind that it would increase domestic employment. Hollywood always opposed such urgings. MPAA head Eric Johnston said the imposition of any such measures by the U.S. government would be contrary to their "free-trade principles." Strongly advocating unencumbered world trade, MPAA members publicly argued that the imposition of any such measures by America "could also seriously injure the film industries in the countries involved. This would run counter to the MPAA doctrine of open competition on a world-wide basis." While such pronouncements may have sounded principled and idealistic they were really simply self-serving. Hollywood knew that any such measures would not work because the presence of foreign movies on American screens was so negligible. Also, Hollywood worried that if the U.S. government initiated any restrictions, affected foreign nations might enact even tougher measures of their own against Hollywood's very dominant presence on offshore screens.[141]

Johnston spoke before the Motion Picture Industry Council (a group comprising labor and management interests and worried about unemployment in Hollywood) in 1954 and said any attempts to place restrictions on the exhibition of foreign films in the States would be a "grave mistake." Such a move, he felt, would result in more retaliation from abroad and lead to even more unemployment in Hollywood.[142]

Because it had such a stranglehold on the world's cinemas, Hollywood likely had very good reason to worry and to pretend its opposition was not rooted in maintaining its own hegemony and profits, but was a principled stand for free trade. Figures released in 1953 by the U.S. Department of Commerce revealed that U.S. films took up 74 percent of total playing time around the world, broken down by region as follows: Europe, 63 percent of screen time; South America, 64 percent; Mexico and Central America, 76 percent; Caribbean, 84 percent; Far East, 48 percent; Middle East, 57 percent; South Pacific, 65 percent; Africa 63 percent; and Canada, 75 percent.[143]

Arthur Mayer, a one-time foreign movie importer, estimated in 1959 that the percentage of the U.S. market taken by foreign product "is still negligible"—probably less than five percent. And that was better than it used to be. Mayer thought much of that increase in patronage was attributable not to a shift in audience preferences but to the reduction in Hollywood output that caused cinemas to abandon the double feature, hold movies over for a longer time and sometimes look elsewhere for product.[144]

According to Department of Commerce data, in 1953 U.S. film producers took $176,200,000 from foreign sources; this was the amount received in New York after all expenses, while the earnings of British movies in America, net after all expenses and distributors' share, were $4.4 million, described by a reporter as a "surprisingly low figure." U.S. payments for all foreign movies shown in America that year amounted to $5.2 million (the world other than Britain earned only $800,000) up from $4 million in 1952, but down from an estimated $11 million in 1951.[145]

Feature film grosses in America in 1956 for foreign product broke down as follows: Mexico (all ethnic, no English subtitles or dubbing), 107 pictures, $3,016,695; Italy, 52, $2,318,753; France, 38, $2,229,965; Britain, 50, $1,746,800; Germany, 74, $282,482; Japan, 6, $247,637; Russia, 31, $194,0000; Sweden, 3, $80,060; and Greece, 12, $16,000. The total for the nine nations was 373 movies, for $10,132,392 gross (gross is the distributor/producer share of the box office—very roughly half. About half of the gross, after deducting expenses and distributor share, was remitted to the foreign producer). That $10 million represented only about five percent of the approximately $190 million that the U.S. remitted home in actual dollars from foreign screenings. Only about $5 million of the foreign total would eventually be remitted. In fact, the films from four of those countries, Mexico, Germany, Greece and Russia (224, $3,509,177), were virtually all ethnic product. Germany remained alone among the European producers in not achieving at least one post-war hit in America. However, the number of imports that could reach a modest $100,000 gross (a hit marker for imports) were small in relation to the overall total of movies released.[146]

Similar figures for 1957 estimated that 832 imports from 10 countries grossed $15,907,769 for the year. (Chinese features were fairly numerous, all ethnic, but no figures were available.) Japan had 301 films, for $932,702 gross; Italy, 160, $1,768,120; Mexico, 116, $3,205,753; Britain, 93, $6,347,201; France, 61, $3,176,146; Germany, 51, $266,412; Greece, 35, $88,435; Russia, 9, $75,000; Sweden, 3, $36,600; and Spain, 3, $12,400. Mexican, Japanese, Greek, and many German and Italian films played only in the ethnic houses. Generally, most of the earnings going to one of the foreign countries were accumulated on perhaps just four or five of the titles exported to America.[147]

For 1958 the breakdown for 661 films from 12 countries, which grossed $41,992,225 was as follows: Britain, 76 films, $27,167,250; France, 46, $8,345,825; Mexico, 116, $3,301,000; Italy, 48, $1,508,450; Japan, 296 $933,000; Germany, 52, $509,200; Sweden, 3, $97,000; Finland and Denmark, 7, $48,000; Greece, 2, $34,000; Russia, 12, $30,000; and India, 3, $18,500. One film, *Bridge on the River Kwai* (U.K.), grossed over $14 million, yet many thought of it as an American product. Even then it could be difficult to define the parentage of a movie, with co-productions, offshore shooting, subsidiary companies, the poaching of personnel, and so forth. France's big jump in earnings was mostly due to Brigitte Bardot—*And God Created Woman* was released in late 1957 but counted in 1958 totals. Numbers for France indicated the remittance to that nation should have been about $4.2 million in 1958. Yet the French Centre National du Cinema in Paris said the remittance to French producers that year was only $600,000. Reason for the discrepancy was reported to be unknown.[148]

From 1957 to 1958, Germany remitted $18 million to the Hollywood cartel from its film earnings, while German movies remitted $208,000 from America.[149]

The U.S. share of film and television tape rentals, derived from the showing of U.S. film and television programs abroad, according to the U.S. Department of Commerce rose from $120 million in 1950 to $215 million in 1955, then declined to $184 million in 1960. Almost all of it went to cartel members. Estimates for payments from the U.S. for foreign film and television tape rentals rose from $4 million in 1950 to $15 million in 1960.[150]

Figures for the earnings of foreign films in America were made to look especially puny when compared to earnings in America of domestic product. Blue chip U.S. productions (those grossing $1 million or more in U.S. and Canadian rentals) numbered 135 in 1953 and garnered a combined gross of $311,950,000. A year earlier, 119 movies in that category combined for $253,510,000. To that date, only a handful of foreign productions had ever grossed $1 million in the States, not per year, but across time.[151]

Some indication of the weak position held in America by foreign movies could be seen from a dispute revolving around the Oscar awards at the end of 1959. The Independent Film Importers and distributors of America (IFIDA) corresponded with the Academy of Motion Picture Arts and Sciences over its rules for nominations for the Oscar for best foreign film. What irked IFIDA was that foreign films were then nominated by groups in the countries of origin, which sometimes resulted in nomination for movies that had never been shown in America. IFIDA suggested the rules be changed so that only foreign movies that opened for public viewing before November 30 in the year in question be eligible. Declining to change the rules, Academy executive director Margaret Herrick replied, "The number of foreign films released in the United States is limited, and some countries do not have any product at all on American screens. It would therefore, in the opinion of the governors, be unfair to confine awards eligibility in this category to films released in the United States."[152]

Banging on the door for nearly a decade had produced virtually no progress for foreign films in America—their penetration continued to be negligible. British movies had always done better than other European product simply because they did not have the added handicap of a different language. The main producers of foreign-language film, countries such as France and Italy, struggled along, with each being able to lay claim to a few modest hits. Germany, which continued to be shut out, was an exception. The situation changed a little late in the 1950s when the continental foreign product got some notoriety and some extra bookings through some more openly explicit product and personalities that drew attention, notably France's Brigitte Bardot and Italy's Gina Lollobrigida. Mainstream media, often for the first time, paid attention to offshore product. One effect was the branding of all the continental product as sexual in content and more criticism of the imports—too arty before, too sexy now.

6

The Golden Age Ends, 1960–1965

> It is a known fact that many of the foreign films are with-
> out doubt detrimental to the morals of the young and old,
> but especially the young.
> —*The Rev. Eugene E. Geiger, 1960*

> I am most gravely concerned at the influx of foreign films
> that evidence a sense of moral values so remote from ours
> as to be completely repugnant to the historic American
> sense of cultural and social values.
> —*Representative Kathryn Granahan*
> *(Democrat, Pennsylvania), 1961*

Europe's golden age of filmmaking, which began right after World War II, continued into the 1960s. More and more it became apparent that Hollywood's tendency of blanket rejection of all offshore product as being essentially worthless was and had always been a lie. Still, these films made little headway in America, remaining largely confined to their art house ghetto. The flurry of interest and extra publicity and bookings that foreign product received late in the 1950s had less to do with the growing critical acclaim and stature of European movies and more to do with vehicles from the continent that exploited sex and featured the likes of Brigitte Bardot and Gina Lollobrigida. But whether Europe launched its drive to increase its screen penetration on the backs of critical raves or on the backs of sex symbols, Hollywood was able to beat it back.

As an example of the growing influence (if not screen penetration) of foreign movies, the magazine *Saturday Review* devoted several articles in one 1960 issue to the topic. In one of those pieces in praise of offshore product, Hollis Alpert said that until recently movies of impact came from Hollywood and that kept alive the belief that Americans were pre-eminent in the motion picture field. He remarked, "We could also rest on the vaunted superiority of our technical resources." Alpert felt all that had changed with the films of impact then coming from Europe. He mentioned several filmmakers from the U.K. who, under the general heading of "angry young men," had produced movies such as *Room at the Top*, *Saturday Night and Sunday Morning* and *Look Back in Anger*. Also mentioned was the French New Wave then at its peak (Jean Luc Godard's *Breathless* for example), the much-respected Italians (led by Federico Fellini), Ingmar Bergman of Sweden, and others. Alpert concluded that the prestige of American films had started to decline with its influence on the wane. It was a situation brought about by too much concentration on a slick surface and by the neglect of meaning. "Our movies today suffer by comparison with the best made elsewhere. The innovators of the screen are no longer to be found in Hollywood.... The foreign challenge may soon be to the box office as well," he explained. "From block-booking to the present policy of block-busters, Hollywood may be heading toward bust." Although such sentiments were a long way from being in the majority they were no longer absent to the degree they had been in earlier periods.[1]

With an increasingly positive critical reception, foreign producers spoke less often about tailoring their product for America, although that urge had not completely vanished. Nat Cohen, a U.K. producer and head of Anglo Amalgamated, back in London after a visit to the States, felt a great opportunity awaited the British industry if it could structure itself to meet the needs created by a decrease in American domestic production. Cohen admitted he was impressed by recurring complaints from U.S. exhibitors that British films had a tendency to include too much Cockney dialog and provincial dialects. Convinced that those items hurt the earning potential of several good British pictures, Cohen had modified the use of North Country dialog in his current production.[2]

With a number of hits in the late 1950s, foreign producers and distributors once again hotly debated the question of whether to dub their output. Theoretically, a dubbed item had a much greater potential earning capacity. On the other hand, dubbing was an expensive prospect, considering the gross take of the average foreign item, and often did nothing but increase a loss. Herman G. Weinberg was, in 1960, a long-time subtitler of foreign films into English. Working out of New York, he had done the titles for over 300 movies in his 30 years in the business. Reportedly the first film, *Two Hearts in Waltz Time*, that had simultaneous translation (dialogue in subtitles) was done by him in 1929. He spent three weeks doing that picture and received a fee of $1,000. Of all the foreign movies shown in America, Weinberg said, about one-third were titled in the country of origin (where it was cheaper but where the job might be poorly done), another third were done by Weinberg and the rest by a handful of competitors, mostly based in New York. Back in 1926, he had a job at the Fifth Avenue Playhouse transcribing the symphonic scores that came in with German silent pictures; then sound movies arrived. At first they tried the technique used for silents: Every few minutes a full-screen title announced that "Eric has left Maria to go to Switzerland with Hedwig. We shall see what happens." However, that method did not work as too much content was lost and there were always people in the audience who knew the language; they would laugh at jokes and so forth, leaving everybody else annoyed because they thought they were missing something.[3]

La Dolce Vita (Italy) was one of those rare foreign movies that did well at the U.S. box office in its subtitled version. Predictably, it was said to be breaking down exhibitor resistance to subtitled product in general because it got bookings in venues that had never before played a subtitled picture. The Legion of Decency "separately classified" the film with the understanding that the qualified approval would only be applicable to the subtitled version. Presumably a dubbed version of the film would have been condemned.[4]

Besides a debate on the financial aspects of dubbing, there was an equally heated and long-lasting debate on the artistic merits of dubbing versus subtitling. Leading the way on that debate was film writer Bosley Crowther, who expressed his belief that the convention of using subtitles should be abandoned for the U.S. market and replaced by the use of dubbed English dialogue. Prepared to be blasted by critics as a "former purist," Crowther argued that subtitles diverted attention when a viewer should be looking at the rest of the screen and weren't always accurate. He said, "It is foolish to hobble expression with an old device that was mainly contrived as a convenience to save the cost of dubbing foreign-language films when they had limited appeal." Dubbing was then very accurate, he said, and synchronization was so efficient that you could barely notice anything. Also, in a subtitled version he thought the foreign tongue could be distracting. Concluded Crowther: "Anyhow, it is time we abandon the somewhat specious and even snobbish notion that foreign-language films are linguistically inviolable.... Subtitles must go!"[5]

La Dolce Vita (Italy, 1960, Marcello Mastroianni, Anita Ekberg).

Two weeks later Crowther reported he had received an "immense volume" of mail in response to his article on dubbing, with the full range of opinion expressed. Because of that, he felt there was a core of foreign film buffs who did not want such films dubbed. Again, he argued that dubbing was the most satisfactory way—or the least objectionable way—to convey the necessary information. Resistance to dubbing, he said, seemed to hinge on two basic arguments: Dubbing was phony and it deprived the audience of the original actor's voice. In response, Crowther observed that in some movies, Italian for example, the original dialogue was recorded later in the studio, and not always by the original actors. Crowther also believed dubbing was valuable because it could lead more Americans to be exposed to foreign movies.[6]

Writing in *The Nation*, Robert Hatch authored a piece opposed to dubbing and Crowther's views on the topic. Agreeing that dubbing had reached a fairly high technical standard Hatch felt there was still no way you could put the words "thank you" into the mouth of someone saying "merci," especially in a close-up, without being very noticeable and distracting. Though admitting to the dubber's skill, he said, "The device is all wrong psychologically and logically. In the first place there is something repellant about putting words into someone's mouth; it reduces the performer to a puppet.... More important, what kind of voice are you to use?" For example, should one use one with an accent, or one without? Hatch thought subtitles were a compromise and while they were never the equal of knowing the language being spoken, they had their virtues. He said, "They are openly added and do not tamper with the internal structure of the picture. Dubbing is fakery, and unlike makeup and the other illusions of the screen and theatre, it is fakery performed on a finished work."[7]

Crowther returned almost a year and a half later, late in 1961, to declare again that dubbing was the only method to use, although he allowed there would be and should be a "limited number" of cinemas across the country that would continue to show foreign films with subtitles. He thought a dubbed movie would draw five to 10 times as many people to see it as the subtitled version of the same film. As examples he cited *Two Women* (Italy), with 85 percent of its engagements being for the dubbed version (star Sophia Loren did her own dialogue for the dub in English— an unusual event) and Ingmar Bergman's Swedish feature *The Virgin Spring*.[8]

Nearly three years after that, Crowther returned yet again, during the second New York Film Festival, to promote the virtues of dubbing: "It seems to be desirable and in line with the advancement of cinema art that quality dubbing should be encouraged by the showing of well-dubbed films at the festival." He hoped that if two or three well dubbed movies were shown at the festival the next year it might help to break down a resistance to dubbed product that was "archaic and unreasonable."[9]

Others also opposed Crowther and his crusade for dubbing. Arthur Knight, in *Saturday Review*, declared himself to be a subtitle man although he conceded that with respect to reaching a wider audience, dubbing was more effective. But if that wider audience was exposed to an inferior product then there was no gain. Dubbing was bad, he felt, because the dubber was most concerned with picking a word that matched the lips, rather than one that best expressed an idea. Knight concluded that as a rough rule of thumb, "the greater the artistry in the original work, the greater the violence wreaked on that conception by a dubbed version."[10]

Also opposed to dubbing was Stanley Kauffmann, writing in the *New Republic*. He told of Richard Davis, head of a firm that distributed the Italian comedy, *The Big Deal on Madonna Street*. At a New York screening of the movie, the first reel was run with subtitles and was then run again in a dubbed version with English dialogue. At that point a vote was taken to see how the audience would prefer to see the rest of the feature. The vote was "overwhelmingly" in favor of subtitles. Because of that vote and because of reactions from patrons of the cinema where it was playing, who made their views known before the opening, Davis initially released the feature in a subtitled version. Kauffmann added, "Mr. Davis is to be congratulated on his resistance to the crusade led by Bosley Crowther of the *New York Times* to abolish sub-titles." Arguing the authentic voice was important, Kauffmann said it was necessary to preserve a performance whole in preference to "artistic bastardy." Although he agreed more people would go to see a film if it was dubbed, he dismissed the idea "that the number of people who see a work is the paramount criterion, whether or not the work is debased to attract them." He declared, "This is an admirable democratic impulse but it is not necessarily a sound artistic standard at all."[11]

French producer Paul Graetz felt, in 1961, that the days of subtitled foreign features for the U.S. market were just about over. He said he usually immediately dubbed his films, despite the cost of $15,000 to $20,000. At other times he shot a second version of the film, directly in English, along with the French one. As to how to crack the American market, he suggested a producer should get a U.S. director and a U.S. writer, plus a French writer for the domestic version.[12]

Art houses, especially those in New York, remained the key venues for foreign movies in America. Vincent Canby wrote that British product and Hollywood product together dominated playing time at New York's first-run art houses. It was a situation of serious concern to independent distributors and foreign producers of foreign-language features because "a successful booking at one of New York's 15 firstrun arties [was] still the main if not the only gateway to the U.S. market for non–American film producers," said Canby. A survey of 14 such venues for June 1, 1959 to May 31, 1960, and June 1, 1960 to May 31, 1961, revealed that a total of 591 weeks were devoted to first-run art films in the first year and 740 weeks in the second year (all the cinemas did not play first-run art films all the time). British films had 252 of those weeks in 1960–1961 (154 in 1959–1960); U.S., 233 (170); France, 85 (124); Italy, 45 (15); Germany, 19 (22); Russia, 45 (20); Japan, 0 (23); Sweden, 40 (61); Denmark, 0 (2); Argentina, 4 (0); India, 16 (0); and Poland, 1 (0). Canby concluded that if you were an Indian, Japanese, Argentine or Polish producer looking for a New York venue for that "all-important New York booking," you would have had a hard time, but if you were a Spanish, Norwegian, Brazilian, Hungarian, or Yugoslav producer, to mention a few, you would have great difficulty. Of these last, he said, "You might as well give up entirely, if you base your hopes of the experience on the last two years. No pictures of these nationalities have played a New York first-run artie in the period covered by this survey."[13]

By the summer of 1962, Manhattan had a reported 17 art houses but a boom was underway with nine new ones slated to be opened in the near future. Importers and independent distributors who had often been forced to delay a national release of their movies, said Canby, because a suitable New York art house was not available were, naturally, happy over the prospect of more venues. According to reporter Mike Wear the number of art houses in the U.S. had increased from 50 to 60 in 1950 to 350 to 400 in 1962 (these were houses that played art films—some of which were American—regularly but not necessarily exclusively). Wear said the Manhattan expansion would be to 21 by the end of 1962, not the 26 mentioned by Canby. In any case, he wondered where the product would come from. Most cinema operators felt that eight to 10 films were needed per house per year (long runs for some items). Thus, when cinema expansion was complete, a total of 168 art house movies a year would be needed (21 times eight). Said one exhibitor, "Where are they going to get the 168 worthwhile pix? Somebody is going to suffer."[14]

Canby did another survey of the art house playing time statistics for first-run movies in which he compared data for 1962–1963, 898 weeks (573 weeks for foreign films) from September 1 to August 31, with data for the same dates in 1961–1962, 742 weeks (512 foreign) in total. The percentage of playing time for foreign slipped to 64 percent from 69 percent in the earlier year. Twenty-five venues were surveyed in 1962–1963, 20 in 1961–1962. For individual countries, the breakdown was as follows: U.S., 325 weeks in 1962–1963 (230 weeks in 1961–1962); Italy, 168 (105); France, 160 (162); Britain, 125 (147); Japan, 55 (11); Greece, 25 (14); Sweden, 10 (28); India, 10 (2); Russia, 8 (14); Argentina, 7 (3); Mexico, 3 (5); Germany, 2 (0); Spain, 0 (11); Poland 0 (4); Yugoslavia, 0 (3); Czechoslovakia, 0 (2); and Switzerland, 0 (1). Japan moved to 55 weeks from 11 mainly as a result of the opening in January 1963 of the Japanese producer Toho's showcase Toho Cinema. Canby concluded, "The arties which used to be the exclusive outlets for overseas product are now geared more and more towards the prestige release of the commercial U.S. industry."[15]

In the following year (September 1, 1963, to August 31, 1964), 25 art venues devoted 1,006 weeks to first-run art product, as follows: U.S. 375 weeks, Italy 180, Britain 166, France 108, Sweden 55, Japan 54, Germany 19, Russia 13, Poland 10, Spain 9, India 6, Denmark 5, Mexico 4, and Brazil 2. A total of 179 movies were screened, as follows: U.S. 77, Italy 26, France 24, Britain 20, Japan 16, Sweden 5, Germany 2, Russia 2, India 2, Poland 1, Spain 1, Denmark 1, Mexico 1, and Brazil 1. Most of the U.S. films were released by the majors. All but two of Japan's weeks were at their own venue, the Toho.[16]

For the one-year period running from September 1, 1964, to August 31, 1965, 25 art houses devoted 904 weeks, as follows: U.S. 357 weeks, Britain 163, Italy 142, France 135, Japan 48, Russia 15, Canada 14, Greece 8, Denmark 7, Spain 6, Sweden 5, Argentina 2, and Germany 2. A total of 146 movies were exhibited: U.S. 51, Britain 25, France 25, Italy 18, Japan 16, Canada 2, Denmark 2, Spain 2, Argentina 1, Germany 1, Greece 1, Russia 1, and Sweden 1.[17]

In June 1965, the Toho cinema, which had been a showcase for Japanese movies for more than two years and had originally enjoyed at least some success, closed down. Reportedly it found the local interest in contemporary movies from Japan too feeble and unreliable to keep the showcase going.[18]

When a foreign film finally did get a booking at one of New York's art houses—the necessary prelude to a possible national release—it still had to face the critics who, with a bad review, could destroy any such chances. *Variety* noted, "[*New York Times* critic Bosley Crowther] still makes or breaks most imports."[19]

Agitation for censorship of foreign films was heavier than usual during this period; relatively more attacks were directed against them (bearing in mind their still negligible presence) than against American product. It was all to the benefit of Hollywood for it was another indirect control method as such attacks and agitation undoubtedly worked to limit their bookings and screen penetration. Typical, perhaps, of some of the outrage was what took place in 1960, when Fort Lee, New Jersey, expressed concern the morals of its citizens would be impaired if a film art house was allowed to open there. The mere announcement that Pax Films (headed by Mal Warshaw) had taken a lease on the Grant-Lee Theatre with the intention of operating it as an outlet for art films brought about a storm of protest from the Borough Council, which had apparently been influenced by three local Roman Catholic priests. Also, that Council indicated it would join with three Catholic parishes in an effort to bar the cinema from bringing in what it described as "indecent foreign films." All this furor took place before Warshaw had applied for a license and before he had booked a single film. Warshaw stressed that nobody had asked him what movies he would play and that just the fact that he had said he would operate an art theater appeared to have immediately been interpreted as "obscene." Council President Julius Balestri exclaimed, "I would not hesitate to pass an ordinance barring all future theatres from Fort Lee if that's the only way to keep this one out." However, the Borough attorney urged caution in light of court decisions on censorship.[20]

Fort Lee's Borough Council got into the controversy as a result of protests from the pastors of Holy Trinity, Madonna, and Epiphany Roman Catholic churches, who cited newspaper stories about the plans to convert the Grant-Lee (a legitimate house) into an art cinema. The clergymen asked the Council to investigate the type of films to be shown and to refuse a license if the programming could be considered indecent. Reverend Eugene E. Geiger, pastor of Holy Trinity, declared, "It is a known fact that many of the foreign films are without doubt detrimental to the morals of the young and old, but especially the young." The Council attorney warned the body it had no right to ask an applicant what type of films would be shown before granting a license. He said the Borough needed an ordinance to protect the public from indecent films but it would require careful study to draft one that would pass the scrutiny of the Supreme Court. Other religious groups in Fort Lee (Protestant and Jewish) quickly registered their opposition to the position of the Borough Council.[21]

A couple of weeks later an ordinance was introduced by the city council of Fort Lee to protect the community from the "danger" of foreign art films. Under its terms, the council had the right to ban in films, stage shows, and other public performances the use of profane, lewd, lascivious, or indecent language, and so forth.[22]

Independent Film Importers and Distributors of America (IFIDA) executive director Mike Mayer sent a letter to the Fort Lee city council expressing "shock and alarm" over "the misapprehension, apparently common in Fort Lee, concerning the nature of foreign motion pictures and their receptivity in the United States." Mayer asked the city council to look at some of the top foreign product currently in New York and said his group was willing to make prints of such films as The 400 Blows and Wild Strawberries available to the council at no cost.[23]

Still seeking a license, Mel Warshaw had to submit to fingerprinting by the local police. He said he had operated and managed cinemas in various parts of the U.S. but this was the first time that local authorities requested his fingerprints as a requisite for a cinema license. However, the Borough Council was no longer determined to block Warshaw from receiving a license. After other groups, both religious and civic, rallied to Warshaw's side and charged the council with trying to institute prior unconstitutional censorship of films, that body changed its position. Also, the Council postponed hearings on its proposed ordinance, allowing it to fade away. And so Warshaw got his license and the controversy disappeared.[24]

Former film importer Arthur Mayer said, in 1960, that in all his 40 years in the business he had never encountered such widespread and vehement criticism of films. He thought it was part of a societal battle to resurrect censorship or if that was not possible then to introduce some classification system. Mayer thought that in some unnamed high echelons of the industry (presumably the majors), an effort was under way "to make it appear that such proposals are not the consequences of dissatisfaction with American films, but are a spontaneous public revolt against those 'obscene foreign movies.'" However, he commented, foreign movies occupied only about three percent of screen time in the States. Nonetheless, Robert Selig, president of Fox International Theatres declared, "Much of the present criticism of films has been fomented not by Hollywood product but by foreign and art films." Charles Einfield, vice president of 20th Century–Fox, asserted that "the advertising of foreign movies was bringing criticism upon the industry as a whole." Even more explicit, and damning, was the statement of James A. Fitzpatrick, counsel for the New York State Joint Legislative Committee Studying the Publication and Dissemination of Offensive and Obscene Material, who said, "The industry has the machinery for effective self-regulation for most of the domestic product—unfortunately, foreign films, which are among the most flagrant offenders, refuse to subscribe to the industry's Code."[25]

The opening of the Westwood Art Theatre in the west side Cleveland suburb of Lakewood in 1961 caused a protest even before its debut. The first movie booked there was Brigitte Bardot's *La Verite.* Two other art houses on the east side of Cleveland were owned by the same man. One of those, Heights Art, ran into trouble in the previous year when it screened the French feature *The Lovers.* It was banned by the Shaker Heights Police Department and led to the indictment of the cinema manager. Those responsible for the protest over the Westwood were described as ministers, mothers, and PTAs. Orlando L. Tibbets, pastor of Lakewood Baptist Church urged the mayor to deny the Westwood a permit but the latter said he had no legal way to stop the Westwood from opening.[26]

In Washington, D.C., that same year, a House Post Office subcommittee, chaired by U.S. Representative Kathryn Granahan (Democrat, Pennsylvania), was planning hearings into the distribution of Communist literature through the mail. Rumors arose that she would add the issue of lewd imports of foreign films into the States to the agenda. She wanted to root out loopholes through which "filthy" foreign product entered the U.S. to "degrade our moral values." Already the congresswoman had sounded the call for a "special Movie Morality Code" to block out the "invasion" of "sex-laden" offshore product. She mentioned specifically the French feature *Les Liaisons Dangereuses* and fretted that it was free "to work its insidious propaganda of immorality on the American motion picture public." She opined, "It would verge on criminal neglect of public interest—and it would be an unthinkable and indefensible breach of public trust—if this dirty movie were to be permitted by our responsible public officials and motion picture executives to be foisted on the American public." Believing that such a storm of protest had arisen at the time of a trend toward overemphasis and distortion of sex in some movies, she felt that the problem could not be ignored in the public interest. Representative Granahan concluded, "I am most gravely concerned at the influx of foreign films that evidence a sense of moral values so remote from ours as to be completely repugnant to the historic American sense of cultural and social values."[27]

The MPAA made an offer to the IFIDA to scrutinize and pass on all the advertising material for foreign films used by the independents. It was suggested that those importers submit their advertising campaigns to the cartel's Advertising Code Administration for approval—the body that passed on all advertising material from the majors. Supposedly, the suggestion was made as a response to a common problem of allegations being made around the country about violence and immorality in films. Until recently, said a reporter, it "seemed to be MPAA policy to 'discreetly' blame the importers for the industry's bad public relations." In response, the IFIDA politely but firmly declined the cartel offer.[28]

As the foreign producers continued to try to improve their presence on U.S. screens, more and more of their movies were sent to and passed by the Production Code Administration. Foreign movies approved by that arm of the cartel rose from 73 in 1959 to 112 in 1961. However, of those 112 approved movies made abroad in 1961, 58 were produced by American studios and the rest (54) by foreign producers.[29]

Data from the Legion of Decency did indeed reveal that offshore product was treated more harshly than was domestic product. In 1960 the Legion rated 222 domestic movies and gave three of them (1.35 percent) the dreaded C (condemned)-rating. That same year the group rated 53 foreign features and gave five (9.43 percent) a C-rating. For 1961, two films (0.81 percent) of 248 domestic pictures rated were given a C, while eight (19.51 percent) of 41 rated foreign films were condemned. While a C-rating in the 1960s had lost some of the power it once had, it still carried enough weight that a film so rated was a commercial liability in that many circuits and individual cinemas refused to book such a feature.[30]

Public agitation for applying some type of classification system to movies—as opposed to the blanket "approval" bestowed on a production by the cartel's voluntary Production Code Seal—was generally opposed by the U.S. distributors (the cartel members). They tried to get public acceptance of another voluntary service called "The Green Sheet"—it gave capsule evaluations on the suitability of films for the young. It was financed entirely by the MPAA but the evaluations were made from outside the industry, by representatives from a group of 10 civic organizations. Monthly distribution of the Green Sheet had reached 60,000 with copies sent to various groups which, in turn, reproduced the copies and circulated them locally. What was still true at the end of this period was that all foreign films shipped into America had to first pass a form of censorship imposed by the U.S. Customs, an arm of the Treasury Department. Intermittently, movies had been denied entrance or delayed because Customs inspectors had felt they were, or might have been, obscene. Several states (New York, Maryland, Kansas, and Virginia) and municipalities (Atlanta; Birmingham; Lowell and Lynn, Massachusetts; Chicago; Denver; Detroit; Memphis; Milwaukee; Pasadena; Omaha; Seattle; and Portland, Oregon) maintained censorship systems of various kinds. However, many of those were dormant or inactive. In addition, there were occasional one-off attacks in various places, the individual harassments of movies, and so on. Also, of course, there was the Code Seal. But censorship in general had suffered a number of defeats in the U.S. Supreme Court and as of the mid-1960s was, as an official influence, notably less potent than it had been in the past.[31]

Distribution problems continued to bedevil offshore product and to limit its presence. U.K. director Tony Richardson, who directed *Look Back in Anger* (partly financed and distributed in the States by Warner Bros.), complained that Warner "virtually abandoned" his film because it was unable to exploit it according to its normal pattern.[32]

Some foreign producers complained about the expenses deducted by the distributors and they pointed out a contract signed for a 50/50 split in reality turned out to be split more like 25/75 in favor of the distributor. Also annoying was the amount taken off the top by art cinemas as "house expenses," as well as the amount of money going to sub-distributors. Although producers agreed they should pay some of the expenses—such as prints, shipping charges, a portion of advertising and publicity costs, and so forth—many felt they were paying all of everything. Many foreign producers accepted flat rate sums for their movies in which they received a fixed sum of money and nothing more, with the expenses borne by the distributors. Such contracts were a sign of weakness in the foreign producers, an indication of the low market share attained by offshore product. Hollywood's majors always signed percentage of the take contracts.[33]

Despite worries expressed by U.S. independent distributors that the Hollywood majors might move in on them and take away their foreign art film distribution, it did not happen. By the mid-1960s the cartel members were only barely involved in handling foreign product. Only Columbia—through its association with Davis-Royal Films—was servicing the art house market with a continuity of "specialized" movies. United Artist's subsidiary Lopert Films, once one of the most active foreign film distributors when it had been independent, put only three films into release in the last half of 1962. One of those was Jules Dassin's *Phaedra*, which had actually been set for UA handling until it received a condemned rating from the Legion of Decency. Fox had just formed its own art subsidiary, International Classics, but it had not handled any product to that date. MGM was described as being "lethargic" in marketing its art films, of which it had "a few." Neither Universal nor Paramount were said to be showing any signs of getting into the handling of art films again, while Warner "occasionally" picked up an art release.[34]

Russian cabinet minister Sergei Romanovsky, chairman of the State Committee on Cultural Relations with Foreign Countries, said the Soviet Union would buy no more U.S. films until American distributors accepted Russian features under the film exchange program agreement signed the previous year by the two nations. Romanovsky charged Russian movies were not widely distributed in the U.S. However, the majors claimed almost all of the pictures were money losers. In the face of a perceived refusal by the majors to distribute Soviet films under the exchange program, the Soviet export agency had been marketing them through the small Artkino distributors, but were able to reach only small audiences in art venues. American films, though, were widely distributed in Russia, and like other foreign movies, were successful.[35]

Independent distributor Jack Hoffberg reported that, according to U.S. Customs House figures for 1964, the following number of motion pictures were imported: Italy 86, Britain 56, France 51, Scandinavia 10 (for a total of 203 in this subgroup); Hong Kong 157, Greece 70, Mexico 68, Germany 57, Spain 24, Japan 20, U.S.S.R. 14, Austria 11, Argentina 11 (for a total of 239 in this subgroup—most of which were destined for ethnic houses with no English dub or subtitles. For example, all the Hong Kong and all the Mexican features were so destined). Of the 203 pictures in the first subgroup, all for the art house market or more commercial bookings if they could be had, Hoffberg said less than 20 achieved any kind of success while another 20 broke even for the distributor. All the other 163 lost money. "There is no market in the U.S. for all these 203 pictures which were imported in 1964," said Hoffberg. "The maximum number of pictures from the four leading European producing countries, Italy, Britain, France and Scandinavia, which have some chance of achieving financial success, is about 60."[36]

Exhibitors continued to be a stumbling block for foreign producers. While the cinema owners continued to talk about foreign fare, they mostly did not book it. At the Theatre Owners of America (TOA) 1960 convention, a report was tabled by M. Levin, chairman of the TOA's Foreign Film Committee. One point made in the report was that the time would soon come when the majority of cinemas in the States would be showing foreign films as a matter of course—due to lack of sufficient product from Hollywood. A second point from the study was that art houses, which had tended to specialize in foreign fare—would be showing the best of American films as well as the top foreign movies. Art houses would continue to show those films in their original language (with subtitles) while regular houses would show those same imports, but dubbed into English, predicted the report. Some worried that the market for foreign might actually decline if Hollywood squeezed more and more of its own output into the art venues. Around the time of the convention a number of films debuting in New York had opened in an art house as well as in a Broadway theater (a regular commercial outlet)—*The Apartment* and *Elmer Gantry*, for example.[37]

Harry Feinstein, area manager for the Stanley-Warner cinema chain, said in 1963 that he was introducing art films into all the small houses in the circuit. He said he had experienced great success in cities like Lima, Ohio, and would soon extend such programming to towns like Punxsutawney, Pennsylvania, with a population of only 9,000. He declared, "Now we are showing Ingmar Bergman in Lima and plan to show his pictures all over, including Punxsutawney."[38]

In Minnesota, the Minneapolis-based Ted Mann circuit itself had five cinemas in that city that screened foreign fare—four were neighborhood houses that screened them regularly. Another chain had two Minneapolis theatres offering foreign movies occasionally. Most of the better foreign product, from all over, reportedly played Minneapolis. Yet across the Mississippi River, in St. Paul (population over 300,000), which had an influential Catholic clergy, only British comedies and some of the serious movies from the British Isles were welcome. *Never on Sunday* (Greece) was a smash hit in several Minneapolis outlets but never played St. Paul. One neighborhood house there tried to operate as an art house with foreign films but soon shut down.[39]

Melvin Brown of B&B Theatres, owner and operator of the 825-seat Peachtree Art theatre in Atlanta, Georgia, claimed his venue was the first art house to do business as such south of Baltimore when it opened in 1946; he found import product to be "skimpy." For the first 10 years he got his customers used to foreign movies as he performed what he called "spade and missionary work." Favored film-making countries at his outlet were, in order, Britain (especially comedies, such as the *Carry On* series, and mysteries), France, Italy, and Sweden. However, he said that Ingmar Bergman's work "is beyond the ken of his clientele and that German movies were, for the most part, a puzzlement to his patrons." Brown did not like to screen pictures with subtitles because some of his customers complained that they were "an annoyance."[40]

In the middle 1960s the average foreign film still drew something like 35 to 40 percent of its receipts from the New York market. Those average foreign productions, whether they came from the U.K. and were made in English or were released with subtitles, were usually limited to bookings at 150 to 200 cinemas in the U.S., of which 50 to 60 were in New York. For pictures like these, said Cyrus Harvey, president of the independent distributor Janus Films, the bulk of his returns came from just five cities— New York, Boston, Los Angeles, San Francisco, and Washington.[41]

Estimated gross film rentals in the U.S. by foreign films in 1959 totaled $39,626,486 from 824 movies (708 of them were foreign language items that grossed $21,500,000. Excluded were 116 Hong Kong films, all destined for ethnic houses, with grosses unknown). The country breakdown was as follows: Britain, 116 films, $18,644,190 gross; Italy, 96, $9,720,060; France, 78, $5,187,508; Mexico, 106 $3,200,970; Japan, 218, $1,160,480; Germany, 81, $662,160; Sweden, 9, $477,168; India, 2, $200,000; Russia, 59, $175,000; Greece, 53, $107,050; Norway, 1, $50,000; Denmark, 4, $32,000; and Israel, 1, $9,900. Just four Italian films (two starring Steve Reeves) earned a total of $9.2 million, which meant the other 92 Italian releases combined for a gross of $520,060. The French total was down significantly from the previous year because of substantially lower earnings for Bardot films. The British totals included "pure" British product but also those films in which U.S. majors had important financial participation but which still were classified as U.K. movies by the British government. Excluding such British movies as those, 87 "pure" British movies took in $3,618,190 in 1959, while the 29 financed and/or released by the U.S. majors took $15,026,000. Most of the German, Japanese, and Mexican films went to ethnic houses, as did 50 of the 53 Greek productions.[42]

For 1960, the estimated film rentals from a total of 875 films were $50,291,105, which divided as follows: Britain had 135 movies, and a gross of $22,974,986; Italy, 116, $12,265,913; France, 105, $5,190,000; Mexico, 96, $3,277,000; Japan, 226, $2,014,000; Russia, 50, $1,833,481; Germany, 72, $1,233,375; Sweden, 15, $635,000; Belgium, 1, $475,000; Greece, 31, $110,000; India, 5, $103,350; Spain, 15, $89,000; Denmark, 3, $44,000; Norway, 1, $30,000; Finland, 2, $10,000; Argentina, 1, $3,000; and Israel, 1, $3,000. Almost all the revenue earned by films from Mexico, Japan, Greece, and Spain came from ethnic houses. Nine British comedies (star-

Look Back in Anger (U.K., 1958, Richard Burton and Mary Ure).

ring the likes of Peter Sellers and Alec Guinness) took in $6,659,000 while four of Steve Reeves's Italian beefcake spectacles earned $4,640,000. Excluding British product, 740 foreign-language movies took in $27,316,119. In that year the Hollywood majors distributed 67 movies that took in $32,207,555. Of the revenue earned by the foreign-language pictures, $14,720,069 was earned by 37 films released through the majors—Columbia, MGM, Paramount, Fox, Universal, United Artists, Warner Bros., Buena Vista (Disney), Allied Artists, and American International. Vincent Canby estimated that 99 percent of the total income was earned by just 80 films, those handled by the majors and the four or five leading independent distributors.[43]

In 1961, 942 pictures earned $69,178,045, with 796 of those being foreign-language and taking $28,211,445. (As for other years, the data included U.S.–financed movies in whole or in part made in other countries, which were either in a foreign language or qualified as a "domestic" product under the laws of the nations where they were made.) Country breakdowns were as follows: Britain, 146 films, $40,966,600 gross revenue; Italy, 79,

$11,148,570; Mexico, 104, $3,427,000; Greece, 56, $3,113,000; France, 90, $3,040,050; Sweden, 20, $2,104,300; Germany, 69, $1,857,000; Japan, 274, $1,772,000; Russia, 61, $767,000; Spain, 13, $502,425; Philippines, 2, $150,000; Denmark, 3, $130,000; India, 4, $102,800; Czechoslovakia, 1, $50,000; Argentina, 15, $32,000; Poland, 2, $12,000; Cuba, 1, $1,800; Norway, 1, $1,000; and Yugoslavia, 1, $500. Mexican, Japanese and Argentine product again went almost totally to ethnic houses. Just three of the British films (actually American), *The Guns of Navarone*, *The World of Suzie Wong*, and *Swiss Family Robinson*, took in $24.8 million. A single Greek movie, *Never on Sunday* (financed by United Artists and released in the U.S. by its affiliate Lopert), earned $3 million, leaving the other 55 Greek items to share $113,000. Taking out the swollen totals for Britain and Greece (really U.S. movies) and those aimed at ethnic houses (not available to the general American public) reduced the $69 million to an amount that was half at best, probably less. Hollywood's 10 majors handled 62 of those movies ($46,755,000) with 34 independent distributors handling the other 880 movies ($22,432,045). Close to half of that latter amount ($10,410,000) was earned by just six titles. Breakdown for the majors' share was as follows: Britain, 33, $34,266,000; Italy, 12, $5,188,000; Greece, 1, $3,000,000; France, 3, $846,000; Sweden, 1, $1,100,000; Germany, 5, $1,205,000; Japan, 2, $425,000; Spain, 1, $400,000; Philippines, 1, $150,000; Denmark, 1, $125,000; and Czechoslovakia, 1, $50,000.[44]

For 1962, 840 films took in $49,427,611 (excluding British items, 718 foreign-language releases earned $25,400,177). Hollywood's 10 majors released 79 pictures ($27,341,620) with 38 independents handling the other 761 films ($22,085,991). Nation breakdowns were: Britain, 122, $24,027,434; Italy, 89, $8,884,862; France, 77, $6,424,139; Mexico, 101, $325,000; Japan, 176, $1,694,611; Denmark, 5, $1,119,000; Germany, 63, $1,020,000; Spain, 24, $964,000; Greece, 38, $895,565; Sweden, 17, $519,500; Russia, 89, $384,000; Argentina, 9, $113,000; India, 4, $75,000; Czechoslovakia, 2, $55,000; and Poland, 4, $17,000. Only a handful of 1962 imports exceeded $1 million in U.S. rentals, with about 14 more bringing in receipts of more than $300,000 each. Majors' share of the above figures were as follows: Britain, 22, $18,381,000; Italy, 14, $4,880,000; France, 2, $665,620; Mexico, 20, $700,000; Japan, 1, $290,000; Denmark, 3, $1,100,000; Germany, 3, $600,000; Spain, 13, $700,000; and Czechoslovakia, 1, $25,000.[45]

In 1963, 805 movies earned $69,342,000 with 728 foreign-language items taking in $31,887,000. Nation breakdowns were: Britain, 77, $37,455,000; Italy, 93, $17,233,000; France, 91, $4,567,000; Mexico, 88, $3,330,000; Japan, 156, $2,359,000; Spain, 13, $1,400,000; Greece, 83, $964,000; Germany, 55, $483,000; Sweden, 22, $451,000; Argentina, 15,

Kwaidan (Japan, 1964).

$380,000; Russia, 98, $354,000; Philippines, 2, $150,000; India, 6, $70,000; Yugoslavia, 2, $65,000; Poland, 2, $43,000; and Denmark, 2, $38,000. About $100,000 of Greek earnings came from ethnic houses, as did $175,000 of Germany's take, $300,000 of Spain's and $250,000 of Argentina's (from 12 films). Approximately $12.5 million of the Italian total was generated by a dozen or so sword and scandal epics such as *Duel of the Titans* and *Barabbas*. Four British pictures earned $18.7 million. Hollywood's majors handled movies that year that earned $53,265,000.[46]

For 1964, a total of 728 films earned $70,902,000 with 645 of those being foreign-language features and taking $21,804,000. The nation breakdown was: Britain, 83, $49,098,000; Italy, 60, $9,396,000; Mexico, 93, $3,340,000; France, 60, $2,951,000; Germany, 55, $1,930,000; Spain, 18, $1,481,000; Japan, 165, $1,124,000; Sweden, 18, $557,000; Yugoslavia, 2, $325,000; Argentina, 9, $200,000; Greece, 55, $152,000; Russia, 108, $104,000; Poland, 1, $82,000; India, 7, $60,000; Denmark, 1, $47,000; Philippines, 2, $45,000; and Brazil, 1, $10,000. British totals were increased by a few blockbusters: *Tom Jones* ($14.5 million), James Bond's *From Russia with Love* and the Beatles' *A Hard Day's Night*. All of Mexico's earnings came from ethnic venues, as did one-third of Spain's, half of Japan's, all of Argentina's, and almost all of Greece's. The 35 independent distributors earned $15,908,000 while the majors took $54,994,000. Majors' share was: Britain, 42, $44,060,000; Italy, 13, $3,000,000; France 4, $603,000; Mexico, 93, $3,340,000 (Azteca—defined as an 11th major in this account, was the main Spanish-language distributor to U.S. ethnic houses); Germany, 3, $1,730,000; Japan, 1, $500,000; Spain, 17, $1,311,000 (Azteca for some); Argentina, 9, $200,000 (all Azteca); and Yugoslavia, 1, $250,000.[47]

Despite the numbers listed above, one industry observer wrote that payments from the U.S. for foreign films and television tape rentals rose from $4 million in 1950 to $15 million in 1960, and then ranged between $10 million and $13 million all through the 1960s. They were amounts, said Joseph Phillips that were "certainly insignificant amounts when compared with U.S. film rentals abroad." He estimated the rentals obtained by the distribution of foreign films in the U.S. at $40 million in 1959 to $71 million in 1965. Payments made to foreign film producers were much smaller than their rentals because the distributors' share and various other expenses had to be deducted from the gross. Phillips estimated there were about 85 distributors of foreign movies in the States. About 500 cinemas screened such product regularly as did a larger number on occasion. "It is evident from these data that foreign film producers have not succeeded in making a very big dent in the U.S. market," concluded Phillips. "There is no evidence that foreign film companies play any significant part in the production, financing, or distribution of films in the United States."[48]

For 1961, Hollywood's majors grossed $616 million worldwide, $326 million in the domestic market and $290 million from foreign locations.[49]

7

The Modern Era,
1966–2002

The American public learned to like our [Brazilian] music
and it will learn to like our films.
—*David Haft, 1970*

I feel that Americans have been perverted by the stupidities of *Dallas* and *Dynasty*.
—*Sergio Leone, 1985*

The sad fact is that foreign-language films no longer matter. Americans absorbed in their junk culture are shuttering a window to the rest of the movie world.
—*Richard Corliss, 1997*

As this period began, movie showman Joseph E. Levine (responsible
for the Italian sword and sandal Hercules epics, among others) captured
the sad state of foreign films in America when he declared that only five
percent or less of moviegoers went to see the pictures of Federico Fellini
and other famous foreign directors. "Also, Antonioni, Truffaut, Resnais,
Fellini are known to only maybe 1% of film goers," he complained. "Antonioni is getting to be better known because of *Blow-Up*. But, before that,
mention the name Antonioni and most film goers would think it was some
kind of Italian cheese." Levine's point was that you could not stay in the
motion picture business if you just made art films.[1]

161

And it was not because there was a lack of product in general in the world. In fact, in 1969, the U.S. produced about 300 movies, a small part of the estimated worldwide total of 4,100 features. Asia led the way with 1,837 productions, Europe (including Soviet Russia) had 1,315 and the Middle East produced 374 movies. Top 10 film-producing countries were as follows: Japan, 494; India, 308; Italy, 301; U.S., 300; Taiwan, 246; Korea, 229; Turkey, 224; France, 173; Hong Kong, 169; and the Philippines, 169.[2]

Individual countries tried to increase their share of the American market but nothing ever seemed to work, for any of them, at any time. Within those countries some of the industry personnel had various levels of insight into the nature of the problem. Alfredo Burla, president of the Italian Film Exporters Association, said, in 1969, that sales of Italian movies to the States had fallen dramatically in the previous two to three years. Reports to him from various U.S. film executives attributed the slump to items such as "the dubbing problem," "subject matter alien to U.S. filmgoers," and "U.S. trade union pressure to limit programming of foreign pix." However, Burla was not convinced those reasons were responsible and contended the majority of Italian movies were then filmed in English with at least one American actor in the cast. Also, he said the most successful Italian features in America were precisely those with national or Latin themes. Concluded Burla, "The problem is that the films are rejected by the majors or independent importers without giving audiences a chance to warm up to them."[3]

Italian producer Carlo Ponti argued in 1971 that Italy could not produce movies for its home market because costs were too high and it was "no longer possible" to recover those costs from the domestic market. "The Italian industry," he said, "without America does not exist. We need American capital, we need the U.S. market and we need the American companies to release our films in the whole world." Until such time as other world distribution channels appeared on the scene, Ponti saw no alternative "to Europe's dependence on the American distribution companies." Sale of product market by market, with various independent distribution companies, was not a solution in his eyes.[4]

Cinema Italia, a film series sponsored by the Italian public broadcaster RAI and its sales arm Sacis, had an eight-month deal to screen its movies at the Carnegie Screening Room in New York. However, when that deal expired in June 1988, it was not renewed by the theater and Cinema Italia organizers were not able to find another venue. Thus, said Sacis president Gian Paolo Cresci, the Italians were forced to lower the flag they had so recently raised to show New York and the U.S. that there was a visible Italian motion picture industry. The Carnegie had 78 seats, with the Italians looking for one in the 200-seat range. Of that futile search Cresci said, "It was impossible [to find another Manhattan venue]. It was like a plot against Italian cinema."[5]

At the start of the 1990s two Italian films opened in the States— Guiseppe Tornatore's *Cinema Paradiso* and Maurizio Nichetti's *Icicle Thief. Paradiso* producer Franco Cristaldi noted that in recent years at least 90 percent of Italian producers had been making strictly local comedy films. "Attempts to imitate American films result in a picture that can't be exported," he said. Nichetti remarked, "I will not do films in English or copy American films. It is better to work seriously to tell our own stories and use our own actors to make something people will want to see everywhere." Reporter Lawrence Cohn said that during the 1960s an average of 40 Italian movies were released annually in America and that Lina Wertmuller films were strong in the 1970s but since then interest had dropped off. During 1989, only two Italian features opened in the U.S., plus a half dozen more that had been shot in English.[6]

An agreement was struck in July 1999, in Taormina, Italy, by the Italian Minister of Culture Giovanna Melandri, the Hollywood majors and the American Film Marketing Association (an organization of U.S. independents). One result of the deal was to be the creation of a committee that was to meet twice a year to continue the dialogue started in Taormina. An information exchange was promised, whereby the American experience was to "benefit" the Europeans. Said a reporter, "Wringing out a bland pledge of cooperation is one thing, but what the Italians want is to somehow muscle their way into more U.S. release space."[7]

French producer Raymond Danon wondered about the difficulties French films faced in obtaining bookings in America. He did so after a U.S. comment that many movies that were successful in France (or Italy, or the Netherlands, and so forth) did not travel well. Speculation was that local humor, situations familiar only to the home market, and so on, made them "hard to savvy" in foreign countries. Danon argued it was too simplistic to dismiss French product as "too French" for the States. Instead, he suspected that there remained a rigidity of attitude by U.S. showmen and bookers. Musing that more co-productions might be the answer, Danon observed that French producers "rarely count on U.S. revenues in their fiscal prognosis." If by chance a movie did click in the States, it was a bonus.[8]

During 1975, 26 French films opened in first-run cinemas in Manhattan, easily outpacing the product of any other nation. However, French output that year totaled 222 features—meaning that only one in ten French movies crossed the Atlantic. After a period of minor flirtation by the Hollywood cartel in investing in French filmmaking, the money had dried up. Over the previous decade, United Artists's special relationships with Francois Truffaut and Claude Sautet, Columbia's with Eric Rohmer and Claude Berri, and Universal's with Claude Chabrol and Claude Zidi had all fizzled out. Journalist Tom Allen declared, "One of the glories of the French film is that no Gallic director has consistently hit it big by aping American trends."[9]

Daniel Toscan du Plantier, production chief of France's top production, distribution, and exhibition company, Gaumont, declared he had the blueprint for having French films attain success in the States. By that he meant having a say in the handling of Gaumont movies in America through a local office. Gaumont's strategy was based on choosing the right distributor for each feature and it was easier to implement that strategy if Gaumont had an American office. Also important was having a say in the handling of Gaumont films in the U.S. One example was The Lacemaker, which started out slowly. Du Plantier made the decision to spent $8,000 on a three-quarter page advertisement in the New York Times focusing on star Isabelle Huppert. It was a plan that worked.[10]

Figures from the French government indicated that revenue earned on French pictures in the U.S. market moved from 431,000 francs in 1970 to 15,108,000 francs in 1975.[11]

Claude Lelouche's A Man and a Woman arrived in the U.S. in 1966 and quickly went on to become the top-grossing ($6.3 million) French feature ever released here, a position it held for decades. (As of 2000, it was eighth on the list of all-time foreign-language films in the U.S., at $14.3 million.) Twelve years later, in 1978, Lelouch was convinced his own lack of screen penetration since then and, with a few exceptions, the narrow range of success received by most European filmmakers in America was "less a function of audience reception than of distributor reluctance and/or inability to handle foreign fare." Since A Man and a Woman, he had made a dozen films, yet only half of them had received any distribution in the States. Lelouch remained convinced there was a large U.S. audience for European films; he claimed, "American distributors work under the assumption that subtitled films have little or no chance of broad popular success outside of the large cities." About 75 percent of the A Man and a Woman prints were subtitled, not dubbed.[12]

French Culture Minister Jean-Philippe Lecat promised more money in 1978 for Unifrance Film, the national industry organization charged with publicizing French movies abroad and studying ways of obtaining better access to American screens. Unifrance, like Gaumont, then had an office in New York. According to a study prepared by the French, their movies took 1.5 percent of the U.S. market while all foreign films combined took 2.3 percent. Since that report noted that the American box office got 45 percent of its receipts from the under-20 crowd, it was felt that more youth-oriented movies, without copying U.S. efforts, might be helpful. Other suggestions that had been popping up for years included renting a theater for exclusive use, forming their own distribution company, and so on. Gabriel Desdoits, a longtime New York agent for French films then turning more towards handling U.S. independent product abroad, said, "[The] costs of launching a

A Man and a Woman (France, 1966, Jean-Louis Trintignant). This Claude Lelouch feature was the top grossing French film released in the U.S., a position it held for decades.

French or foreign film in the U.S. are enormous when compared to the limited outlets. But there is always hope for the one big hit."[13]

Reporter Ted Clark wrote in 1979 of a French "renaissance" on U.S. screens. Still, he admitted there were limitations. One was that a French movie had to make 80 percent of its earnings in the U.S. playing in subtitled format in "sophisticated east and west coast cities" and that there were few exceptions "outside the accepted foreign-language markets of New York, Los Angeles and San Francisco." He remarked, "Nevertheless, the day when dubbed versions hit screens the length and breadth of the subcontinent, and are networked on tv, is far away." Clark credited the improved success of French films to the opening of the Gaumont office in New York and the personal attention given to its operation by du Plantier. It reportedly led to a considerable improvement in critical and public awareness of French films. Credit for starting that renaissance was given to a 1976 Gaumont release, *Cousin, Cousine,* followed by *The Lacemaker.* Gaumont made almost no money from *Cousin, Cousine* because it sold the film outright "for a modest sum" to a U.S. distributor, only to see it go on to gross about $6 million. Independent distributor New Yorker Films and Gaumont each owned, in 1979, a half interest in a New York twin cinema.[14]

Early in 1982, Columbia and Gaumont launched a joint venture, Triumph Films. Some 18 months later Gaumont agreed to keep the organization going even though it was unhappy with it. A disenchanted du Plantier remarked, "The principal obstacle for triumph in the U.S. is that

My Life to Live (France, 1962, André S. Labarthe and Anna Karina).
Directed by Jean-Luc Godard.

America is still a closed situation for foreign films. The U.S. film companies now recognize the value of foreign films but the public has not
changed." He added, "The negative reaction of American film audiences
has been a barrier for 30 years. You cannot hope to change that mentality
overnight."[15]

Later in 1983, du Plantier wondered, "Why shouldn't Americans like
foreign movies? They like foreign cars, foreign food. Film is a good food."
Gaumont was the leading distributor and exhibitor in France, the largest
producer in Italy, had operations in Brazil, and so forth. And because of
that, its size and experience, Gaumont was particularly vexed by its inability to attract a mass market in the States for its films. Until recently, said
reporter Louise Lief, most foreign films screened in American had been
picked up haphazardly by independent distributors at foreign film festivals
and marketed piecemeal to cinemas. Gaumont was trying to change all
that, she added, "but the endeavor [was] clouded by a history of failure broken by only occasional success." Du Plantier exclaimed, "Our talent wants

to exist, to be shown in America. We want to reach America. We love it, we hate it, we need it." Nicholas Seydoux, Gaumont president and chairman, thought one reason for the lack of success was because "the most important European cinema is built on the portrayal of psychological relationships." He explained, "American films are films of action and adventure. The two operate on different cultural levels." European films, reported Lief, took only two percent of the total U.S. film market. Gaumont struggled with a language barrier because its experience had shown that, unlike Europeans, American audiences did not like to see dubbed films, and subtitles limited the films to an elite audience. With regard to the Triumph Films venture, du Plantier said the deal with Columbia would be worth the price if it opened Gaumont up to a cable audience. "Cable TV is showing only a few foreign movies, but to millions, and that is a forward step," he explained.[16]

At the second Sarasota, Florida, French Film Festival in 1990, the French complained, as they had a year earlier, about a lack of reciprocity and they hinted about retaliation. Following the first festival, French industry representatives were invited to Hollywood to discuss the situation with studio heads. They went, said journalist Fred Hift, "with considerable hopes, heard much sympathetic talk, and got absolutely nowhere." As a result the French concentrated on dealing with independent distributors. No representatives from the MPAA cartel were at either festival, while the U.S. Commerce Department sent a representative to the first festival but not the second one. That prompted Dominique Wallon, the chief of the French National Cinema Center, to describe that situation as "something of an insult." Jack Lang, France's culture and communications minister (who was at Sarasota) remarked that French films took only about one-half of one percent of the U.S. market and then added, sarcastically, "At least we're on top of the list of European movies at the American box office." Lang repeated his assertion that the Americans had no right to complain about a French quota since "the U.S. virtually shuts out foreign films." More outspoken was French producer Philippe Carcassone who said, "Perhaps we could prevail on the Americans to cut down on the number of inferior American pictures they pour into our French market. They would then stop cluttering up our screens and give our industry a better chance at home." Jean-Charles Taccella, who directed *Cousin, Cousine* (which as of 2000, still stood at number 21 on the list of all-time foreign-language grossers in North America) and then spent months trying to get a U.S. distributor to take it, said, "How can the American public appreciate our pictures if neither distributors nor exhibitors will offer them?"[17]

As of 1991 the Unifrance Film office in Los Angeles had been the

French government's outpost in Hollywood for a decade, a tireless promoter of French movies and filmmakers. However, in April 1991, the French shut the office in favor of a much more modest office housed in the French consulate; it was a definite scaling back. Head of that French film office was Catherine Verret, who explained that it no longer made economic sense to maintain a separate office in Los Angeles, "given the number of [French] films actually bought in Los Angeles." Though Americans spent $5.1 billion at the box office in 1990, only about 1.5 percent of that sum was spent on foreign-language pictures. Given that situation, reporter Larry Rohter was moved to remark that the days when a foreign-language film like *La Dolce Vita* or *La Cage aux Folles* (numbers five and six, respectively, on the 2000 list) could earn $18 million at the box office "and compete with home-grown offerings" were long past. Also gone, he thought, was the notion that a hip, educated young audience could be relied on to provide traditional support for foreign-language films. Said Steve Rothenberg, vice president of theatrical distribution with the Samuel Goldwyn Company, "For the most part, the young audience has been drifting away. There's a whole generation of college students that hasn't been weaned on top-notch foreign-language films the way people in the 60's and 70's were, and that affects the grossing potential of these films." Rohter added that since the mid–1980s, the centralization of cinema ownership in the hands of a few giant national chains, often affiliated with Hollywood studios, had resulted in fewer and fewer movies screened in more and more houses at the same time, "a situation that does not favor foreign-language films." Specialty divisions of the Hollywood majors (through which they handled the foreign product they distributed) had all been closed by this time, leaving distribution of offshore items to independent firms. During 1990, the majors spent an average of $11.6 million on advertising and publicity costs for each of the movies they produced.[18]

In a 1996 interview, French director Bertrand Tavernier said the total of world cinema screened in America was less than two percent of the total. "Americans don't buy foreign books. They don't listen to foreign songs," he said, continuing, "As [German director] Wim Wenders says, among all civilized countries, the U.S. is the one where the lowest percentage of people own a passport. Ignorance is the worst protectionism in the world." Tavernier added that MPAA cartel head Jack Valenti had said many times that the American audience did not want to see subtitled films, and it did not want to see dubbed films either: "With an attitude like that, you don't need any official protectionism." Asked about the attitude of the American press to foreign movies Tavernier replied, "There's less and less space being given to foreign films in many magazines and newspapers."[19]

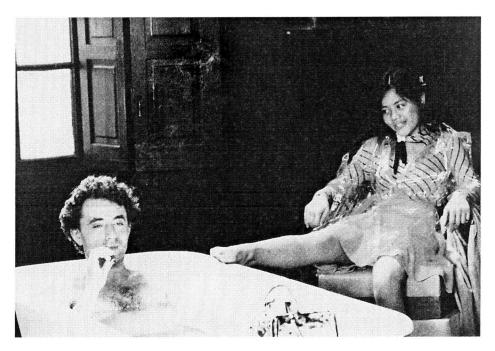

Diva (France, 1981, Richard Bohringer, Thuy an Luu).

By the end of the 1970s, it was still true that no postwar German film had ever grossed more than $200,000 in American art houses. Werner Herzog's *Aguirre* and Rainer Werner Fassbinder's *Despair* (an English-language movie with Dirk Bogarde in the lead) were in that range while Wim Wenders's *American Friend* took about $100,000.[20]

Just a few months later, in 1980, a breakthrough was achieved by German movies when both Volker Schlondorff's *Tin Drum* and Fassbinder's *The Marriage of Maria Braun* hit gross rentals of $1 million. Later in 1980, the foreign-language box office king was *Cousin, Cousine* ($5.5 million to that point), then *La Cage aux Folles* ($4 million), both French. The Italian leader was *Bread and Chocolate* ($3 million). By then the two German breakthrough pictures had each reached $2 million. During 1979, film distributors in Germany received $155 million in total; U.S. distributors took $75 million of that. Some German directors were upset that foreign investors already had their hands in the pie of the first successful German postwar films to appear on the screen. It was the German branch of United Artists that reinvested foreign ticket tax funds in *Maria Braun* and *Tin Drum* during the production stage and then negotiated the North American rights.[21]

Still, success did not last. One executive in the German film industry

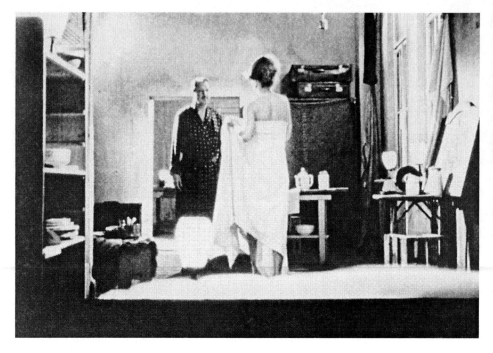

The Marriage of Maria Braun (Germany, 1979, Ivan Desny, Hanna Schygulla).

described an all-too-familiar reaction, in 1994, when he pitched his films to the American market: "They just look at the film and say 'Too German.'"[22]

During a speech in 1986 in Los Angeles, Pierre Viot, with the Cannes Film Festival, remarked that the film imbalance between the States and Europe could be a long term problem. Suggestions he made to change the situation included co-productions and common actions between European countries, and greater promotional efforts by European filmmakers in the U.S. market. There were about 21,000 screens in America in 1985, 23,000 in Europe; admissions totaled 1.11 billion in the U.S., 700 million in Europe; and 300 features were made that year in the States while 400 were produced in Europe. Despite those roughly equal markets, in most European nations, American films took around 50 percent of the box office revenues (47 percent in France in 1985, compared to 43 percent for French movies). Viot estimated that "at most, 1% of the box office revenues in the U.S." came from French films.[23]

In 1970, David Haft was the U.S. agent for Embrafilms, a new promotion and export agency that was a joint venture of the Brazilian government and Brazil's motion picture industry. Until that point movies from that country had next to no impact in the States. Reportedly Brazil was considering renting its own cinema in Manhattan as a showcase for its features. Haft felt a significant precedent was to be found in the popularity in the U.S. of bossa nova music: "The American public learned to like our music and it will learn to like our films."[24]

The government of India announced in 1971 that it would not renew its contract with the Hollywood cartel's MPAA, an organization that held something that was close to a monopoly on the foreign movies shown in India. The government explained that it was not renewing because of the failure of the American organization to import, promote and popularize Indian pictures in the U.S.—which, according to the Indians, had been promised under the deal. Through its foreign arm, the MPEA, the MPAA declared that no such promise had been, or could be, made because "this is a free economy and...there are no ways of forcing Indian films into American theaters even if we wanted."[25]

Export earnings for Indian films in the year 1976-1977 totaled $8,128,689. The largest single market was the U.K., which contributed $1,458,733 of the total. Next came Dubai at $1,264,204. In sixth spot was the U.S. at $223,137; seventh was Kenya at $209,400. Slightly ahead of the U.S. was Mauritius in fifth place, $255,303.[26]

When MPAA president Jack Valenti was in Moscow in 1973, as head of the U.S. delegation to the Moscow Film Festival, he said that if Soviet filmmakers wanted to do better in the West they would have to make some changes. He added, "Many countries seem unable to understand why if they take 10 American films, we can't take 10 of theirs and show them in theatres." He cited a recent deal between the Russians and Columbia Pictures, in which the latter acquired a number of Russian films in return for Russia taking some Columbia product; Valenti said that was the type of deal he wanted to stop. "What I am trying to do is negotiate for the first time on the basis of no reciprocity," he explained, stating, "It can't be on a reciprocity basis. It has to be on the basis of films we think we can sell."[27]

Michael Thornhill, Australian film director and producer, argued in 1978, "American audiences are both provincial and parochial.... The evidence to date would suggest that American audiences wish to see American films." Attempts in his part of the world to make carbon copies of American product had, he thought, "failed dismally." One approach he suggested to take to try and improve the penetration by Australian movies was to spend a lot of money in America publicizing and promoting those features.[28]

In order to spearhead its effort to crack the U.S. market, the government-funded Australian Film Commission (AFC) opened an office in Los Angeles in 1980. Some six years later, the AFC could report only "limited success." Richard Guardian, the AFC's Los Angeles representative, said all foreign films (not just Australian) had a tough time in the States because they were "still foreign films." "The subject matter, the sensitivities of the films are culturally different from American films," he explained. With regard to Australian movies specifically, Guardian commented, "In many cases, the subject matter is not pertinent to American audiences, and the pacing is a bit slower than what Americans are used to." He thought producers should assess the U.S. market needs before filming, instead of following a "shoot first, ask questions later" policy.[29]

Distributor Orion Classics announced in 1985 that it would handle Akira Kurosawa's *Ran* with a selective release plan, mindful of the "traditional resistance" to Japanese films in America. David Owens, assistant director of the Japan Society's Japan Film Center in New York City, said the market for Japanese movies had been "very limited" in the past because U.S. audiences had the idea that Japanese pictures were "difficult." Owen explained his view of that perception by saying, "Most Japanese pictures are paced differently than American films, they develop character and atmosphere at the expense of plot and action. U.S. audiences don't want to wait."[30]

Figures from Tokyo revealed that America was Japan's biggest foreign customer, importing in 1986 some $4.7 million worth of Japanese features, out of a worldwide export total of $9,244,764. Fifty countries imported Japanese movies that year. During that same year, Hollywood's majors took $137 million in film rentals out of Japan—independent U.S. producers took another $33 million for a total of $170 million, a ratio of 35:1 in favor of the U.S. For years U.S. films had taken 40 to 50 percent of the Japanese market.[31]

One tactic used by foreign producers in this period, as in the past, was to try and Americanize their product. Some continued with this strategy despite the fact it had been attempted sporadically for decades—never with any success. Author and producer James Clavell declared in 1968 that in order to export more movies more successfully, Britain had to increasingly make them "Yank style" which was, he argued, "the most internationally successful combination of content and development." Even though British movies could not recoup their costs on the home market and had to rely on export earnings—notably from the States—Clavell believed that few U.K. filmmakers were geared to U.S. tastes. "Quite apart from the technical factor that the soundtrack must be understood across the pond," he said, "it is the choice of story and more notably the style of their telling

Kagemusha (Japan, 1980, director Akira Kurosawa on the set).

that can spell the difference for a U.K. pic between a limited artie success and a smash in the mass markets."[32]

Around that same time, Polaris Productions was a fairly new American distribution firm. Cofounder Vernon Becker contended that while U.S. movies were made with the international market in mind, there were commercial films made for the home markets of other nations that were produced with "a necessarily nearsighted and parochial view." Unsuitable for America, those items could be made suitable if only changes could be made to put them in a "palatable form." Simple cutting of the film was not

seen by him as a solution. An example he gave was the Danish feature
I, a Marquis that was about a local Danish scandal. Becker went to Copen-
hagen and convinced the director and scriptwriter to write and shoot five
day's worth of new scenes with the same actors, to explain things more
clearly. That was done months after the film was released in Denmark.
Another example was the children's feature The Princess and the Swineherd,
based on a Hans Christian Andersen story. Becker felt a few new scenes
were needed, preferably with an American star. Again he approached the
principals and they agreed to take out three songs, create a new character
(to be played by Burl Ives) and write new songs for that character. Persua-
sion of all parties, in both cases, was said to be "easy."[33]

Walter Manley, a New York importer, in 1970 felt that European producers had taken to heart too much of the advice to Americanize their output. Selling a foreign-language movie was hard, explained Manley, so the
word went out: "Shoot in English if you want the American dollar. Make
films that look like American pictures if you want that sale." The results
lately, he added, had been "laughable, with directors working with split
scripts, actors mouthing gibberish to allow for post-sync work, etc." "It's
not the kind of atmosphere a creative director can function properly in,
and the results show it," he said. One thing that had not changed was the
power of the New York Times to break (but not make) a foreign-language
film, said Manley. While a good review in the Times would not help sales
that much, a bad review could hurt the possibility of getting bookings outside New York.[34]

Speaking of the difficulties of getting foreign movies exhibited on the
art house circuit reporter Addison Verrill noted that they had to compete
against U.S. product as well as against foreign for screening time; the odds
of winning were very low "unless a foreign item [had] something special
about it or [was] directly geared to the American market." Over the years,
the ranks of independent distributors had shrunk with a trend on both
sides of the Atlantic for packagers to concentrate on putting together elaborate productions, stressing action-adventure with big names.[35]

Australian director Peter Weir, speaking to a motion picture industry luncheon in Australia in 1978, complained there was "scant chance"
for Australian filmmakers to crack the U.S. market unless they agreed "with
established Yank attitudes," which were not stated. Weir added, "The Yanks
aren't interested. The Americans make their own entertainment. Sure,
they'll poach! But the editing pace of our films just isn't right for that market."[36]

To dub or not to dub foreign-language product remained a contro-
versial and confusing issue. Peter Riethof, an American living in Paris who

was a veteran in the field of dubbing for export, said in 1974 that in the past European producers who did not consider the U.S. market easily accessible had commissioned English dubbed versions for countries "less demanding" than the States. "These versions were produced at a minimum fee" and aimed at such markets as South Africa, Hong Kong, Latin America, Australia, New Zealand, and so forth. Although they weren't expected to surface in the U.S., increased sales sometimes meant those cheap dubs did get exhibited in the U.S., a result Riethof thought might lead to disappointments. For Riethof it was evident that the American market could only potentially lead to box office success if the American-dubbed version of the film had "been done with such care that the public [would] for all practical purposes not see any difference between an 'American language' foreign version and a regular film produced State side."[37]

Los Angeles exhibitor Max Laemmle said, with regard to dubbing, that it helped to broaden the market for a foreign movie, but only after the film's reputation had been built through subtitle-version screenings in major markets. "Our audience would stone us if I brought them dubbed films," he added.[38]

Jeremy Irons studied French for his lines in Volker Schlondorff's *Swann in Love*. However, his French was not good enough to pass muster so French actor Pierre Arditi dubbed him. But that was unacceptable in the States where Irons's voice was recognized, so he had to work on his French some more so he could redub his own lines. Fassbinder's *Querelle*, which starred America's Brad Davis, was shot in English with actors Jeanne Moreau and Franco Nero using their own voices. Other actors—mostly German—were dubbed. But the entire foreign cast did so badly in English that the preview audience in New York giggled at their delivery. Thus, the movie was dubbed into German—including Davis's lines—with English subtitles added. Journalist Dan Yakir said the foreign film audience in America preferred to see those movies in their original language. When they were dubbed in English, remarked Yakir, they generally fell "flat on their face at the box office."[39]

Lawrence Cohn reported in 1992 that distributor Miramax hoped to introduce European cult movies to a wider American audience by dubbing them into English, starting with the French horror film *Baby Blood*—for which Miramax had allocated $20,000 for a "first-class" dubbing job. Miramax cochairman Harvey Weinstein noted his company had dubbed *Cinema Paradiso* into English after its subtitled theatrical playoff, in the hope of generating income in the ancillary markets (such as cable, television, syndication) with it. "But there's a prejudice against dubbed and foreign films in general on the part of TV syndicators and stations," noted Weinstein, concluding, "Despite its Oscar and success we couldn't crack the syndication barrier."[40]

Cohn returned a year later to recall a sort of heyday of dubbing in the late 1950s, when many of the dubbed pictures of Brigitte Bardot moved beyond the art house circuit. After its big success in 1961, *La Dolce Vita* was reissued at the start of 1966 by American International Pictures in a dubbed version that performed very well, grossing more than $8 million that year. However, wrote Cohn, in the decade before 1993 dubbing of foreign films had almost ceased for the U.S. market "due to audience resistance." Both *Das Boot* and *La Cage aux Folles* were issued unsuccessfully in dubbed versions after the original subtitled prints had attracted a wide audience. Recent foreign hits of the time such as *Cinema Paradiso* or *Women on the Verge of a Nervous Breakdown* never played dubbed in U.S. cinemas. According to Cohn, the last significant attempt to use dubbing in addition to subtitling was on the Russian/Italian production *Dark Eyes*, starring Marcello Mastroianni. A test release of the English dubbed version reportedly "flopped miserably."[41]

Later in 1993, exhibition chain AMC declared its intent to make its circuit available to dubbed French movies. That plan was born following the Sarasota, Florida, French film festival in 1992. After that, some 12 months of discussion with the French film export board, Unifrance, led to a loose agreement by which AMC would make its screens available; Unifrance would pay for dubbing and prints while both parties would contribute to marketing costs. At the 1993 Sarasota festival, French Culture Minister Jacques Toubon announced $2.5 million would be made available to Unifrance to support the project. "Thanks to dubbing, a French film should be able to be considered a regular movie and break out of the art movie ghetto," enthused Toubon. However, one distributor pointed out that the subtitled version of Luc Bresson's *Nikita* outsold the dubbed version by a ratio of four to one. Many American industry observers believed that dubbing would not cause foreign product to make significant inroads into the States. Peter Riethof, who had produced dubbed American ver-

Das Boot (Germany, 1981, Jurgen Prochnow).

sions of over 400 European films, said when quality dubbing became a rarity, the market collapsed. He dated that to the mid–1970s when Asian companies started doing the dub work cheaply. Riethof felt that if two versions were to be used, then the subtitled and dubbed items should be released simultaneously. If the dubbed version was released later, it lost all the marketing benefits of the original launch. Unifrance head du Plantier agreed that if high quality was not achieved for the AMC plan, the dubbed French movies would be buried forever and with them the French hopes of breaking out of the art house circuit. "We have to prove it can be done with dubbed films," he declared. Du Plantier thought dubbing would cost $50,000 to $100,000 per film, while Riethof felt that for excellent quality the cost would be closer to $200,000 per film.[42]

Leonard Klady reported in 1994 that, according to the trade, fewer and fewer non–English language features were being acquired in North America but the ones selected were drawing a bigger audience. Opinion on whether such a movie should be dubbed was still said to be split in the trade. One belief was that Americans did not go to the movies to read, and therefore subtitles were out. "I don't think the public cares if a picture is dubbed or not," said one exhibitor. "These films have other hurdles to clear. Most don't come with movie stars, and they may have a cultural perspective that simply doesn't translate to the masses." He added that their greatest sin was that "millions are spent on making a film and some goon spends two days in a recording studio to make the English version." In Europe most films were dubbed; it was hard to find an original language version (with subtitles) of American movies in Germany or Italy. Less than one year after the deal between AMC and Unifrance was announced, it collapsed when French producers and distributors were asked to financially contribute to the dubbing project. They all declined.[43]

Famed film critic Stanley Kauffmann mentioned the potential revival of dubbing in 1995, when a number of French distributors were said to be interested. Kauffmann declared that he opposed dubbing back at the start of the 1960s, when dubbing received a flurry of publicity, and in 1995. Subtitles, he felt, were much the better of the two methods. French distributors argued that every country in the world, except the U.S. and the U.K., saw foreign movies dubbed in the local language, so why not America?[44]

Il Postino became, in 1996, the first foreign-language film since the 1973 Swedish drama *Cries and Whispers* to win an Oscar nomination for best picture, but relatively few Americans were likely to see the Italian comedy. To that date it had grossed $11 million at the box office—impressive for its type, but not much more than a single weekend take for an above-average Hollywood product. (It was in second place on the 2000 all-time list, at $21.8 million.) That film was subtitled and distributor Miramax had no plans to dub it. Miramax had planned to release a dubbed version of *Les Visiteurs*, a 1993 French farce that took in $90 million at the box office in France, believing that a well-dubbed version could expand the potential audience from 20 cities to 100. Some $500,000 was spent by the producer on the English-language version, dubbed by Mel Brooks's firm, Brooksfilms. But that version was scrapped after test screenings proved disastrous with the result that Miramax released the movie with subtitles. Commented du Plantier: "I think it's a pity. For once we had a very strong commercial movie, and it was made for an extremely young audience, the kind of audience that will never accept subtitles."[45]

Leonard Klady declared in 1999 that Americans hated dubbed films, even those who liked foreign films. On the other hand du Plantier maintained that industry resistance to dubbing was the primary barrier to getting French films on U.S. screens. Miramax had just issued a dubbed English-language version of its Italian Oscar-winner *Life Is Beautiful* with the hope the new version would be sold to network television—which had not happened to past hits such as *Il Postino* or *Like Water for Chocolate* in either dubbed or subtitled form. Klady thought the re-release of *Life*—at $57 million in box office receipts, the top-grossing foreign-language film of all-time in North America (number one on the 2000 list)—was taking place too late to capitalize on its fame. He said there had not been a foreign art house hit in a dubbed version since *La Cage aux Folles* in 1978. A national poll of moviegoers by Marketcast in August 1999 revealed that 31 percent of the audience said they would be more likely to see foreign-language films if they were dubbed in English, while 27 percent said they definitely would not. A turning point for dubbed pictures came in 1984, said Klady, with

the release of "a meticulously produced and excellent" dub of *Das Boot*, the Oscar-nominated film about life in a German U-boat. Still said to be one of the finest examples of the dubbing process, *The Boat*, as it was retitled for U.S. audiences, "was shunned by audiences despite aggressive marketing."[46]

Art houses remained the mainstay of exhibition possibilities for foreign films in the States, especially those in New

Camille Claudell (France, 1988, Gerard Depardieu).

York. Reporter Addison Verrill commented in 1973 that the launching of foreign-language product in New York was still necessary for any hope of an exhibition potential outside of that city. Almost 20 years later, journalist Lance Loud said little about that situation had changed and, because imports had to open in New York, the *New York Times* inadvertently had what *Los Angeles Times* film critic Michael Wilmington described as a "veto power" over a foreign film's future in America. Yet getting screening time in New York could be difficult, even for world-famous filmmakers. In 1990, directors Federico Fellini and Jean Luc Godard each released a new film that did not make it to the States. Fellini's *Voice of the Moon* and Godard's *Nouvelle Vague* were limited to the festival circuit in the U.S.A. As well, Fellini's 1987 *Intervista* did not get a U.S. cinema release.[47]

In 2002, New York reportedly still accounted for more than 60 percent of an average foreign film's take in America. The next best market, but a distant second, was San Francisco.[48]

Hollywood, throughout this period, continued to use the same tactics it had used in the past to limit foreign film penetration, and continued to enjoy success. Poaching continued as one of those strategies. As European directors achieved greater acclaim during that golden era from roughly 1950 to 1965, Hollywood's majors moved in to sign contracts with some of that foreign talent. By the end of the golden era the majors had signed up directors such as Michelangelo Antonioni, Francois Truffaut and Roman Polanski.[49]

Charles Schreger reported in 1978 that Louis Malle was the latest in a long line of foreign directors trying to crack the American market with an English-language film done for the majors, in his case *Pretty Baby* (Paramount). Schreger listed failures in that category over the previous 12 months: Lina Wertmullers' *A Night Full of Rain* (Warner—poor reviews, poor box office); Ingmar Bergman's *The Serpent's Egg* (Paramount) and *The Touch* (1971 release by ABC Films), both of which died commercially; Claude Lelouch's *Another Man, Another Chance* (United Artists) bombed, as did Fellini's *Casanova* (Universal); and Antonioni's *Zabriskie Point* failed in the early 1970s, as did his more recent *The Passenger* (1975—MGM). Successes listed by Schreger were limited to Milos Forman, Roman Polanski and Francois Truffaut, with the latter described as having a "mixed" outcome. Arguing that there had been foreign directors who successfully made the transition from auteur to commercial American filmmaker, Schreger had to reach far back in time to find them, to Hollywood's beginnings, to the likes of Fritz Lang, Ernst Lubitsch, and so forth. Undoubtedly Hollywood hoped that any talent it poached would lead to greater profits for itself but even if that did not happen, it was not a complete loss for the

The Serpent's Egg (Sweden, 1977, Liv Ullmann, David Carradine).

cartel. When a foreign director was producing for Hollywood he was, obviously, not contributing to his native film industry. If, after a failure, Hollywood cut him adrift and he returned home, he might have been less able or willing to accept the limitations and conditions of his native industry again. For example, he would have to return to working with much smaller budgets.[50]

Censorship provided less obstacles to offshore product as censorship faded into the background of a more sophisticated and tolerant society. The old Production Code gave way in 1968 to a new voluntary system when the MPAA implemented ratings for movies: G for general, M for mature, R for restricted and X, a rating that usually meant a movie would not be shown in a regular cinema but limited to porn houses. When the MPAA implemented its rating classification system, the independent's organization, the International Film Importers and Distributors of America (IFIDA), announced it supported the plan and that it would participate in the voluntary plan, but its members were not obliged to do so. Within a few months, however, some IFIDA members were not submitting their films to the MPAA's Code and Rating Administration. As far as mainstream, regular cinemas were concerned, a film without an MPAA rating carried an X by default, even if the movie had no sex or nudity. The MPAA charged the independents $150 for assigning a rating to a picture. As in the past, the art houses continued to screen foreign items, and domestic for that matter, with no concern over what rating a movie had, if it had one at all.[51]

Tariffs and other government regulation remained a non-issue in the States for foreign films. There was no agitation for them and there were hardly any of them in America. Speaking in Canada, where he argued against any type of government intervention in the film industry, in any country, MPAA head Jack Valenti beat the drum for free trade and said, "The American market is totally free. A Canadian film, a Zambian film, an Australian film, a Brazilian film ... any film enters the marketplace on the same basis as an American film."[52]

A newer tactic involved cutting the foreign films. If they were "diffi-cult" or hard to understand in the first place, then imagine the impression they must have made after Hollywood cut them. Journalist Dan Yakir reported in 1985, "To maximize commercial potential, foreign films are often recut and shortened in a way that will be most palatable to the Amer-ican moviegoers." Sergio Leone's *Once Upon a Time in America* was forced to shed one hour and 32 minutes; Michel Lang's *The Gift* lost five min-utes; Fassbinder's *Querelle* lost about 30 seconds. *Once Upon a Time in Amer-ica* was not just shortened but it was also recut. Originally it was supposed to be 4.5 hours long, planned as a film in two parts but the Americans would not buy it. Said Leone, "I feel that Americans have been perverted by the stupidities of *Dallas* and *Dynasty* and so they can't respond to real cinema. The cinema I love is dying, and in the United States it is no longer possible, because money has become the sole consideration." Yakir men-tioned many other foreign movies that had been cut. Fima Noveck had altered foreign features such as Lina Wertmuller's *Love and Anarchy* and *Swept Away* as well as the works of other Europeans, for U.S. release. A self-proclaimed troubleshooter, Noveck declared, "European films lack an emotional punch. They tend to linger on a point that's already made and overstate things. Their pace is too leisurely."[53]

The use of remakes was increasing as a strategy used by Hollywood. Why distribute a foreign film if one could buy the underlying rights and remake the feature with U.S. stars, an American writer, a changed plot, and so on? *Cousins* was a remake of the 1975 French hit *Cousin, Cousine*. *Three Fugitives*, the two-men-and-a-baby comedy from Touchstone Pictures, was equally indebted to its French inspiration *Les Fugitifs*. In the latter case, Touchstone also bought up the American distribution rights to the French original that, wrote reporter Gregg Kilday, "it promptly put in mothballs" before asking its director, Francis Veber, to do the remake himself. A novel by Fay Weldon, *The Life and Loves of a She-Devil*, was produced as a four-hour miniseries by the U.K.'s BBC, in conjunction with Australia's the Seven Network and the American A&E Cable network. Despite that, it was made into a U.S. film. One of the writers of that screenplay, Barry Stru-gatz, said, "We liked the book a lot, but we had to Americanize it, setting it in New York and Long Island. It was a very bleak, black comedy. We brightened the tone a bit and made it a little more hopeful."[54]

Reporter Josh Young commented in 1994 that, increasingly, French films could not be seen in the States, even on video, because a growing number of those films were "providing fodder for Hollywood remakes." Those French films had only been screened in the U.S. at film festivals. Recent remakes cited by Young were *True Lies*, *Mixed Nuts*, and *Nine Months*,

Lola (Germany, 1981, Barbara Sukowa). Rainer Werner Fassbinder directed.

which were remakes of the following French originals, respectively, *La Totale, Pere Noel et un Ordure,* and *Neuf Mois*—none of which had ever played in the U.S. Hollywood's studios, said Young, had concluded that audiences would rather hear Steve Martin deliver jokes in English than see the French original and read jokes in subtitles. Film critic Molly Haskell said, "I don't think there was ever a case where the remake was better." Haskell attributed the remake craze to a lack of ideas in Hollywood and added, "Studios don't want the original competing with the remake, which is invariably inferior." When *Variety* reviewed the French movie *Grossesse Nerveuse* earlier that year, when it screened at a festival in Switzerland, the trade journal gave it a good review and added the thought it "could lend itself to a U.S. remake." Disney had two remakes of French features on its shelf, *My Father the Hero* (*Mon Pere le Heros*) and *Three Fugitives* (*Les Fugitifs*). Neither of the French originals got U.S. theatrical release nor were they available here on video. Francis Veber had no less than five of his films remade. In *Hero,* Gerard Depardieu played the same role in both films. Young pointed out that foreign films took in fewer than two percent of American box office receipts, with French films taking less than one percent. He also said, "Of course, if there is no theatrical release, the film almost certainly won't go to video." Fine Line Features (a distributor of imports) president Ira Deutchman said, "Foreign films do notoriously badly on video, so I wouldn't hold out any hope that these films will be released on video." In conclusion Young complained, "So clever French comedies end up being used an animated scripts."[55]

In a 2001 article, reporter David Edelstein said it would be terrific to report that Hollywood did not, contrary to popular belief, "have a coarsening effect on the foreign properties it remakes." He remarked, "Terrific, but wrong. In this area as in few others, studios live up to their reputation as titanic forces of philistinism. Remakes don't, from the outset, attract artistic adventurers." It was easier to borrow a story than it was to invent your own. Edelstein said that over the previous few months, he had spent close to 100 hours watching foreign features and their U.S. remakes "without finding one—not one—remake that measured up to the original."[56]

With the arrival of the videocassette at the start of the 1980s, hopes were raised (at least in some quarters) that foreign movies would benefit. As early as 1982, one account argued that foreign films on videocassettes would potentially perform better than they would in cinemas. One reason being that it was cheaper for customers to rent a foreign movie than going to the theater. Also, a foreign film was only one title out of hundreds or thousands on a video store's shelves; that is, a foreign movie on cassette could go places that a celluloid version could not, and at less financial risk.

Even Dwarfs Started Small (Germany, 1971, director Werner Herzog on the set with the Schneider Midgets).

Supposedly that cassette could either be dubbed or subtitled; neither format was foreclosed. With such a potentially bright future, the reporter concluded, "Instead of having to settle for the table scraps of their theatrical counterparts, foreign features on homevideo can nab at least part of the monetary main course."[57]

Of course, nothing remotely like that happened. Blockbuster Video, with some 2,400 stores worldwide in 1994, said that European films were most popular in affluent, white-collar areas and college towns, especially in the northeastern U.S. The typical European film-watcher was educated, well-off financially and did not mind reading subtitles. In deciding what films to stock, Blockbuster looked for indicators that the film would be recognized, such as having had a U.S. cinema release, magazine and/or newspaper reviews, and famous actors. Such criteria, of course, automatically excluded many foreign films. French and Italian features were the foreign features generally most rented from Blockbuster.[58]

According to a 1996 report from the Video Software Dealers Association, foreign-language films made up only two percent of the video rental market. And that was very, very close to their take at the cinema box office.[59]

As had always been true, the Hollywood cartel's control of the distribution system remained the single most powerful tool in limiting foreign penetration of American screens. Foreign producers complained in 1968 that more often than not their financial returns from the U.S. rarely seemed to match the reports of the performance—with the same outcome whether distribution was through a major or by an independent. It was almost a universal belief among independent European filmmakers, said reporter Harold Myers, that if they sold one of their productions on the basis of a guarantee against percentage, "the actual sum guaranteed [was] usually the sum total of what may finally be expected." That is, the minimum became the maximum and the foreign producers, in a polite way, were claiming they were being ripped off.[60]

That same year, French filmmaker Francois Truffaut could not understand why his compatriot and friend Jean-Luc Godard had been recently cautioning against making deals with the U.S. majors, even though he noted that Columbia, in its three-picture deal with Godard, retained the right to final cut "but never exercised it." Truffaut's deal with United Artists, however, gave the director complete control over the final form of each film.[61]

An idea of the power of the majors could be seen in the share of the domestic box office controlled by the films they handled. The top 16 U.S. distributors took 90 percent of the 1970 market's $340 million gross. Share of the seven (RKO was by then defunct) Hollywood majors was as follows: Fox, 16.57 percent; Columbia, 11.85 percent; United Artists, 11.23 percent; Paramount, 10.4 percent; Universal, 7.0 percent; Warner Bros., 4.84 percent; and MGM, 4.52 percent. Thus, the majors took 66.4 percent of the total U.S. domestic market that year.[62]

In 1971, MGM formed a separate entity for the domestic distribution of foreign-language films, for the urban U.S. openings of selected imports. If those features caught on, said Metro, they would be shifted to regular domestic channels for widespread release. This was a strategy revived by other majors as well. Prior to the new film rating system that went into effect in 1968, nearly all the majors had, at one time or another, a separate division, with its own name, to handle the few foreign items they distributed and, more importantly, to circumvent the old Production Code requirement. It was generally felt handy, said one account, "to have another legal entity available just in case some corporate images otherwise might be bruised by certain product." After the new rating system became effective, rules called for all films released by any MPAA member company under any name to be submitted to receive a rating. All the majors then deactivated their other names. In this case MGM was revising its old name, Premier, for its new releasing strategy. When the majors handled foreign films in some sort of "special" way, compared to the way they handled their own releases, they went a long way to ensure that the foreign item was thus handicapped and did not do that well.[63]

Reporter James Monaco, because of what he called the "arbitrariness" of the film import business, started a new column, or service, in a Canadian film trade journal in 1975. Called "Holding Pattern," the column was dedicated to films that to that point had been forgotten—they had no distributor although they may have appeared at film festivals and private trade screenings. They all had, thought Monaco, at least adequate market potential if handled correctly. Set up to be a recurring feature, that original column contained a list and reviews of 13 films, all foreign except for one produced by a U.S. independent studio.[64]

Akira Kurosawa's *Dersu Uzala* (a Japanese and Russian co-production) won the 1975 Academy Award for best foreign film, the Moscow Film Festival's grand prize, and was shown at the New York Film Festival in 1976. Yet it did not open in New York City until January 1978.[65]

When film writer Stanley Kauffmann looked at the number of foreign films released in America and compared that with worldwide production in 1977, he became depressed and concluded, "You come up with a list of films floating out of figurative reach that makes any statement of ours about the 'best' this or that of the year, or of the decade, simply silly. We just don't know." Agreeing that some of the foreign movies released in the U.S. were not all that great, he said the point was that many foreign films sounded interesting "and in a rational world we ought to have the chance to find out about them." However, it then cost $50,000 to $150,000 to open a foreign film in New York, he said, and things would only get worse. "Self-evidently, we need a system of international exchange outside the usual commercial channels, or cinematic isolationism is going to increase and petrify," he concluded. But Kauffmann then added he had not "the slightest hope" that anything was going to be done about this matter—"prospects are black." He said his article was partly to let the reader share his depression and partly "to help [him] scoff a bit more at the cant about 'film the international language.'" He concluded bitterly, "Not unless the whole vocabulary is *Stars Wars* and *The Godfather*."[66]

Journalist Frank Segers stated in 1979 that the majors generally shunned foreign film distribution on the grounds that their distribution systems, geared to the country-wide release of big U.S. features, did not easily accommodate foreign-language items that required "more modest and specialized handling." It was an argument that made economic sense to Segers since to support a large distribution overhead, "a steady flow of product of broad national appeal is required." "Foreign pics just don't fit that category," he remarked. Outlining some of the costly items involved in opening a foreign movie Robert Shayne (of the distributor New Line) mentioned print costs, subtitling, trailers, an advertising campaign, arranging for radio advertisements (television advertisements were almost never used because of their high costs), hiring a publicist, clearing import duties, paying in advance the preopening and first-week advertising costs. He complained, "All this to distribute a film with generally little value in subsidiary

Fear of Fear (Germany, 1975, Margie Carstensen). Directed by Rainer Werner Fassbinder.

sales [such as to television and videocassette] and that can playoff theatrically in a limited number of U.S. cities." To penetrate the key New York market could cost a distributor in the neighborhood of from $60,000 to $100,000. As always in the past, New York remained the main market. One independent distributor said a foreign film earned 20 to 40 percent of its total take in New York. During 1978, the four top-grossing foreign films in American were also the top four in New York. *Madame Rosa* grossed $2,562,312 nationally ($551,000 from New York), *Bread and Chocolate* made $1.6 million ($400,000), *Donna Flor and Her Two Husbands* made $1,303,669 ($351,000), and *Cat and Mouse* made $1,165,305 ($325,000).[67]

Canadian academic Bruce Mallen said that, in 1979, U.S. production groups spent some $780 million on production costs alone, to produce about 340 movies. Of that total no more than $125 million was spent on pure independent features; the rest was expended by the majors. It was that small group of majors in whom the Canadian film industry, as a whole, had to rely on for effective U.S. distribution. "In other words," said Mallen, "Canada's biggest competitors in the U.S. market will also have to be Canada's biggest distributors." He felt that all evidence pointed to the

La Mortadella (Italy, 1971, William Devane at left, Sophia Loren, others unidentified).

increasing power, share of films produced and share of revenue generated by those few firms. Christmas releases in 1979 in Los Angeles were all from the majors; not one feature from an independent was on a major screen in that city. Every first-run house in Los Angeles at that time was screening a major studio theatrical release.[68]

A 1980 account argued that American films or American-style features dominated the world market. It reported, "Whether the pictures are made in Hollywood, Canada, Europe, Africa or the Far East, it's more than likely that the package will be partly or wholly assembled here [Hollywood] as will the arrangements for distribution." All the deal makers, producers, financiers, distributors, and so forth, from everywhere, reportedly did their deals in Hollywood.[69]

The New Yorker theater opened its doors in 1960, running retrospectives of American films. Its outgrowth, New Yorker Films, functioned as a distributor for foreign films and introduced filmmakers such as Bernardo Bertolucci, Werner Herzog, and Rainer Werner Fassbinder. In 1960, Dan Talbot convinced the owner of the Yorktown theater to rename it and make it a repertory house instead of turning it into a Spanish-language cinema, as the owner had intended. After a brief stint as an employee, Talbot bought the venue in 1962. In the mid–1960s, having shown most of the American films he wanted to screen, Talbot moved toward exhibiting European cinema. He began to distribute more or less by accident. Shortly after he saw Bertolucci's *Before the Revolution* in 1964 at the New York Film Festival, he wrote to the producer asking to screen it at the New Yorker. However, the producer wrote back to say that he did not want to make an exhibition deal, but he was prepared to sell Talbot the distribution rights. After paying a $500 advance against a percentage, Talbot was in business as a distributor, New Yorker Films. In 1973 Talbot sold the cinema to the Walter Reade organization to concentrate on distribution.[70]

Talbot declared the American film market was not especially hospitable toward foreign product. Of the thousands of theaters in America at the time, only 200 played art films. Of that 200, said Talbot, "There are less than fifteen three-star theaters—to use the Michelin system—that are a proven known quality in major cities and attract a sophisticated, urbane audience. Only fifteen!" Some of them were: the Orson Welles in Cambridge, Massachusetts; the Clay in San Francisco; and the Biograph in Chicago. That small group of prestige art houses were responsible for 50 percent of the income from a foreign movie, explained Talbot. There was a possibility, he admitted, of crossing over into the fringe of the commercial market in large cities, but warned, "There are many cities in America where a whole generation of moviegoers has literally never seen a foreign film!" Talbot then paid, in 1980, a maximum of a $35,000 guarantee for a German film, and as high as $100,000 for a French or an Italian picture. An average price for a film that had commercial possibilities was $50,000, but a risky project could command substantially less than $20,000. To open a foreign film in New York cost Talbot about $100,000. He usually opened a film with just two prints, on a modest budget, and waited for critical and audience response. If it looked like it had a chance then he made a dupe negative and spent more on promotion. New Yorker's deal with Gaumont had the former distributing Gaumont's films for a commission with the studio paying for prints and advertising.[71]

Writing in 1983, Stephen Klein repeated a common complaint that European producers had over-inflated expectations in Europe over how much money they could get from the U.S. theatrical market and also overly-high expectations about what they can get from ancillary markets—such as pay television rights. One executive from a major said the Europeans were going to be unpleasantly surprised when "they tried selling paycable themselves on a one-shot basis, without a steady relationship and some domestic 'locomotive' films." Klein added that the majors, through their "classic" units, were controlling more of the foreign film distribution as more of the independents were leaving the business, or at least foreign distribution, because of the prestige and purse strings of the majors.[72]

Reporter Harlan Jacobson said in 1983 that all the majors, except Paramount and Warner Bros., then had a classics unit, whereas only United Artists had such a unit in 1980. Those units handled domestic features as well as foreign items, anything that required so-called special handling. A couple of such units had existed in the 1950s, said Jacobson, mainly to handle sexually explicit films—subsidiary firms to get around the MPAA Production Code restrictions. Also, United Artists had a classics division in the mid–1970s. Jacobson stated that New York counted for about 35 percent of a foreign film's potential gross, compared to about 10 percent for Hollywood product. *Blade Runner* earned about $15 million in 1982, about equal to the entire yearly take for all foreign films in 1982, excluding the U.K.'s *Chariots of Fire*. Jacobson estimated that for conventional foreign films there were only 150 to 200 cinemas in the country that would play them, out of some 18,000 theaters in total. After the expiration of Gaumont's three-year distribution deal with New Yorker Films, Gaumont signed an agreement with Columbia's classics unit, Triumph, perhaps hoping to move into the big leagues as well as hoping to get Columbia pictures for Europe.[73]

Lawrence Cohn argued in 1984 that the foreign film that made it to America was a "rare commodity." Even movies that were big hits in their home markets, with a few exceptions, increasingly did not travel to the U.S. It reflected, thought Cohn, "changes in popular tastes and different distribution patterns." Cohn said it all contrasted sharply with the 1960s when the majors released over 200 new films per year "and among them were numerous foreign comedies, thrillers and romances of popular rather than art-house appeal." From 1961 through 1970, said the reporter, a total of 32 films starring or featuring Jean-Paul Belmondo were released in the U.S. However, as of 1984, none of his previous 12 films had been released in the U.S., some of which were huge hits. Alain Delon appeared in 17 features released in the States in the 1960s (five of those were British or U.S. productions with original English-language soundtracks). His last French-made American release was eight years earlier, in 1976, as was the case with Belmondo. Delon's last 14 features remained unreleased in the U.S. "The difficulty of arousing U.S. interest in the films of Delon and Belmondo is mirrored in the careers of many other foreign stars," wrote Cohn, adding, "In some cases, whole popular national cinemas are written off as not suited for the U.S. market, such as Japan, India and other prolific filmmaking countries." Adriano Celentano, an Italian actor and comic, had starred in many record-breaking hit movies in Italy, yet all 25 of his features since 1972 had bypassed America. Italian comic Renato Pozzetto, another big star domestically, had made 38 films since 1974, yet none were released in the States. Enrico Montesano had starred in 24 Italian movies since 1979, but only a single feature, *I Hate Blondes* (1980), played America. Alberto Sordi appeared in 16 movies shown in the U.S. during the 1960s, yet of the 19 films he had made since 1971, only *Viva Italia* was released here. Monica Vitti had a total of 13 of her pictures released in the U.S. in the 1960s. Since 1975, only two of her vehicles had been released in the U.S. while 18 other Vitti vehicles produced since that date had not been.[74]

Cries and Whispers (Sweden, 1972, Liv Ullman). Directed by Ingmar Bergman.

Reporter Richard Gold noted in 1986 that the classics units of Columbia, Fox and Universal had all disappeared, while the classics unit of MGM/United Artists lay dormant as the parent company reorganized. One reason for the demise of those units was said to be the lack of ancillary money from foreign films with no cable television interest and a U.S. market for foreign homevideo described as "very, very limited."[75]

Very near the end of 1996, the number of foreign-language films released in New York City stood at 55. About 90 percent of those features made less than $1 million at the box office nationally, a cutoff point, said reporter Linda Lee, below which few distributors made money. A serious national release then cost large distributors about $500,000 for prints and advertising. Added to that was the approximate $200,000 needed to acquire a film for American distribution; the break-even point (distributors received about 50 percent of the gross box office receipts) was a box office take of around $1.5 million. In answering her own question as to why foreign movies failed, Lee attributed it to the fact those features had next to no ancillary markets; U.S. independent production had taken over the subject

Women on the Verge of a Nervous Breakdown (Spain, 1988, Carmen Maura).

matter, style, and ultimately the audience of the foreign films. She also pointed out that the explicit sexual content once uniquely associated with foreign films was not unique any more. Since foreign titles usually had small advertising budgets they were remembered less often when customers went to the video store. Most foreign films never sold more than 10,000 to 15,000 videocassettes to the video rental stores. Judith McCourt, director of research for *Video Store Magazine*, said the average video store dedicated just 1.2 percent of its space to foreign titles. Another factor working against foreign pictures was a loss of cinematic culture among college students, said Serge Losique, director of the Montreal World Film Festival. "Now, it's action films and Clint Eastwood," he lamented. During the 1960s, students regularly went to see foreign films at the Brattle, off of Harvard Square. But then, in 1996, Alex Fitzsimmons of the Brattle said, "We don't really get students. If we show a French film, we get French people."[76]

Italian director Gianni Amelio's *The Way We Laughed* took the Golden Lion top prize at the 1998 Venice Film Festival. Despite winning that award, it did not get any U.S. distribution until November 2001, when it finally opened in New York. Journalist Stuart Klawans thought one of the reasons it took so long to arrive was that a review in *Variety*—"the publication that most strongly influences potential United States distributors"—defined it as an "art film," something he thought was close to "sure death" for a movie. Klawans concluded, "The structural problems of foreign-film distribution, which doomed *The Way We Laughed* in advance as an art film, have not improved since 1998."[77]

Exhibitors also continued to be more of a roadblock than an opportunity for foreign films. As of 1968 there were about 14,000 cinemas in the States, plus another 4,000 drive-ins. "Some 15 years ago there was still a considerable prejudice on the part of many circuit bookers to all imported product," said reporter Robert Landry. "Even British films were passed by sometimes on the grounds that British actors didn't speak American English." About 3,000 of those theaters produced 75 percent of the total box office revenue in America. A popular U.S. movie could get 10,000 play dates yet even foreign films of merit, said Landry, were hard pressed to reach as high as 900 dates. If foreign producers asked for higher advances from distributors, Landry thought it might be "on the reasoning that the advance cash was all they might ever see."[78]

Charles Teitel was a second generation Chicago foreign film exhibitor and importer who commented that "expressions of discontent toward the European and Asian film have been rampant through the years." Over the years, he said, the number of people objecting to foreign movies had been "astounding." Reminiscing in 1971, Teitel recalled that when Chicago's World Playhouse booked its first French film with subtitles in 1933, the theater was picketed by a group labeled as "Patriots of America." The cinema and its owner (Teitel's father Abe Teitel) were denounced as Bolshevik and "thoroughly damned for advocating the overthrow of American enterprise." The cause of all the furor was Rene Clair's *À Nous la Liberté*, now considered a classic. Around 1953, Sergei Eisenstein's Russian film *Ivan the Terrible* arrived in Chicago, where William Randolph Hearst's newspaper, the *Chicago American*, refused all advertising for the feature. In 1956, Teitel presented Italian filmmaker Vittorio de Sica to a Chicago audience that was attended by only one member of the press. During a question and answer session, that media representative reportedly said, "Mr. de Sica, do you mean to imply that films made in our country are inadequate? I will have you know that Hollywood produces the greatest films ever. Actually we do not need pictures from you to be brought to this country. We have enough films."[79]

During the early 1970s, the short-lived and ill-fated Jerry Lewis Cinema chain launched a nationwide survey (with questionnaires available at the Lewis venues) to determine public opinion about such things as the types of films most popular with audiences—to better program the new Lewis chain. On that survey form, patrons were asked to choose three types of movies they preferred from a pre-selected list of 13, including comedy, romance, western, horror, and so forth. Apparently the only categories missing from the list, said an account, were "foreign-language pix and pornography." Jerry Lewis Cinemas were widely publicized as centers for "family entertainment."[80]

Since the summer of 1977, all of southern New Jersey had been without a foreign film house, at least through early 1979. The last one had been the Springdale Theatre in Camden that Allen Hauss had run as an art house from April 1976 to the summer of 1977. Earlier, he had been involved with the Carlton Theatre in Moorestown, which lasted for two years as an art house. Said Hauss, "There just wasn't enough art-oriented film buffs in South Jersey to sustain a theatre." He added that the only time he sold out his 250-seat venue was when they showed "a Monty Python film that appealed to the college kids." "With other films, we did consistently bad business—eight to ten people a night," he added. The nearest option for South Jersey residents wanting to see a foreign film was one of the five art screens in Philadelphia—two of which were on college campuses. Although most of those five were heavily involved in exhibiting foreign movies, none showed them exclusively.[81]

Harlan Jacobson stated in 1980 that the number of cinemas that played first-run foreign movies on a regular basis was no more than 100, and the theaters that were the real trend setters for offshore product may not have numbered "more than 20." New York remained the key launching area for foreign features with a constant refrain heard by U.S. import distributors from exhibitors in smaller centers—"After it plays New York, we'll talk." Fassbinder's *The Marriage of Maria Braun* hit $2 million in U.S. rentals at this time, which was a lot for Fassbinder, a lot for New Yorker Films (the distributor) "and a disaster for any U.S. produced film."[82]

Everyone agreed that New York was the most important exhibitor market for a foreign film. Next most important were five key cities; Los Angeles, Boston, San Francisco, Seattle, and Washington, although there was disagreement on how those five should be ranked. After those came a third tier of centers, led by Chicago and including Philadelphia, Pennsylvania; St. Louis, Missouri; Houston, Texas; Dallas, Texas; Santa Fe, New Mexico; and Coral Gables, Florida.[83]

Walter Manley, an importer and distributor, believed the market for foreign movies in 1991 was likely only half of what it was 20 years earlier and might be no better than just one percent of the overall market. Film booker Jeffrey Jacobs estimated that, with regard to the regular venues for offshore product, there had been a shrinkage of 10–20 percent in the U.S. since the mid–1970s. In New York City, for example, eight of the 20 theaters showing foreign, independent American, and repertory films in the 1970s had closed or shifted to first-run domestic fare by 1991. Those losses were partly offset by the addition of two outlets screening foreign films.[84]

Cinema chain AMC announced in 1996 that it planned to open a 25-screen multiplex in New York City in the coming year. Supposedly the plan involved devoting six or seven auditoriums to "specialty" or foreign films. Said Earl Voelker, AMC vice president, "We are going to dedicate a portion of our facility to the launching of international film fare." However, a similar plan had been announced when AMC built its 24-screen multiplex in 1995 in Dallas. When they booked foreign or independent American fare, it was said that nobody came so, a year later, only mainstream Hollywood fare was available on those 24 screens. Reporter Ann Hornaday observed that "the all–Arnold [Schwarzenegger], all-the-time schedule of blockbusters is common in multiplexes."[85]

Foreigners had been trying for many decades to increase their presence on U.S. screens, basically without success. Still, Hollywood stood ready to offer them advice on how to increase their chances, and improve their product. At the same time, some insisted the problem was that those foreign films just weren't very good, to put it mildly. *Variety* reporter Jack Pitman lamented, in 1972, the eclipse of the U.K. movie. "A natural English reticence with the buck and promotion razzmatazz (too vulgah, dear chaps) has effectively removed them from the international film orbit," explained Pitman, concluding, "But even if they were primed to commit risk coin, they would still be looking for the style and pace of material that could cut it in today's offshore markets. As the Yank majors complain, the wide appeal stuff isn't to be had in England."[86]

Richard Gold reported that the overall poor performance of foreign movies in America in 1985 "reflected a dearth of high-caliber product, according to industry observers." Orion Classics marketing vice president Michael Barker complained that it was a really difficult year for offshore product—"the quality of European pictures has not been as good as in the past." Jeff Lipsky, theatrical sales vice president at Goldwyn pictures, said, "The U.S. audience these days has little tolerance for foreign language films because of their caliber."[87]

Journalist Peter Besas offered advice from a few quarters but spent more time in pointing out how difficult it was for a foreign film to succeed in America. In fact, he said, "The chances for a big breakthrough in the U.S. market are a million to one for a simple reason—the Yank market is the toughest in the world to crack." Those foreign producers who dreamed

Farewell, My Concubine (China, 1993, director Chen Kaige).

of hitting it big in the States, he thought, were largely unaware of "how limited" the market for foreign product was in the U.S. and how high the costs and risks involved in releasing foreign films, even just in New York. "To paint a foreigner's chance as anything but slight would be foolishly sanguine," he remarked. Besas also observed the foreign producers sometimes asked "unrealistic prices" for the U.S. distribution rights for their movies, especially for those that were hits at home. "Sometimes they try to play off distributors and agents against each other and shop around for the highest prices," explained Besas, "the result often being disastrous from their own standpoint, with an ultimate 'no-sale' rung up." Robert Shayne, of distributor New Line Cinema, remarked, "The majority of foreign films have a very limited audience. Even dubbing a film doesn't enable it to reach wide audiences. The problem is that films not made in English, when dubbed or subtitled, are simply not of interest to many filmgoers.... Also, most films don't deal with universal themes of interest to Americans." Shaye thought one solution would be for the foreigner to co-produce with U.S. independent firms such as his own. His firm would go as high as to pay up to $250,000 as a minimum distribution advance and start a release with 25 prints and an exclusive run in New York. If that was successful—meaning the film got good reviews and did well at the New York box office—then New Line would dub the movie for release to other U.S. venues.[88]

Another distributor, Herbert Steinmann, told Besas that a major obstacle to the distribution of foreign movies was the high cost of release, at least $100,000 to market an item in the U.S., with New York alone costing about $75,000 for prints, advertising, and other expenses. "Due to high release costs," he said, "most distributors wouldn't take on a foreign film even if it were given to them free." Steinmann agreed with the idea that films often had to be tinkered with after their arrival in America. The Italian film *Love and Anarchy* had a prolog added to it by Steinmann for its U.S. release because he felt the U.S. audience had to be told who Benito Mussolini was. Ben Barenholtz, of the distributor Libra Films, said the average price paid by his firm for an offshore item was $25,000 to $50,000, "since the foreign pic potential is really very small." A usual procedure for his company was to start with just two prints and if that indicated a potential then 25 to 30 prints were put into release. He agreed that the New York reception was critical for a foreign film and if it did not do reasonably well both in terms of the box office receipts and critical reviews, then it became virtually impossible to get the movie released in other parts of America. Barenholtz advised foreign producers not to go to a major to distribute their films but to use an independent firm because the latter did not have the high overhead costs of a major and could thus turn a profit on a smaller box office gross.[89]

Around that same time another foreign distributor commented that the U.S. was a difficult market for offshore product, "limited in playoff opportunities (to perhaps a dozen major cities) and with little or nothing of promise in the way of television or cable exhibition." That caused reporter Frank Segers to advise foreign producers, somewhat facetiously, that the best thing they could do was "to make a comedy with luscious location backgrounds with perhaps a name or two thrown in for marquee value." He added, "Then shop around for as much upfront money in a distribution deal as possible."[90]

A more formal "help" system was set up for foreign producers by a New York company in 1986, International Film Exchange (IFEX), which developed an "international film survey" market research procedure. Based on some 10,000 responses, the preliminary survey revealed New York audiences preferred films from France, Italy, Germany, and Spain, in that order. With its mailing list of 10,000 foreign movie buffs, whom it claimed it could invite to theatrical test screenings of new foreign films, IFEX offered to do so for a fee of $3,000. That fee covered the cinema rental and staff salaries. IFEX promised it would promote and conduct two theatrical test showings of a feature before a full audience of interested filmgoers.[91]

At a world sales and distribution conference organized by the Munich Film Festival, in that German city in 1989, Los Angeles marketing consultant Andrew Fogelson stated, "There is no grand plan to keep European pictures out of the U.S." New York sales agent Walter Manley told the conference: "We're not as xenophobic as you think we are. The quality of the picture is what really matters. Quality will somehow make its way." Brad Krevoy, an executive with the independent Concorde Pictures who was looking for foreign films to handle, "urged foreign producers to shoot in

English, select scripts that had potential in the U.S., and engage the help of American casting directors and talent agencies." Peter Rawley, executive vice president of the International Creative Management agency, advised European producers to avoid historical subjects because Americans were not very knowledgeable about the past and to avoid stories that were "culturally demanding because (U.S.) audiences are not culturally educated."[92]

Many articles in this period, especially in the 1990s, dealt with the declining audience for foreign films and the reasons for that decrease. A certain amount of revisionist history was first necessary, though. In order to discuss a decline it first had to be postulated that the audience for foreign films was greater in the past than it really was. One of the first such articles appeared in 1973, when reporter Paul Gardner wrote about the decline of the foreign film, compared to the 1960s. He thought a major reason for that decline was a change in Hollywood features as many of them became more explicit and darker (*Midnight Cowboy* and *Carnal Knowledge*, for example), thus usurping the offshore features, as well as a disappearance of art houses. European producers were still making pictures with established star players such as Catherine Deneuve, Jean-Paul Belmondo, Alain Delon, and Romy Schneider, but many of their films were increasingly no longer screened at all in the States—limited to festival showings only. Cinemas once committed to foreign movies booked more and more "arty" U.S. films. Emanuel Wolf, president of Allied Artists, declared, "The public's fascination with just anything foreign is over." Wolf added, "American movies, dealing with serious themes related to us, are more meaningful for audiences here." Once Hollywood got more sophisticated, studio executives agreed, the foreign-language market was in trouble. Leading that upsurge in interest in the 1960s, thought Gardner, were *And God Created Woman* (Brigitte Bardot), *Les Liaisons Dangereuses* (Gerard Philipe and Jeanne Moreau), *La Dolce Vita* (Anita Ekberg), and *The Lovers* (Jeanne Moreau). Films such as those arrived in America and contrasted sharply, thought Gardner, with a Hollywood output epitomized by Rock Hudson chasing the ever virginal Doris Day, hoping for a kiss after the tenth date. One year earlier, Ingmar Bergman's *Cries and Whispers* was passed on by the majors and finally picked up for distribution by Roger Corman's New World Pictures (then mainly known for dealing in cheap horror and drive-in schlock) for "under $150,000."[93]

Just a few months later, respected film writer Vincent Canby remarked that the market for foreign-language movies that seemed so vibrant and financially rewarding in the late 1950s and 1960s had "more or less collapsed." A film like Yasujiro Ozu's *Tokyo Story* (Japan) played New York, then a dozen other cities (but not doing very well in most), then played about 200 16mm engagements in college houses and film societies, with distributor Dan Talbot thinking the feature might earn $50,000 in two or three years. While that was said to be "fairly typical" for a foreign movie, it was less than a major spent just to advertise the New York opening of an average Hollywood movie. In explaining why audiences were less interested in foreign movies, Canby cited the usual reasons of more sophisticated American films and a decline in the number of art houses. Eric Rohmer's *Claire's Knee* considered a hit in the U.S., earned $410,000 while Francois Truffaut's *Bed and Board* took in $372,000 from 425 houses (there were then 10,000 to 12,000 cinemas in America). By comparison, the American-made *The Poseidon Adventure* earned $40 million and *The Getaway* took in $17.5 million. Audiences were also said to strongly resist black-and-white movies. Dan Talbot added, "Young audiences today don't like subtitles. They don't want to read. And they're absolutely hooked on color."[94]

Some 15 years later, Arnie Baskin, associate professor at New York University's film school, observed, "Americans are only interested in themselves. So they're only interested in foreign films if there's an American lead in the foreground and a foreign locale in the background." Distributors said that U.S. films had a faster pace and "catchier soundtracks" than their offshore counterparts. Because of their limited appeal, they did not receive widespread advertising, which of course, limited their appeal. Subtitles were also said to be a "big deterrent for American moviegoers."[95]

A 1990 article in *Newsweek* about the decline in foreign films in America recalled the good old days of the 1960s and 1970s, when "it was often foreign movies that really seemed to matter." David Ansen thought less of them were arriving in 1990 because of the rising costs of marketing, because many of the independent distribution firms had gone, and because many of the art and revival houses had disappeared, victims of home video. Foreign films did not often go to home video, but when they did, reported Ansen, the subtitled version was preferred to the dubbed format by a ratio of five to one.[96]

Researcher Christine Ogan agreed in 1990 that a European film renaissance in the U.S. began shortly after World War II and ended in the late 1960s; of the following years, she said, "The art theater has become a rare commodity in the United States, and foreign-language films are extremely difficult to find in first-run theaters." According to Ogan, the number of art houses rose to 549 in 1966 (5.9 percent of all indoor theaters) from 25 in 1955 (1.5 percent). "In any case," she added, "the art theater is virtually unknown today." She also argued, "Quality in foreign filmmaking has been on the decline for the last twenty years." The most important determinant of the availability of foreign films to consumers in the U.S. then, she found,

Life Is Beautiful (Italy, 1997, Nicoletta Braschi).

was "the oligopolistic nature of the film industry." Those Hollywood majors controlled 84 percent of the U.S. film market and increased that dominance to 92 to 94 percent between 1975 and 1989. Just 10 exhibition companies owned about 65 percent of all cinema screens in America. "So what appears to be a climate for success, in which a shortage of domestic films might allow foreign films to enter the market, is instead a controlled environment that prevents easy entry by independent companies," she explained. A similar control was exercised in the videocassette field where, in 1989, eight firms had 66 percent of the market; all but two of them also dominated film distribution. The public could make its decisions based only on what distributors and exhibitors made available. Ogan thought globalization might lead to an increased supply of foreign films but was "more likely to lead to Americanization of the European media industries." She concluded the future of the foreign film in the U.S. was "bleak"; its only hope lay in "breaking the oligopolistic structure of the domestic film industry," allowing for increased distribution of offshore product. However, she felt there was next to no chance such a break-up would occur as American policy favored protecting industries with a trade surplus.[97]

Reporter Patricia Thomson thought, in 1991, that the shrinking number of viewers for foreign fare was a reflection of the aging of the baby-boom generation and that the 1980s generation of college students had shown little interest in alternative film fare. Mark Lipsky, executive vice president of distributor Miramax's Prestige division, said, "I blame Ronald Reagan for a lot of my problems. His decade created a tremendous lack of interest in the arts generally and in anything that wasn't cash-producing." Lipsky added, "We're at a low in the acceptance of alternative media.... It's a constant tug-of-war, getting the press to pay attention to what we're doing. That wasn't the case 15 years ago, and it may be the lack of notable names in foreign film—the Truffauts, and so on." Importer Walter Manley remarked, "There's not the same intellectual following today."[98]

A flurry of articles about the decline of the foreign film appeared in the late 1990s. Richard Corliss, in *Time* magazine, said foreign-language film earnings in 1996 amounted to less than one percent of the total U.S. box office take, down from four to five percent in the 1960s. "Few foreign-language films are released in the U.S. these days, and those that are attract few customers," commented Corliss. Bingham Ray of the distributor company October Films agreed it was the lowest point for such fare: "The sad fact is that foreign-language films no longer matter." Declared Corliss, "Americans, absorbed in their junk culture, are shuttering a window to the rest of the movie world." Miramax Films cochairman Harvey Weinstein said, of current foreign directors, "The auteurs are there, the American marketplace is just not accepting them." Political films were no longer wanted. Weinstein added, "The real problem is our boredom with anything outside ourselves." Said Tom Brueggeman, a booker for Loews Theatres, "Americans are obsessively and exclusively interested in American culture. Even college students now tend to like the same films everyone else likes."[99]

Even the U.K. business magazine *The Economist* commented on the decline; it said that back in the 1960s foreign-language films took "up to a tenth" of the North American market. As recently as 1986, it went on to state, the figure was seven percent, but only 0.75 percent in 1997 (the first two figures were highly exaggerated). Only 250 cinema screens, it was reported, out of a total of 30,000 in the States and Canada, regularly played foreign-language films in 1997. The article guessed at one reason for the decline, saying, "That there has been a general downgrading of the cinema, compared with the theatre and the other arts, in American minds."[100]

Critic Andrew Sarris also wrote about the decline, after discussing the glory years and directors of the late 1940s through the early 1960s. Wondering what had happened, he guessed "[No one] wants to admit it today, but the fashion for foreign films depended a great deal on their frankness about sex." But then Hollywood got more sophisticated and young Amer-

Emmannuelle (France, 1974, Sylvia Kristel and Umberto Orsini discover Frederic Lagache taking a bath).

ican audiences increasingly embraced independent domestic movies as that fare came to take over the niche formerly held by imported features. Sarris felt great foreign films were still being made; they just weren't being well-promoted or well-attended.[101]

In a 2000 piece, reporter Phillip Lopate mentioned a Film Forum series of foreign classics screened in New York, made in the years 1945 to 1965, which Film Forum called the Golden Age of Foreign Films. Lopate agreed with the name because of the high quality of the movies and because of the "receptivity" of U.S. audiences. Explaining the decline, he, too, mentioned the increased sexual sophistication of American films. He added, "Hollywood has done a good job of capturing an increasing market share worldwide, stifling the local product and discouraging the distribution of foreign films stateside." However, he was forced to admit, "European cinema has sharply declined since its postwar heyday."[102]

Patricia Thomson argued, in 2001, that the decline was due to the disappearance of the baby boomers from the cinemas and the lack of ancillary markets for foreign features—which made it more difficult for distributors to handle them with any chance of a profit. Videocassettes had caused the death of many art and repertory houses without giving them the sort of exposure in video stores that they had received in the disappeared theaters. Thomson noted, "Foreign films have smaller ancillary markets than their English-language counterparts." Wendy Lidell, who had distributed foreign movies for 15 years, said, "There are so few subtitled films shown on television, there's basically no television licensing." Normally on a U.S. feature, television licensing could amount to 15 percent of revenues. Without that money, said Lidell, "you've eliminated an essential revenue stream. So immediately the theatrical distributor doesn't have that money to spend on marketing." Foreign films faced a similar disadvantage when it came to home video and cable television markets. "The small screen was less hospitable than the big screen to subtitled films," Lidell declared. Subtitling then cost $3,000 to $3,500 for the first print, and up to $4,000 or $5,000 for an especially talkative film. That price dropped 50 percent for additional prints but still totaled up to $9,000 for a modest run of five prints or $31,500 for 20 prints, at the low end.[103]

Any discussion of foreign film earnings in America should be put in context of the U.S. gross box office receipts, which were as follows: 1963, $904 million; 1964, $913 million; 1965, $927 million; 1966, $964 million; 1967, $989 million; 1968, $1.045 billion; 1969, $1.097 billion; and 1970, $1.175 billion.[104]

In 1970, 87 films grossed more than $1 million each; 330 took in $100,000 or more each, and the top 25 earning movies (two percent of the number released) took 41 percent of the total receipts. That left 98 percent of the films released that year to compete for the remaining 59 percent of the market.[105]

During 1971, only 12 subtitled features placed in the top 350 films that played domestically, and half of those finished below the top 200. Total gross for all 12 was $4,970,314. Topping the group were *Bed and Board* (distributed by Columbia, #108 on the list, $759,055 gross) and *The Conformist* (Paramount, #109, $752,004).[106]

Worldwide theatrical billings for the U.S. majors hit a new peak in 1974 of $1,047,418,375, up from $819,376,624 in 1973. Of the receipts in 1974, domestic earnings (roughly 50 percent of gross box office receipts) were $545,867,286, while the foreign take was $501,551,089.[107]

In 1987, according to reporter Rob Medich, foreign-language films accounted for less than half of one percent of the $4 billion spent that year for movie admissions.[108]

A comparison of the number of films imported to the U.S. for 1968 and 1988 indicated a significantly smaller number entered the U.S. in the later year, for most of the major film-exporting nations. From the U.K., 91 films were imported in 1968 (62 in 1988); from France 48 (24); Canada 4 (17); West Germany 20 (14); Spain 15 (13); Italy 62 (12); Japan 24 (8); and Australia 0 (13).[109]

For each of the years 1991 to 1993, foreign movies took less than two percent of the U.S. box office gross. Total domestic box office receipts in 1992 were $4.9 billion, with foreign-language films grossing just $22 million of that. English-language foreign imports grossed another $44 million that year (excluding such releases as *Lawnmower Man*, nominally a U.K. product but filmed in the U.S. with American financial involvement). Thus, the true import box office gross was $66 million of the $4.9 billion domestic gross, just 1.3 percent, which, said *Variety*, was "a typical result over the past decade."[110]

Journalist Leonard Klady reported in 1995 that between two-thirds and three-quarters of the entire foreign film box office was derived from just four metro areas—New York City, Los Angeles, Montreal, and Toronto (historically and traditionally Canada has always been statistically counted as part of the U.S. domestic film market). And, he said, when Boston, Chicago, San Francisco, Seattle and Minneapolis were added, "the picture was virtually complete." Foreign-language films remained almost entirely a theatrical phenomenon. Revenues from cassette and cable sales generally lagged 75 percent to 80 percent behind comparably grossing English-language pictures. For example, *Il Postino* (an Italian hit that took in $19 million at the box office) was thought unlikely, by Klady, to sell as many cassette units as *Priest*—an English-language feature that had a domestic box office of $4 million. Later, Klady reported that for 1999, foreign films generated some $100 million at the box office, two percent of the domestic gross. Klady did not make clear if this report included films partially connected to Hollywood.[111]

Reporter Roger Smith stated that in 2000 foreign movies accounted for 3.9 percent of the U.S. box office, but that included Hollywood-connected U.K. movies such as *Chicken Run* and *Billy Elliott*. "Take those two out, and the number is closer to 2 percent," said Smith.[112]

Hollywood's contempt for the foreign film could be clearly seen in the treatment of offshore product in the Oscar ceremonies. The first Oscar for best foreign film went to Italy's *Shoe Shine* in 1947. Nations then sent in their own list of nomination with the Academy of Motion Picture Arts and Sciences (responsible for the Oscars) voting for the final short list of five—with a one-film-per-country maximum restriction. For example, the list of five could not contain three French and two Italian items. It was still done that way in 1982 when French director Bertrand Tavernier blamed

High Heels (Spain, 1991, director Pedro Almodovar).

the rules on the "protectionism and provincialism" of Hollywood. "It's as if the Americans are saying to the rest of us, 'You are entitled to produce one good film a year,'" complained Tavernier.[113]

Just after World War II, while he was manager of the 50-person International Department of MGM, Robert Vogel was called in by the Academy of Motion Picture Arts and Sciences (AMPAS) Board of Governors. "There were some great pictures out there," recalled Vogel, "but it didn't mean anything to Hollywood. Particularly great stuff from France, Italy, Japan. We'd be accused of provincialism if we ignored them." He was told by AMPAS to keep his eyes open and look for something outstanding. Believing it would be presumptuous to do that on his own, Vogel contacted his opposite numbers at two other studios. The three of them made recommendations for an Honorary Award. The first went to Vittorio de Sica of Italy. By 1956, Vogel said, to avoid the arrogance of America telling the world what its best films were, the committee decided to have the foreign films nominated by the foreign countries themselves. Then AMPAS executive director Margaret Herrick made two trips to Europe to "find or create selecting bodies." The system remained the same at the end of the 1980s. Most of those foreign organizations existed for the sole purpose of selecting Oscar contenders. Some 33 movies were entered for the best foreign-language Oscar in 1989. In 1956, the award moved up from the honorary category to become a part of the regular Oscars. Originally, in order to vote, Academy members had to sit through 80 percent of the foreign films screened. Because so few were willing to commit themselves to some 12 or 13 double-bills, the committee embarked on an experiment, splitting the voters into "red" and "blue" teams. "We felt that more people would commit to seeing 80 percent of 15 films than 80 percent of 30," said Academy executive administrator Bruce Davis. After a member had seen his quota of roughly 12 films, he could vote for any films he had seen, red or blue. AMPAS rules stipulated that the foreign films screened had to be identical to the version released in the country of origin, except with the addition of English subtitles. The five movies with the highest vote totals were certified as the nominees, screened twice more and presented to the entire Academy.[114]

When the 1999 Oscar ceremonies produced three Oscars for the Italian film *Life Is Beautiful* (actor, dramatic score, and foreign-language film), reporters Benedict Carver and Dan Cox heralded it as an "endorsement of Europe's film industries" and as marking a "new acceptance" of foreign-language films. It also caused them to reflect that for many in the international community the Academy seemed to "harbor a curious, anti-foreign sentiment." Those feelings reportedly went back as far as 1948, when Academy president Jean Hersholt "exposed an attempt by the biggest studios to pull funding for the Academy when Laurence Olivier's *Hamlet* became the first non–U.S. favorite for best picture." *Hamlet* went on to win that year.[115]

A list published in *Variety* in 1992 listed the top grossing foreign films of all time in the U.S. (apparently only those with no Hollywood connections). That list (see Appendix A) had 26 films with a total gross of $249.2 million. A similar list published in 2000 listed 54 films with a total gross of $513.9 million (all films that had grossed $4 million or more in their lifetimes). By comparison, the yearly domestic box office take in that time period was around $5 billion annually. Thus, all of the top grossing foreign films, over their lifetimes (some were decades old), could manage no more than 10 percent of the receipts of any average single year in America. In contrast, *Spider-Man* opened in the U.S. in May 2002, on 7,500 screens, grossing $115 million in ticket sales in its opening weekend. Six months earlier, *Harry Potter and the Sorcerer's Stone* had opened on 8,200 screens in its first weekend, grossing $90 million, $317 million after six months in release.[116]

United Kingdom director Mike Leigh complained in 2002 that the British film industry was being badly damaged by Hollywood; he explained, "Sadly, folks in the U.K. tend to think of a movie as a Hollywood movie." He thought Britain would be better off it if made more serious and indigenous films "and did not try to ape what it perceives to be commercial." "There is pressure, particularly on young filmmakers, to deliver products of a formulaic kind," Leigh added. Timothy Spall, who had acted in half a dozen of Leigh's films, agreed that U.K. filmmakers were too concerned about trying to please audiences on both sides of the Atlantic; he remarked, "That can dilute the truth of what they're trying to say."[117]

8

Conclusion

The prevalence of foreign films on the cinema screens of the United States, whether in terms of percentage of screen time or percentage of box office receipts received, is currently in the range of one to two percent and has been in that area for something like 90 years. These numbers refer to foreign films that are truly at arm's length from the Hollywood cartel. Their zenith was in the late 1950s and through much of the 1960s, when the share for foreign films may have risen to five percent, if even that high. One had to go back in time a full century to find a period when foreign movies enjoyed a substantial presence on American cinema screens. In fact, they even dominated those screens for a brief spell.

Foreign producers, especially the French, were able to hold a dominant position in pre–World War I America for a variety of reasons. They were technically advanced, structurally well-organized, and usually received good reviews from the media and the general public for their movies. In short, they won the competition battle in the United States motion picture market at a time when that market was truly open, a condition quickly foreclosed by the Americans. Prior to World War I, the U.S. film industry was very chaotic, anarchic, and competitive. Domestic cartels came and went; producer sued producer over alleged patent violations; producer stole from producer and sold pirated movies. In such an atmosphere, domestic film producers spent more time battling each other than dealing with the penetration of foreign filmmakers. By 1910, one of the cartels—the Motion Picture Patents Company—while it did not last for very long, did manage to bring a certain amount of order to the domestic industry. One of the reasons for establishing that cartel was to limit the presence of foreign films

208

in theaters and to increase the U.S. presence. Various tactics used by the cartel, such as block booking of films into cinemas and the vertical integration of the industry whereby producers made movies, distributed them, and owned the theaters in which they were screened, allowed the cartel to drastically lower the foreign presence in the period immediately before World War I. Working in conjunction with those efforts were reviews of foreign movies in the trade press that suddenly went from good to bad. Additionally, all of the foreign nations that had a film presence in America at that time were combatants in World War I and had their economies devastated. It meant there would be no quick recovery for their film industries, giving Hollywood a huge advantage domestically and internationally.

Throughout the remainder of the silent film era, Hollywood moved swiftly to dominate the film screens of the world and to consolidate their hold on the domestic screens. Cartel members owned all of the important screens in America and continued to block book their product, both at home and abroad. Hollywood also poached talent wherever it found it. These tactics increased their wealth and allowed them to buy more theaters, spend more on making movies, poach more talent, and advertise more, which gave their product more widespread appeal. That made them wealthier still and led to a repeat of the cycle. When talent was poached from, say, a European film industry struggling to re-establish itself after World War I, it had a devastating impact on that industry. No sooner had an actor or director established himself, perhaps having built a small following at home, than he was lured to Hollywood by more money.

Just how much foreign film had disappeared from U.S. screens in 10 years could be seen from a minor national furor that arose in America in the early 1920s, when a few German films attracted attention. There were almost no foreign movies playing the U.S. then, but when a few German movies played in a small number of U.S. cities it caused a national worry over an "invasion" and the German "menace." Over and over again the question was raised as to why foreign films had no presence in the States. Over and over again, Hollywood's cartel members and the U.S. media, and even independent U.S. importers of foreign films, explained that it was so because virtually all foreign films were of a terrible quality. Europeans who raised those questions, though, did not usually accept such arguments. They understood that the situation was due to the nature and structure of the Hollywood industry—it was a cartel designed to limit foreign presence to as low a degree as possible. Along with that went the argument that European filmmakers did not produce product suitable to the tastes of the "unique" American audience. Left unsaid by that argument was why

Hollywood, which successfully produced movies for that unique crowd could export them all, successfully, to most other countries.

When sound films arrived at the end of the 1920s, foreign films were almost non-existent in America, a position unchanged when World War II arrived. In the 1930s, a new quandary arrived for foreign filmmakers—whether to dub their movies or subtitle them for the U.S. audience. It was an issue that remained unresolved through to the present. Throughout the world, U.S. movies were usually dubbed, and reportedly were always accepted by audiences in all those nations. Yet Americans were different: they did not like subtitles since they did not go to a movie to read, but they did not like dubbed movies either. For the first time, in the 1930s, foreign filmmakers started to make efforts to distribute their films in the States themselves, instead of contracting with a U.S. firm, and to control cinemas either through ownership or a lease. However, many of those efforts were little more than token affairs and none succeeded. An art house circuit became a reality in the 1930s. On the one hand, it provided a specific market for foreign films, although such venues were few and far between. On the other hand, it tended to put severe limits on offshore product since only rarely did they get bookings in other than art houses. More and more foreign producers fell into the trap of trying to "Americanize" their movies in one way or another, while never really knowing what that term signified. It was all in a vain hope of cracking the lucrative U.S. market. World War II had the same effect on foreign film industries as had World War I. Film industries again had to struggle to recover from again devastated economies.

During the postwar 1940s, the best-organized and best-financed attempt to break into the U.S. film market was launched by the British producer J. Arthur Rank. Other U.K. producers such as Alexander Korda were also involved. Yet little success was achieved and that expensive campaign was one of the reasons the Rank organization ran into financial difficulties at the end of the 1940s. Rank, and other U.K. film people, had to suffer the humiliation of having Hollywood tell them that one reason their films had little success in America—besides the usual one that they were of low quality—was because of their funny accents.

Recovering more rapidly than expected, the European film industry entered what came to be known as its "Golden Age" in the late 1940s (and lasting until around 1965), during which time it gained greater and greater critical acclaim, even from a few literate American sources. Producers in countries such as France, Italy, Germany and the U.K. all launched major efforts to increase their screen presence in America. None succeeded in more than a marginal way. There was still a trend to "Americanize" offshore output and more efforts to self-distribute. Hollywood's censorship regime also caused great difficulties for foreign product. Offshore product had to run a gauntlet of censors that included the U.S. Customs department, state censors, local censors, the Roman Catholic Legion of Decency and the cartel's own Production Code Administration. Foreign movies were usually treated more harshly than were domestic ones. More and more it became apparent that Hollywood's distribution control was the key element in keeping foreign product out. If a film did not get a pass from the Legion of Decency and the Production Code—and foreign movies usually did not—then it had no chance for regular cinema bookings. Hollywood was able to claim that was the reason, and not its oligopolistic control. If that wasn't enough, it became obvious that exhibitors on their own did not like and would not book foreign—it was Hollywood output good or bad.

As television reduced film audiences and cartel income, less films were produced and a potential product shortage loomed. Some independent distributors hoped that would open the door to their foreign items, as the second half of the double-bill. While Hollywood did drastically reduce its output, it dealt with the gap in a different manner—the double-bill was eliminated.

As a result of the Golden Age, foreign films got a bit more attention at the end of the 1950s. However, much of it fell on the more superficial aspects of European cinema, such as the sexuality of actors such as Gina Lollobrigida and especially Brigitte Bardot. That caused all foreign product to be branded as sexual and led to it becoming a favorite whipping boy in the early 1960s; during this period, censorship was becoming a larger issue in the film business (just before it faded into the background as a result of adverse court decisions) as charges of "immorality" were leveled at Hollywood. It was glad to offload the blame on to foreign product, despite its continuing negligible presence.

In more recent times, some in the industry have explained that foreign films do not do well in America because they produced no ancillary money, such as sales to television and cassette sales. While it was true that foreign films did not make ancillary money, the theory did not explain why foreign films did equally poorly in earlier times when there was no ancillary income for any films. The coming of videocassettes at the end of the 1970s caused a small flurry of hope among some foreign film importers that offshore product might do better on tape. However, it turned out that foreign films' share of videocassette income fell in the same one to two percent range as it did for cinema receipts. One constant is that up to the current time Hollywood has continued to argue that one of the reasons for the poor showing of offshore movies is their poor quality. Apparently they have been bad for close to 100 years.

Sometimes when foreigners gave into urgings to Americanize their output, in response to a complaint they did not meet American expectations, they found themselves attacked by other U.S. elements for being incapable of producing an Americanized foreign film. Those foreign producers were damned for not soliciting and taking advice from Hollywood on how to make films. When they did take that advice, there were dismissed for not getting it right. Hollywood always seemed to have an answer to why the foreigners did not do better in America; usually it involved attributing one or more faults to those offshore producers. When the cartel head, Jack Valenti, was able to say that Americans would not watch dubbed or subtitled movies, it was clear that foreign films were doomed.

If Hollywood always had an answer, it was also true that they never voiced the correct answer. Hollywood's cartel dominated and controlled motion pictures all over the globe and they controlled all three aspects of the industry: production, distribution, and exhibition. Hollywood was very efficient and very ruthless in limiting and destroying any potential competition. Almost every other country regarded making films to be a cultural undertaking, an art form. Among the rich nations, only the U.S.A. did not have such a thing as a culture minister. Those other countries did not want to see their own native industry follow that American model—where a film was simply an item of commerce, a widget—and that made it even more difficult for them to penetrate the States. When all of Hollywood's rationalizations were peeled away, it was apparent that the oligopolistic structure and dominance of the Hollywood film cartel was the overwhelmingly most important reason why the presence of foreign films on U.S. theater screens was negligible, and had been so for close to a century.

Appendix
All-Time Gross
Earnings Leaders

TOP FOREIGN-LANGUAGE FILMS IN THE UNITED STATES, AS OF 1992
(*Grosses in Millions of Dollars*)

Title	U.S. Release Year	Gross
I Am Curious, Yellow (Sweden)	1969	$19.0
La Dolce Vita (Italy/France)	1961	18.0
La Cage aux Folles (France/Italy)	1979	17.0
Z (Algeria/France)	1969	15.0
A Man and a Woman (France)	1966	13.0
Cinema Paradiso (Italy/France)	1990	12.0
Das Boot (West Germany)	1982	11.8
Emmanuelle (France)	1975	11.5
Story of O (France/West Germany)	1975	10.0
Eight and a Half (Italy/France)	1963	9.5
Yesterday, Today and Tomorrow (Italy/France)	1964	9.2
Marriage Italian Style (Italy/France)	1964	9.0
Elvira Madigan (Sweden)	1967	9.0
Dear John (Sweden)	1964	8.8
Cousin, Cousine (France)	1976	8.5
My Life as a Dog (Sweden)	1987	8.4

Title	U.S. Release Year	Gross
Women on the Verge of a Nervous Breakdown (Spain)	1988	7.5
Diva (France)	1982	7.4
Ran (Japan/France)	1985	7.1
Two Women (Italy/France)	1961	7.0
Fanny and Alexander (Sweden/France/Germany)	1983	6.6
Without a Stitch (Denmark)	1970	6.5
La Cage aux Folles II (France/Italy)	1981	6.3
Cyrano de Bergerac (France)	1990	6.1
Napolean (France/Italy/Germany/Spain/ Sweden/Czechoslovakia)	1928/1981	6.0
Swept Away (Italy)	1975	6.0

These 26 films grossed a total of $249.2 million.
Source: *Variety*, August 31, 1992, p. 54.

TOP FOREIGN-LANGUAGE FILMS IN THE UNITED STATES, AS OF 2000 (*Grosses in Millions of Dollars*)

Title	U.S. Release Year	Gross
Life Is Beautiful (Italy)	1998	$57.6
Il Postino (France/Italy/Belgium)	1995	21.8
Like Water for Chocolate (Mexico)	1992	21.7
I Am Curious, Yellow (Sweden)	1969	20.2
La Dolce Vita (Italy/France)	1961	19.5
La Cage aux Folles (France/Italy)	1979	17.7
Z (Algeria/France)	1969	15.8
A Man and a Woman (France)	1966	14.3
Cinema Paradiso (Italy/France)	1990	12.0
Das Boot (West Germany)	1982	11.6
Emmanuelle (France)	1975	11.5
8½ (Italy/France)	1963	10.4
My Life as a Dog (Sweden)	1987	10.1
Elvira Madigan (Sweden)	1967	10.1
Story of O (France/West Germany)	1975	10.0
Red Violin (Canada/Italy/U.K.)	1997	10.0
Shall We Dance (Japan)	1997	9.7
Yesterday, Today and Tomorrow (Italy/France)	1964	9.3
Marriage Italian Style (Italy/France)	1964	9.1

Title	U.S. Release Year	Gross
Dear John (Sweden)	1964	8.8
Cousin, Cousine (France)	1976	8.6
Cyrano de Bergerac (France)	1990	8.0
Belle de Jour (France/Italy)	1967	8.0
Women on the Verge of a Nervous Breakdown (Spain)	1988	7.5
Fanny and Alexander (Sweden/France/ Germany)	1983	7.4
Ran (Japan/France)	1985	7.3
Eat Drink Man Woman (Taiwan)	1994	7.3
Run Lola Run (Germany)	1999	7.2
Two Women (Italy/France)	1961	7.2
The Wedding Banquet (Taiwan)	1993	6.9
Diva (France)	1982	6.5
Swept Away (Italy)	1975	6.0
Garden of the Finzi-Continis (Italy/West Germany)	1971	6.0
Belle Epoque (Spain/Portugal/France)	1992	6.0
Mediterraneo (Italy)	1991	5.8
La Cage aux Folles II (France/Italy)	1981	5.8
Kolya (Czech Republic)	1996	5.8
King of Hearts (France/Italy)	1996	5.7
Indochine (France)	1992	5.7
Central Station (Brazil/France)	1998	5.6
Europa Europa (Germany/France/Poland)	1991	5.6
Jean de Florette (France/Switzerland/Italy)	1986	5.5
Au Revoir les Enfants (France/West Germany)	1987	5.3
Farewell My Concubine (China/Hong Kong)	1993	5.2
Madame Rosa (France)	1978	5.2
Babette's Feast (Denmark)	1988	5.2
La Femme Nikita (France/Italy)	1991	5.0
Wings of Desire (West Germany/France)	1988	4.9
Les Boys (Canada)	1997	4.8
Decline of the American Empire (Canada)	1986	4.7
Manon of the Spring (France/Italy/Switzerland)	1987	4.7
Antonia's Line (Netherlands/Belgium/U.K.)	1996	4.2
Tie Me Up! Tie Me Down! (Spain)	1990	4.1
The Dinner Game (France)	1998	4.0

These 54 films grossed a total of $513.9 million.
Source: *Variety*, February 21, 2000, p. 16.

Notes

CHAPTER 1

1. Charles Musser. *The Emergence of Cinema: The American Screen to 1907 (History of the American Cinema, 1).* New York: Scribner's Sons, 1990, pp. 135–145.
2. *Ibid.*, p. 177.
3. *Ibid.*, p. 364.
4. *Ibid.*, pp. 365, 412–413.
5. *Ibid.*, pp. 450, 488.
6. *Ibid.*, pp. 488–489.
7. Richard Abel. *The Red Rooster Scare: Making Cinema American, 1900-1910.* Berkeley: University of California Press, 1999, pp. xi–xiii, 23, 48, 52–53.
8. *Ibid.*, p. 57.
9. *Ibid.*, pp. 64–65, 87.
10. *Ibid.*, p. 88.
11. *Ibid.*, pp. 88–90.
12. Eileen Bowser. *The Transformation of Cinema, 1907-1915 (History of the American Cinema, 2).* New York: Scribner's Sons, 1990, pp. 22–23.
13. Advertisement. *Variety*, January 12, 1907, p. 24.
14. "Film renters meet in convention." *Variety*, February 15, 1908, p. 10; Advertisement. *Variety*, February 22, 1908, p. 36; "Biograph Co. licenses three manufacturers." *Variety*, February 22, 1908, p. 10.
15. "Lubin has a reason." *Variety*, February 29, 1908, p. 10.
16. "Chicago expects lively times." *Variety*, February 29, 1908; "Kleine Co. answers Edison." *Variety*, February 29, 1908, p. 12.
17. Advertisement. *Variety*, March 7, 1908, p. 39; Advertisement. *Variety*, December 12, 1908, p. 123.
18. "Foreign filmmakers combine to press fight." *Variety*, March 21, 1908, p. 14.
19. "Fight moving-picture rate." *New York Times*, September 13, 1908, pt. 2, p. 6.
20. "Italian Cines out." *Variety*, August 15, 1908, p. 11; "Moving picture peace strongly rumored about." *Variety*, August 15, 1908, p. 11.
21. Ralph Cassady, Jr. "Monopoly in production and distribution: 1908–1915." *The American Movie Industry: The Business of Motion Pictures.* Ed. Gorham Kindem. Carbondale: Southern Illinois University Press, 1982, p. 30.
22. "Manufacturers assume control of all moving pictures." *Variety*, January 16, 1909, p. 13.
23. "Forty-one filmmakers to consider European merger." *Variety*, January 30, 1909, p. 12.
24. "Cut rate war may follow independents' aggressions." *Variety*, March 13, 1909, p. 13.
25. "International film co. has novel distributing scheme." *Variety*, February 20, 1909, p. 13; "Exhibit independent films." *Variety*, February 27, 1909, p. 13.
26. Advertisement. *Variety*, February 27, 1909, p. 31; "Adding American subjects." *Variety*, June 19, 1909, p. 11; "Independents still convening." *Variety*, June 25, 1910, p. 8.
27. "Méliès has Patents license." *Variety*, August 7, 1909, p. 13.
28. "Patents Co. sues independent." *Variety*, September 4, 1909, p. 12.
29. "The moving picture industry." *Variety*, December 11, 1909, p. 33.
30. Méliès suspends releases." *Variety*, December 18, 1909, p. 14.
31. "Independent cleaning house." *Variety*, February 19, 1910, p. 14.

217

32. "Gaumont printing plant goes over to independents." *Variety*, June 25, 1910, p. 8.

33. "Trust and independent line-up for season in picture division." *Variety*, September 10, 1910, p. 12.

34. "G.F. fighting Pathé." *Variety*, March 20, 1914, p. 22; "Pathé in Mutual." *Variety*, October 31, 1914, p. 25.

35. "Picture service prices on the downward slide." *Variety*, February 20, 1915, p. 22; "Pathé to quit?" *Variety*, February 18, 1916, p. 29.

36. "Pathé farming stars." *Variety*, April 12, 1918, p. 48.

37. "The moving picture industry." *Variety*, December 11, 1909, p. 125; "Geo. Kleine leaves G.F. Co. but holds on to his stock." *Variety*, June 26, 1914, p. 17.

38. "Picture service prices on the downward slide." *Variety*, February 20, 1915, p. 22; "Wholesale attempt to corral all exhibitors with Chaplin." *Variety*, June 11, 1915, p. 3.

39. Ralph Cassady Jr. op. cit., pp. 56, 59; Eileen Bowser. op. cit., pp. 210–211.

40. "Feature film men fearful over the road next season." *Variety*, June 12, 1914, p. 18.

41. "Picture service prices on the downward slide." *Variety*, February 20, 1915, p. 22; "Deluge of film productions compels an amalgamation." *Variety*, January 21, 1916, p. 19.

42. "Pathé in new quarters." *Variety*, February 1, 1908, p. 11.

43. "A square deal for all is Thomas Edison's promise." *Variety*, June 20, 1908, p. 12.

44. "Producers' batting averages." *Variety*, November 13, 1909, p. 13; "Producers' batting averages." *Variety*, December 4, 1909, p. 13.

45. "Paris paper warns." *Variety*, November 20, 1909, p. 12.

46. "Better films in Europe." *New York Times*, September 11, 1913, p. 4.

47. "Nothing to it, says Ince." *Variety*, August 14, 1914, p. 19.

48. "Germans are wise." *Variety*, August 14, 1914, p. 19.

49. George K. Spoor. "Judging film subjects for the American market." *Variety*, December 12, 1908, p. 29.

50. Richard Abel, op. cit., pp. xiii, 95.

51. Eileen Bowser, op. cit., p. 50.

52. "Aggressive action possible by major against pictures." *Variety*, March 5, 1910, p. 12.

53. Richard Abel, op. cit., p. 101.

54. "Wm. Fox to drop all the foreign feature films." *Variety*, July 24, 1914, p. 17.

55. "London has big film supply that lacks American mart." *Variety*, February 12, 1915, p. 21.

56. Kerry Segrave. *American Films Abroad: Hollywood's Domination of the World's Movie Screens*. Jefferson, N.C.: McFarland, 1997, pp. 4–5, 14.

CHAPTER 2

1. "Picture sensational draw." *Variety*, December 17, 1920, pp. 1, 45.

2. "Inside stuff—pictures." *Variety*, February 25, 1921, p. 44.

3. "Flood of German features starts action for protection." *Variety*, April 15, 1921, p. 45.

4. "Film tariff fight under way as German imports increase." *Variety*, April 22, 1921, p. 46.

5. "Zukor has bought so far 129 German features for Famous." *Variety*, April 29, 1921, p. 45.

6. "Riot over German feature picture." *Variety*, May 13, 1921, p. 47.

7. *Ibid.*

8. "All Hollywood now lining up against German made films." *Variety*, May 20, 1921, pp. 1–2.

9. "Germany's latest triumph." *New York Times*, April 19, 1921, p. 16.

10. "Film competition." *New York Times*, April 20, 1921, p. 12.

11. Alfred B. Kuttner. "A tariff for the movies?" *New York Times*, April 24, 1921, sec. 7, p. 6.

12. "Menace of German films." *Literary Digest* 69 (May 14, 1921): 28–29.

13. "Don't fear German films." *New York Times*, May 29, 1921, p. 14.

14. "German film feeling reported dying out." *Variety*, June 3, 1921, p. 47.

15. "German-made films now found to be heavy drug on market." *Variety*, June 24, 1921, pp. 1–2.

16. "*Caligari* barred by Albany crowd." *Variety*, December 2, 1921, p. 47.

17. "German director, Lubitsch, regarded unkindly, he says." *Variety*, February 3, 1922, p. 46.

18. Kerry Segrave. *American Films Abroad: Hollywood's Domination of the World's Movie Screens*. Jefferson, N.C.: McFarland, 1997, p. 36.

19. "France and pictures." *Variety*, December 27, 1918, p. 183.

20. "Foreign governments plan to break into U.S. market." *Variety*, August 29, 1919, p. 73.

21. Kerry Segrave, op. cit., pp. 37–39.

22. "Foreign filmmakers combining for break into this market." *Variety*, October 15, 1924, p. 21.

23. "Protest film invasion." *New York Times*, July 16, 1919, p. 13.

24. Kerry Segrave, op. cit., pp. 19–20; "The film situation in America." *Times* (London),

August 10, 1920, p. 8; "The film situation in America." *Times* (London), August 13, 1920, p. 8.

25. "British film men seek market here." *New York Times*, June 10, 1926, p. 28.

26. "Film reciprocity." *Times* (London), July 10, 1926, p. 15; "Calls British film unworthy product." *New York Times*, July 10, 1926, p. 5.

27. "English film opportunities." *New York Times*, July 12, 1926, p. 18.

28. "British film industry organizing for concerted drive on U.S. market." *Variety*, February 23, 1927, p. 9.

29. "Rowland and Cippico's deal with great Italian film co." *Variety*, June 13, 1919, p. 54.

30. "English producers to exploit British films in this country." *Variety*, October 3, 1919, p. 61.

31. "English producers bidding for American film stars." *Variety*, June 30, 1922, p. 38.

32. *Ibid.*

33. "English-made American films novel idea by Geo. Ridgwell." *Variety*, December 24, 1924, p. 23.

34. "English bankers surveying American industry for world-wide films." *Variety*, January 6, 1926, p. 27.

35. "British Nat'l wants stars to make pictures in England." *Variety*, June 15, 1927, p. 9.

36. "Swedish-Biograph planning appeal only to Swedes here." *Variety*, December 9, 1921, p. 37.

37. "UFA plans to open theatre on Broadway." *New York Times*, November 29, 1927, p. 31; "Europe's show window." *Variety*, March 14, 1928, pp. 5, 26.

38. John MacCormac. "London film notes." *New York Times*, December 9, 1928, sec. 10, p. 7.

39. "Poor handling hurts French films in the U.S." *Variety*, October 29, 1920, p. 47.

40. Leon Gaumont tells why Europe can't compete with U.S." *Variety*, October 27, 1926, p. 59.

41. "American and British films coming to grips." *Literary Digest* 90 (August 28, 1926): 23.

42. "Sir Oswald panning us." *Variety*, October 5, 1927, pp. 3, 10.

43. "Sir Oswald sailing: leaves wonder behind." *Variety*, October 12, 1927, p. 3.

44. Andrew Higson and Richard Maltby. *Film Europe and Film America: Cinema, Commerce and Cultural Exchange 1920-1939*. Exeter: University of Exeter Press, 1999, p. 2.

45. "American film invasion abroad starting something." *Variety*, July 4, 1919, p. 3.

46. "English to study filmmaking here." *New York Times*, July 18, 1920, p. 22.

47. "Many imports fail to score." *Variety*, May 21, 1920, p. 35.

48. "Truth about U.S. boycott of British productions." *Variety*, April 14, 1922, p. 43.

49. "In the mail bag." *New York Times*, April 23, 1922, sec. 6, p. 1.

50. "Warns that unions may reform films." *New York Times*, June 9, 1926, p. 25.

51. Frank Tilley. "*Variety* called vitriolic on British films by Beaverbrook's daily." *Variety*, September 26, 1928, p. 6.

52. Andrew Higson and Richard Maltby, op. cit., p. 19.

53. "French actor asserts French films not seen here." *Variety*, February 24, 1922, p. 37.

54. "Why American films are best." *New York Times*, May 20, 1923, sec. 7, p. 2.

55. "Hand kisses spoil films." *New York Times*, February 21, 1926, sec. 2, p. 10.

56. Advertisement. *Variety*, December 26, 1919, p. 198.

57. "Pathé alarmed." *Variety*, March 1, 1918, p. 49; "Warners enforce block booking on entire output of talk films." *Variety*, September 19, 1928, p. 24.

58. "Fight importation of foreign films." *Variety*, June 18, 1920, p. 36.

59. "Acute shortage of features hits trade." *Variety*, April 21, 1922, p. 47.

60. "With Berlin foreign center: Famous shuffling directors." *Variety*, November 25, 1921, p. 44.

61. "German director, Lubitsch, regarded unkindly, he says." *Variety*, February 3, 1922, p. 46.

62. "400 aliens in U.S. films." *Variety*, June 22, 1927, pp. 1, 10.

63. Paul Rotha. *The Film Till Now*. London: Vision, 1960, p. 78.

64. "Equity aiding fight for American films." *New York Times*, June 4, 1921, p. 14.

65. "England and the tariff." *New York Times*, August 7, 1921, sec. 6, p. 2.

66. "Retaliatory action deemed certain if tariff passes." *Variety*, August 19, 1921, p. 38.

67. "Fight foreign film tax." *New York Times*, August 26, 1921, p. 8.

68. "That import tax." *New York Times*, August 28, 1921, sec. 6, p. 3.

69. "High film duty reported out of new tariff bill." *Variety*, October 14, 1921, p. 46.

70. "Film producers ask double tariff duty." *Variety*, December 28, 1921, p. 7.

71. "Agree on film tariff." *New York Times*, April 5, 1922, p. 15.

72. "Picture-making abroad." *New York Times*, December 17, 1922, sec. 7, p. 2.

73. "No cash advances for foreign films." *Variety*, August 19, 1921, p. 38.

74. "Screen: the public be served." *New York Times*, July 30, 1922, sec. 6, p. 3.

75. "Screen: film circulation." *New York Times*, August 6, 1922, sec. 6, p. 3.

76. "Screen: the public rejects." *New York Times*, August 27, 1922, sec. 6, p. 3.

77. "No foreign pictures, new Famous Players sales slogan." *Variety*, December 8, 1922, p. 38.

78. Andrew Higson and Richard Maltby, op. cit., p. 19.

79. "Germany looks this way." *New York Times*, July 17, 1927, sec. 7, p. 5.

80. "Movie house with a past." *New York Times Magazine*, March 28, 1954, p. 39.

81. "Imports and exports." *New York Times*, January 15, 1922, sec. 6, p. 3.

82. "Canada largest importer for American films in 1923." *Variety*, February 14, 1924, p. 19; "Foreign film imports show slight increase." *Variety*, August 12, 1925, p. 22.

83. "Estimate 850 film features scheduled for '25–'26 season." *Variety*, September 2, 1925, p. 25.

84. "$71,000,000 from foreign sales." *Variety*, August 17, 1927, p. 8; "Imports $1,000,000; exports $300,000,000." *Variety*, April 28, 1926, p. 2.

85. "From 400 to 500 foreign pictures made abroad in '28–'29 cutting down U.S. gross." *Variety*, May 23, 1928, p. 10; "555 first-line features with 219 indie full lengths." *Variety*, May 30, 1928, p. 4.

86. Kerry Segrave, op. cit., p. 67.

87. "Europe needs advice." *Variety*, March 7, 1928, p. 3.

88. Paul Rotha, op. cit., pp. 76–77.

CHAPTER 3

1. "French producers over here promoting sale of French-made films." *Variety*, January 23, 1929, p. 6.

2. "Sapene, French quota author, coming to U.S. with ultimatum 'buy film or take exclusion.'" *Variety*, January 30, 1929, p. 6.

3. "Sapene utters downright boycott threat against American trade unless French films are shown." *Variety*, March 27, 1929, pp. 2, 60.

4. "Secret move for French subsidy to push Gallic films in America." *Variety*, Jun 12, 1934, p. 20.

5. "Bernard Natan here viewing U.S. film methods intensively." *Variety*, July 19, 1934, p. 29.

6. "Natan tells what's wrong with U.S." *Variety*, August 14, 1934, pp. 2, 47.

7. "French demands." *Variety*, March 8, 1939, p. 23.

8. Tino Balio. *Grand Design: Hollywood as a Modern Business Enterprise, 1930–1939 (History of the American Cinema, 5)*. New York: Scribner's Sons, 1993, p. 34.

9. "German regulations for issuing of 50 picture export premium permits." *Variety*, March 27, 1929, pp. 2, 60.

10. "Of all foreign-mades over here only German talkers standing up on showings in New York City." *Variety*, April 29, 1931, p. 7.

11. Alexander Bakshy. "The German invasion." *The Nation* 132 (May 13, 1931): 538.

12. "German chains smothering foreign film operation in U.S." *Variety*, June 2, 1931, p. 7.

13. "Berlin hears UFA is sending high official to liquidate U.S. ends." *Variety*, February 2, 1932, p. 11.

14. "Foreigners losing pull for U.S. screen." *Variety*, September 13, 1932, pp. 14, 74.

15. Tino Balio, op. cit., p. 34.

16. "German films get a setback in city." *New York Times*, May 9, 1933, p. 20.

17. "100 German cinemas in U.S. drop to 6." *Variety*, May 23, 1933, p. 13.

18. "Hitler thing deadly." *Variety*, July 18, 1933, p. 31.

19. Tino Balio, op. cit., p. 34.

20. "Camouflaging German pix for U.S." *Variety*, May 1, 1934, p. 1.

21. "Tobis making another attempt to crack Anglo-American markets." *Variety*, April 29, 1936, p. 4.

22. "B.I.'s eye for eye here." *Variety*, October 1, 1930, pp. 7, 64.

23. "English maker's lesson on B'way enough—foreigners no go at Cohan." *Variety*, December 10, 1930, p. 5.

24. "2nd British film invasion." *Variety*, May 1, 1935, p. 5.

25. Ruth Biery and Eleanor Packer. "England challenges Hollywood." *Saturday Evening Post* 206 (July 19, 1933): 12–12+.

26. *Ibid.*

27. "British film group to fight Hollywood." *New York Times*, July 28, 1934, p. 16.

28. "Entertainment." *News-week* 4 (August 18, 1934): 23.

29. Frank S. Nugent. "How fared the English visitors last year?" *New York Times*, March 3, 1935, sec. 8, p. 3.

30. "Behind the G-B label." *New York Times*, December 29, 1935, sec. 9, p. 4.

31. "No room for us in U.S." *Variety*, January 20, 1937, pp. 3, 31.

32. "Ostrer and Hagen join the C. M. Woolf wailing wall." *Variety*, January 27, 1937, p. 7.

33. "GB washes up own U.S. selling org." *Variety*, December 14, 1938, p. 5.

34. "Foresee reciprocity in quota." *Variety*, January 26, 1938, p.13.

35. "Buy British." *Time* 31 (April 11, 1938): 23.

36. "Quota ups Brit., hits U.S." *Variety*, June 15, 1938, p. 13.

37. Arthur Dent. "British films and the American market." *Variety*, January 4, 1939, pp. 5, 30.

38. "French film producers aiming new product at U.S. market." *Variety*, November 22, 1931, p. 11.

39. "Film shortage opens way for foreign here." *Variety*, March 21, 1933, p. 4.

40. Tino Balio, op. cit., p. 34.

41. "Something of a boom for foreign pix into Americanese impends." *Variety*, February 19, 1937, p. 4.

42. "Boyer's caution." *Variety*, February 17, 1937, p. 4.

43. Charles Jahrblum. "With English subtitles." *New York Times*, June 27, 1937, sec. 10, p. 3.

44. Mike Wear. "Foreign pix in U.S." *Variety*, January 5, 1938, p. 57.

45. "Little films." *New York Times*, March 1, 1931, p. 1.

46. "Foreign films over here." *Variety*, December 29, 1931, pp. 13, 178.

47. "U.S. interest in foreigns revives." *Variety*, October 24, 1933, p. 12.

48. "Abnormal bull market for foreign films in America not panning out well." *Variety*, December 28, 1938, p. 11.

49. "Tear bombs injure 9 at foreign films here." *New York Times*, May 7, 1939, p. 1.

50. John Maxwell. "Can reciprocity pay?" *Variety*, January 2, 1929, p. 5.

51. "British producer's views." *New York Times*, May 18, 1930, sec. 8, p. 6; "International resume." *Variety*, September 8, 1931, pp. 5, 30.

52. "Aping Hollywood idea endangering foreigns' chance in U.S. market." *Variety*, September 13, 1932, pp. 14, 74.

53. Cecelia Ager. "How U.S. and Europe differ." *Variety*, February 28, 1933, pp. 3, 41.

54. David Anderson. "Rising to the defense." *New York Times*, November 28, 1943, sec. 2, p. 3.

55. "Variety and the foreign-mades." *Variety*, September 11, 1929, p. 7.

56. Abel Green. "World's screen and stage." *Variety*, July 30, 1930, pp. 3, 18.

57. Cecelia Ager. "Doug Fairbanks, Jr., now a producer." *Variety*, March 4, 1936, pp. 4, 39.

58. "U.S. sees first Japanese movie." *Literary Digest* 123 (April 10, 1937): 28.

59. "Foreign films glut U.S. market; B.O. clicks rare, most of 'em weakies." *Variety*, May 11, 1938, p. 12.

60. "Foreign pix debacle." *Variety*, January 7, 1942, p. 91.

61. Abel Green. "World's screen and stage." *Variety*, July 30, 1930, pp. 3, 18.

62. "America likes European films." *New York Times*, January 28, 1929, p. 22.

63. Douglas Ayer. "Self-censorship in the movie industry." *The American Movie Industry: The Business of Motion Pictures*. Ed. Gorham Kindem. Carbondale, Ill.: Southern Illinois University Press, 1982, pp. 218–219.

64. "Foreign films' sales out." *Variety*, August 8, 1933, pp. 17, 48; David Edelstein. "Remade in America: a label to avoid." *New York Times*, November 4, 2001, sec. 2A, p. 3.

65. "U.S. to combat invasion?" *Variety*, March 18, 1936, pp. 7, 58.

66. Robert J. Landry. "Yankee prudes and foreign films." *Variety*, April 29, 1964, p. 31.

67. "Pash and pinko pix peeve." *Variety*, March 31, 1937, p. 7.

68. "Breen back; foreign, particularly British, pix to submit scripts." *Variety*, April 14, 1937, p. 7.

69. "UFA's future in U.S. in dubious." *Variety*, April 23, 1930, p. 7.

70. "Few foreign films." *Variety*, September 10, 1930, p. 7.

71. "Selling, not sharing new foreign method." *Variety*, June 14, 1932, p. 13.

72. Ernest Marshall. "London screen notes." *New York Times*, June 18, 1933, sec. 10, p. 2.

73. "French producers see American market waning for their pictures." *Variety*, March 8, 1939, p. 23.

74. "U.S. picture firms mull distribution of Latin-American product." *Variety*, February 19, 1941, p. 13.

75. Tino Balio, op. cit., p. 34.

76. "Film imports for five years." *Variety*, January 6, 1937, p. 33.

77. "American films got $26,500,000 in England last year." *Variety*, September 25, 1934, p. 21.

78. "Foreign film coin in '36 at record high." *Variety*, September 8, 1937, p. 3.

79. "Comparative schedules for 3 years." *Variety*, July 15, 1942, p. 5.

80. "Arty and foreign distribs see spurt in U.S. indie pix to make up shortage." *Variety*, September 6, 1939, p. 7.

81. "Plenty of foreign film production but not enough quality for the U.S." *Variety*, November 15, 1939, p. 14.

82. "No foreign pix blackout." *Variety*, February 7, 1940, p. 11.

83. "See Spanish-language pix as solution to the foreign product slack in U.S." *Variety*, May 15, 1940, p. 15; "Big backlog on foreign films." *Variety*, November 6, 1950, p. 13.

84. "Ultimately the war will make U.S. more foreign-film minded—Rosener." *Variety*, August 21, 1940, p. 4.

85. "Indie exhibitors want German and Italian pix kept out of the U.S." *Variety*, March 26, 1941, p. 1.

86. "Despite beefs to Uncle Sam, German pix (oldies) are being shown here." *Variety*, February 18, 1942, p. 7.

87. "GIs in England develop British films and stars for U.S. audiences." *Variety*, June 6, 1945, pp. 1, 28.

88. "Films across the sea." *Business Week*, July 21, 1945, pp. 32, 34.

89. "Movie missionary." *Fortune* 32 (October, 1945): 222, 226.

90. "British filmmakers told U.S. still leads." *New York Times*, November 20, 1945, p. 21.

91. Kerry Segrave. *American Films Abroad: Hollywood's Domination of the World's Movie Screens*. Jefferson, N.C." McFarland, 1997, p. 127.

CHAPTER 4

1. "Rank's prestige pix unit for U.S." *Variety*, June 26, 1946, p. 4.

2. "British pix finally click in U.S." *Variety*, September 11, 1946, pp. 3, 27.

3. "$8,500,000 British b.o. in U.S." *Variety*, November 20, 1946, pp. 3, 38.

4. Alexander Korda. "Is the screen really free?" *New York Times*, December 1, 1946, sec. 2, p. 5.

5. Herb Golden. "Yanks steam at British chill." *Variety*, January 22, 1947, pp. 3, 18.

6. *Ibid.*

7. "Seidelman again warns U.S. must up $ for British films, or else." *Variety*, April 30, 1947, pp. 11, 22.

8. "Rank-Young interviewers evidence that U.S. press seems plenty sold on British pix superiority to H'wood." *Variety*, May 14, 1947, pp. 6, 22.

9. "British b.o. in U.S. NSG—Blumberg." *Variety*, May 21, 1947, p. 5.

10. "Stix still nix British pix." *Variety*, June 18, 1947, pp. 1, 16.

11. "British prefer opportunity to play U.S. market, revenue incidental, Rank stresses to Yank distribs." *Variety*, July 2, 1947, pp. 3, 16.

12. "Brit threatens U.S pix imports." *Variety*, July 2, 1947, pp. 3, 48.

13. "Rank combine hit by B.O. dip in U.S., '47 take only 40% of $10,000,000 dream." *Variety*, December 17, 1947, pp. 4, 18.

14. "Rank thinks Yank distribs never did their best to sell his pix in U.S." *Variety*, March 17, 1948, pp. 3, 22.

15. "Johnston appraises state of film biz on foreign and domestic fronts." *Variety*, July 28, 1948, p. 17.

16. "Aver Anglo-U.S. film relations strained by Korda's television deal." *Variety*, May 5, 1948, p. 9.

17. "Korda's TV threat to exhibs." *Variety*, October 6, 1948, p. 3.

18. "Film time increase is sought by Rank." *New York Times*, October 5, 1948, p. 31; "Johnston denies U.S. movie curbs." *New York Times*, October 16, 1948, p. 8.

19. "British films earn $2,500,000 in U.S. in year." *Variety*, May 25, 1949, p. 19.

20. "Ranks' retreat." *Time* 54 (October 24, 1949): 96–97.

21. "Stresses French inability to compete with British in pitch for U.S. market." *Variety*, January 29, 1947, p. 16.

22. Noel Meadow. "French pictures gain in popularity." *New York Times*, June 8, 1947, sec. 2, p. 5.

23. Bosley Crowther. "Snows of yesteryear." *New York Times*, February 29, 1948, sec. 2, p. 1.

24. "Italo *Open City* freak B.O. in U.S." *Variety*, June 19, 1946, p. 4.

25. "Newsreelers' switch to foreign pix seen as big lift to imported films." *Variety*, May 21, 1947, pp. 5, 20.

26. "Brit. pix bloody but unbowed." *Variety*, May 5, 1948, pp. 15, 24.

27. "Sexacious selling best B.O. slant for foreign language films in U.S." *Variety*, June 9, 1948, pp. 2, 18.

28. "Foreign film bubble bursts." *Variety*, August 31, 1949, pp. 3, 22.

29. Thomas M. Pryor. "Breen's mission to London." *New York Times*, August 18, 1946, sec. 2, p. 3.

30. "Breen's nix on a number of British films straining Anglo-U.S. entente." *Variety*, May 7, 1947, pp. 9, 29.

31. "Mail bag memos." *New York Times*, December 21, 1947, sec. 2, p. 7.

32. Abel Green. "Nix exhib stand vs. British pix." *Variety*, February 6, 1946, pp. 3, 57.

33. Bosley Crowther. "On British films." *New York Times*, November 17, 1946, sec. 2, p. 1.

34. "U.S. life-or-death to Brit pix." *Variety*, December 25, 1946, pp. 9, 22.

35. "U.S. exhibs scored by Jarratt, Korda aide, for shunning British product." *Variety*, December 18, 1946, pp. 1, 29.

36. "U.S. films' peak foreign b.o." *Variety*, February 19, 1947, pp. 3, 48.

37. "20th-Fox's 4-year deal to distribute Korda's product is another step forward for Anglo-U.S. film accord." *Variety*, July 2, 1947, pp. 3, 16.

38. "Britishers' U.S. take only $6,000,000?" *Variety*, March 17, 1948, pp. 4, 18.

39. "U's sales accent on British films for big U.S. keys." *Variety*, July 28, 1948, pp. 4, 17.

40. "U's sales on Rank pix in U.S. to be highly selective." *Variety*, August 18, 1948, pp. 3, 21.
41. Gilbert Seldes. "Are the foreign films better." *Atlantic Monthly* 184 (September, 1949): 49–50.
42. Hayden Talbot. "Rank making serious mistake trying to pressure U.S. exhibs into playing his pix, says Wilby." *Variety*, January 22, 1947, pp. 3, 52.
43. "U.S. exhibs resist Metro's foreign imports, claiming OK for arties only." *Variety*, March 5, 1947, pp. 3, 22.
44. "Caution on any concerted action curbs U.S. majors from jointly agreeing to book British films." *Variety*, May 28, 1947, p. 9.
45. "Par pledges more bookings for Rank but indie circuits still skeptical." *Variety*, June 4, 1947, pp. 3, 22.
46. "Boycott of British films, because of Palestine, spreading in the U.S." *Variety*, August 11, 1948, pp. 1, 55.
47. "U's sales on Rank pix in U.S. to be highly selective." *Variety*, August 18, 1948, pp. 3, 21.
48. "405 films from 11 distribs." *Variety*, January 1, 1947, p. 3.
49. "506 releases in 1948; up 39." *Variety*, November 19, 1947, p. 5.
50. "Sexacious selling best B.O. slant for foreign language films in U.S." *Variety*, June 9, 1948, pp. 2, 18.
51. "Average French or Italian film nets only 20–40G in U.S. market." *Variety*, November 17, 1948, p. 15.
52. Kerry Segrave. *American Films Abroad: Hollywood's Domination of the World's Movie Screens.* Jefferson, N.C.: McFarland, 1997, p. 146.

CHAPTER 5

1. "H'wood whips foreign threats." *Variety*, October 25, 1950, pp. 1, 16.
2. "British in slow but sure headway; U.S. won't accept unknown stars." *Variety*, December 9, 1953, p. 10.
3. "Universal assigns sales talent to push British (Rank) features." *Variety*, January 27, 1954, pp. 5, 24.
4. "Brit. pix get 50% of coin o'seas but Rank's Davis unhappy over U.S. take." *Variety*, July 7, 1954, p. 13.
5. Davis gives figures on how Brit. pix fail to get fair return out of U.S." *Variety*, November 17, 1954, pp. 5, 8.
6. "Rank's $2-mil for American dig in." *Variety*, June 19, 1957, p. 4.
7. "British Lion goes a-huntin' for foreign markets." *Variety*, October 12, 1955, p. 7.

8. "British stars unsold in U.S." *Variety*, December 7, 1955, p. 25.
9. "Drop U.S isolationist anti–British pic exhib policy, pleads O'Brien." *Variety*, September 1, 1954, pp. 5, 22.
10. "Americans accused of British film bias." *New York Times*, February 11, 1956, p. 12.
11. "What British M.P.'s actually said." *Variety*, February 15, 1956, p. 16; "Yanks see quota cry, other angles; view M.P. cracks as muddled logic." *Variety*, February 15, 1956, p. 16; "Careless errata weaken British side of case." *Variety*, February 15, 1956, p. 16.
12. "Europe needy—for U.S. facts." *Variety*, February 22, 1956, p. 7.
13. "If the British are too British for American film tastes how explain Guinness' popularity?" *Variety*, March 21, 1956, pp. 5, 18.
14. Fred Hift. "Deny foreign film prejudice." *Variety*, March 28, 1956, pp. 3, 20.
15. "Brit. pic trade no one-way street, sez Wilcox." *Variety*, March 28, 1956, p. 20.
16. "Brit. unions' forced parity idea labeled unrealistic by Yanks." *Variety*, February 26, 1958, p. 5.
17. "Britain asks U.S. films made there carry Anglo-American identification." *Variety*, October 1, 1958, p. 1.
18. "See dangers in aiming European films for mass Yank audience." *Variety*, March 8, 1950, p. 15.
19. "Italian film invasion." *Life* 33 (October 20, 1952): 107–113.
20. "Italo-U.S. pact may pour $6,000,000 in U.S. pix purse, hamstring IFE." *Variety*, April 1, 1953, pp. 5, 20.
21. "New Italian-U.S. film pact drops principle of subsidy." *Variety*, June 9, 1954, p. 11.
22. Fred Hift. "Italy triples foreign market take but hopes to do better in U.S.A." *Variety*, September 29, 1954, pp. 7, 18.
23. "French prods hit by export mkt. slump, lagging domestic amortizing." *Variety*, June 25, 1952, p. 12.
24. "French-Yanks in two-year deal, subsidizes French office in U.S." *Variety*, December 16, 1953, p. 7.
25. Fred Hift. "French puzzling out U.S. ways." *Variety*, June 9, 1954, pp. 5, 18.
26. "In U.S. Frenchmen go it alone; money doesn't justify cooperation." *Variety*, December 15, 1954, p. 10.
27. "Film center planned." *New York Times*, June 8, 1955, p. 26.
28. "Flaud's theories, not facts, denied; U.S. importers think French fail to evaluate market chances." *Variety*, February 15, 1956, p. 16.
29. "Flaud repeats same points, ignores Mayer." *Variety*, March 21, 1956, pp. 5, 48.

30. "French film problem in United States." *Variety*, March 21, 1956, p. 7.

31. "German daydream: What Italians, French do in U.S., we can, too." *Variety*, June 9, 1954, pp. 4, 16.

32. Fred Hift. "German films too inbred." *Variety*, September 21, 1955, pp. 7, 18.

33. Fred Hift. "Pro-U.S. and it's tough—Schwarz." *Variety*, July 11, 1956, pp. 5, 22.

34. "Hartlieb: Reich must move fast in U.S. market." *Variety*, October 17, 1956, pp. 3, 15.

35. "German film aide here." *New York Times*, April 10, 1957, p. 39.

36. "Export union to boost German product in U.S." *Variety*, July 15, 1959, p. 18.

37. "Russians cool to pix deal with Yanks; ideas on reciprocity a stalemate." *Variety*, September 11, 1957, p. 11.

38. Fred Hift. "Pals no get what USSR got." *Variety*, October 22, 1958, p. 17.

39. "India latest foreign land to badly misunderstand U.S. film economics." *Variety*, February 27, 1957, p. 10.

40. "Emphasize English-language films in foreign prod. with eye to U.S. B.O." *Variety*, October 3, 1951, p. 18.

41. "French producers, with eye on Yank market, strive for U.S. pix slant." *Variety*, December 7, 1955, p. 17.

42. "Protest U.S. actors in British film roles." *New York Times*, June 29, 1950, p. 36.

43. "Brit producers won't slant for U.S. market since TV is glad to get 'em." *Variety*, August 29, 1951, pp. 5, 14.

44. "Europe's new H'wood accent." *Variety*, October 28, 1953, pp. 1, 54.

45. Fred Hift. "Foreign films catering more to U.S. taste." *Variety*, January 6, 1954, pp. 5, 48.

46. "British exhib prez sez producers should gear for U.S. market." *Variety*, February 2, 1955, p. 16.

47. "Goldenson to urge German, British pix slanted for American market." *Variety*, May 19, 1954, pp. 3, 25.

48. Fred Hift. "Foreign stars invade U.S." *Variety*, April 3, 1957, pp. 1, 94.

49. Robert J. Landry. "Unsold in the land of sell." *Variety*, April 24, 1957, p. 5.

50. "Import license, remittance ratio increasingly used by foreigners to force their pix on America." *Variety*, March 24, 1954, pp. 5, 24.

51. "See dangers in aiming European films for mass Yank audience." *Variety*, March 8, 1950, p. 15.

52. "Dubbing of foreign pix still a moot point among distribs in U.S. mkt." *Variety*, April 9, 1952, p. 13.

53. Peter Riethof. "Future of the dubbed film." *Variety*, January 12, 1955, p. 24.

54. "Issue-and-costs-of dubbing foreign films for states again examined." *Variety*, December 4, 1957, p. 25.

55. Robert Shelton. "Movie men of few words." *New York Times*, June 15, 1958, sec. 2, p. 8.

56. Bosley Crowther. "Changing voices." *New York Times*, September 7, 1958, sec. 2, p. 1.

57. Richard Griffith. "European films and American audiences." *The Saturday Review* 34 (January 13, 1951): 54, 85.

58. "Who likes foreign films." *Variety*, September 29, 1954, p. 3.

59. "Warnings vs. foreign pictures come through." *Variety*, November 1, 1950, pp. 3, 23.

60. "Foreign pix spurt toward peak U.S. dates; play half N.Y. arties." *Variety*, April 9, 1952, p. 12; "Stress lack of foreign pix with broad aud appeal for America." *Variety*, January 14, 1953, p. 4.

61. Noel Meadow. "U.S. market on foreign films says due to bad quality." *Variety*, June 24, 1953, pp. 17, 20.

62. "Foreign pix hope for more U.S. dates with curtailment of 'B' productions." *Variety*, September 30, 1953, pp. 3, 8.

63. Fred Hift. "Yanks pick stories for world appeal, British don't, and lose, but squawk." *Variety*, October 12, 1955, p. 7.

64. "British pix industry blamed for lack of U.S. interest in product." *Variety*, June 6, 1956, p. 14.

65. "Yankee fans star fixation retards upbuilding of imported films." *Variety*, May 13, 1957, p. 5.

66. Hy Hollinger. "Foreign pix gain by racy tags." *Variety*, June 30, 1954, pp. 7, 18.

67. "British Lion goes a-huntin' for foreign markets." *Variety*, October 12, 1955, p. 7.

68. "Foreign producers advised by Brandt to develop, not borrow, stars." *Variety*, October 19, 1955, p. 16.

69. "H'wood more 'n' more fills openings for unknown from overseas." *Variety*, July 16, 1958, p. 15.

70. "See dangers in aiming European films for mass Yank audience." *Variety*, March 8, 1950, p. 15.

71. Thomas M. Pryor. "Foreign film distributors organize." *New York Times*, March 19, 1950, sec. 2, p. 5.

72. "Foreign market vital to French pix producers; 20% yearly loss." *Variety*, May 10, 1950, pp. 12–13.

73. "French, Italian delegates see their product's acceptance far off in U.S." *Variety*, May 31, 1950, p. 7.

74. "Foreign pix worst year since '45." *Variety*, January 21, 1953, pp. 4, 20; "Delighted sums up reaction to aliens' U.S. sell." *Variety*, December 5, 1956, pp. 3, 7.

75. "Foreign filmmakers need handbook to warn and guide 'em on U.S." *Variety*, April 7, 1954, pp. 1, 56.

76. "47% of films lack code seal." *Variety*, December 29, 1954, pp. 5, 55.

77. "3 banned unseen." *Variety*, October 6, 1954, p. 16; "State not refunding censor fees." *Variety*, April 8, 1959, p. 7.

78. "Security check on foreign pix." *Variety*, January 14, 1953, pp. 3, 61.

79. "Swede on Yanks' prudery." *Variety*, November 19, 1958, p. 3.

80. Fred Hift. "Censorship by U.S. Customs." *Variety*, April 8, 1959, p. 7.

81. "Foreign filmers form own trade assn.; 50 indies." *Variety*, March 15, 1950, pp. 4, 61; "Foreign pix spurt toward peak U.S. dates; play half N.Y. arties." *Variety*, April 9, 1952, p. 12.

82. "Urges special code class for imports." *Variety*, June 30, 1954, p. 7.

83. "Foreigners sing censor blues." *Variety*, September 8, 1954, pp. 11, 20.

84. Fred Hift. "Europe's a code for a code." *Variety*, October 6, 1954, pp. 1, 16.

85. "Free access to U.S. market." *Variety*, October 6, 1954, p. 16.

86. "Code and Legion again loom high as foreign pix seek commercial coin." *Variety*, March 16, 1955, p. 16.

87. Fred Hift. "French resent American code; taking $10,000,000 globally but almost nothing from U.S.A." *Variety*, June 8, 1955, pp. 5, 24.

88. "Code seal to 305 during 1955." *Variety*, January 25, 1956, p. 7.

89. "European producers should aim to please families—Eric Johnston." *Variety*, July 4, 1956, p. 7.

90. "Point up continued foreign films failure to seek American seal." *Variety*, April 3, 1957, p. 12.

91. "German 08/15 distrib calls imports fated for plush art house ghetto." *Variety*, April 24, 1957, pp. 4, 18.

92. Fred Hift. "Again issue of Hollywood code." *Variety*, August 27, 1958, pp. 7, 16.

93. Henry Brill. "Will we gag films." *The Nation* 175 (August 16, 1952): 132–133.

94. "Foreigners sing censor blues." *Variety*, September 8, 1954, pp. 11, 20.

95. "Of 73 'C' (condemned) films only two with a major U.S. distrib." *Variety*, November 10, 1954, p. 7.

96. "Code and Legion again loom high as foreign pix seek commercial coin." *Variety*, March 16, 1955, p. 16.

97. Fred Hift. "French resent American code; taking $10,000,000 globally but almost nothing from U.S.A." *Variety*, June 8, 1955, pp. 5, 24.

98. "Once dud, N.J. house reaps profits, protests on foreign film policy." *Variety*, November 2, 1955, p. 10.

99. "Arties' tabu on pix with 'C' rating may cue safer themes from o'seas." *Variety*, August 2, 1956, pp. 5, 12.

100. Jack Gould. "Prelate praises radio and video." *New York Times*, December 13, 1957, p. 29.

101. "BB vs. 'C': new boxoffice algebra." *Variety*, July 16, 1958, p. 15.

102. "In ducking Japan's code, U.S. film men echo Europe's peeve vs. H'wood seal." *Variety*, September 28, 1955, p. 7.

103. "Importers in burn at Johnston." *Variety*, October 21, 1959, p. 15.

104. "'51 top prod. year since '44." *Variety*, May 7, 1952, p. 5.

105. "Stress lack of foreign pix with broad aud appeal for America." *Variety*, January 14, 1953, p. 4; "All-time top grosser." *Variety*, January 21, 1953, pp. 4, 20.

106. "Yank exhibs still cool on imports, as Europe strains for U.S. favor." *Variety*, June 1, 1955, pp. 4, 20.

107. "Foreign films' new year for color adds to U.S. importers' hazards." *Variety*, June 30, 1954, p. 7.

108. "Need special approach budget to sell British pix in U.S., sez U. exec." *Variety*, August 12, 1953, p. 16.

109. "Yank distribs increasingly handle foreign pix outside U.S. market." *Variety*, March 16, 1955, p. 15.

110. "Columbia's special dept. to handle foreign features starts Sept. 15." *Variety*, July 27, 1955, pp. 3, 18.

111. "Indie channel or major company poses distrib question in U.S." *Variety*, August 3, 1955, pp. 7, 61.

112. "Ever-hopeful distribs think maybe slump might help foreign films." *Variety*, December 7, 1955, p. 25.

113. Fred Hift. "One world—of film headaches." *Variety*, January 4, 1956, p. 53.

114. Fred Hift. "Mystery of Yank market." *Variety*, October 17, 1956, pp. 5, 78.

115. "Delighted sums up reaction to aliens' U.S. sell." *Variety*, December 5, 1956, pp. 3, 7.

116. "Don't like Europeans' contract terms." *Variety*, April 24, 1957, p. 4.

117. Dan Frankel. "Casting the distribution dice." *New York Times*, October 20, 1957, sec. 2, p. 5.

118. Fred Hift. "Foreign films in America: up from zero." *Variety*, April 9, 1958, p. 25.

119. "America's 40 foreign film importers: don't mistake us for plutocrats." *Variety*, April 15, 1959, p. 91.
120. Harold Myers. "East Berlin can't get U.S. playdates." *Variety*, July 15, 1959, p. 17.
121. Noel Meadow. "TV no threat to film imports." *Variety*, January 24, 1951, pp. 7, 55.
122. "Foreign lingo pix in U.S. wane." *Variety*, November 14, 1951, pp. 7, 10; "Foreign pix spurt toward peak U.S. dates; play half N.Y. arties." *Variety*, April 9, 1952, p. 12.
123. "Shortage vs. closed minds!" *Variety*, June 9, 1954, pp. 5, 18.
124. "Welcome mat for imports." *Variety*, September 29, 1954, pp. 3, 18.
125. "Testing Oklahoma City's taste for foreign features; 8 for $4." *Variety*, October 12, 1955, p. 7.
126. "Wait for fall: can TV put talky British films over with American public?" *Variety*, July 20, 1955, p. 5.
127. "Germans latest to see U.S. video as film market; easier dubbing problem." *Variety*, July 27, 1955, p. 18.
128. "Let 'em eat American cake." *Variety*, December 14, 1955, pp. 3, 25.
129. *Ibid.*
130. "Yank-exhibs criticize British films." *Variety*, December 14, 1955, p. 3.
131. "British accent fine—if in U.S." *Variety*, December 28, 1955, pp. 7, 18.
132. "Beautifully made but too few European films right for U.S." *Variety*, July 11, 1956, p. 5.
133. Bosley Crowther. "Touting foreign films." *New York Times*, September 16, 1956, sec. 2, p. 1.
134. Fred Hift. "British films have best chance; all foreign product handicapped." *Variety*, April 24, 1957, pp. 5, 18.
135. *Ibid.*
136. "In the meantime." *Time* 70 (November 18, 1957): 112–114.
137. "Rank-Yank hits Schine bias." *Variety*, February 26, 1958, p. 5.
138. "Made-in-Europe-for-America." *Variety*, December 24,1958, pp. 5, 15.
139. Fred Hift. "Time favors foreign films in U.S. but Yank theatre men notably timid." *Variety*, April 15, 1959, p. 28.
140. S. H. Fabian. "A money picture is American-made." *Variety*, April 15, 1959, p. 28.
141. "MPAA vs. foreign retaliation." *Variety*, October 22, 1952, pp. 3, 16.
142. Thomas M. Pryor. "Johnston decries foreign film bar." *New York Times*, January 9, 1954, p. 11.
143. "U.S. pix on world scale." *Variety*, June 17, 1953, p. 3.
144. Arthur Mayer. "From Bernhardt to Bardot." *Saturday Review* 42 (June 27, 1959): 8–10+.
145. "Europe's '53 remittables, $78,200,000; British take $4,400,000 from U.S." *Variety*, April 21, 1954, p. 11.
146. Fred Hift. "Foreign films arrive in U.S." *Variety*, January 30, 1957, pp. 1, 62.
147. Fred Hift. "Foreign films find U.S. gold." *Variety*, April 9, 1958, pp. 1, 119.
148. Fred Hift. "U.S. buildup of film imports." *Variety*, April 15, 1959, pp. 1, 30.
149. Kerry Segrave. *American Films Abroad: Hollywood's Domination of the World's Movie Screens.* Jefferson, N.C.: McFarland, 1997, p. 232.
150. Joseph D. Phillips. "Film conglomerate blockbusters." *The American Movie Industry: The Business of Motion Pictures.* Ed. Gorham Kindem. Carbondale, Ill.: Southern Illinois University Press, 1982, pp. 332–333.
151. "135 blockbusters: $311,950,000." *Variety*, January 6, 1954, pp. 5, 66.
152. "Foreign films nominated for Oscar never seen in America." *Variety*, December 30, 1959, p. 5.

CHAPTER 6

1. Hollis Alpert. "Are foreign films better?" *Saturday Review* 43 (December 24, 1960): 43.
2. "Shed Cockney, clean up in U.S." *Variety*, January 30, 1963, pp. 7, 18.
3. "Those English subtitles." *Newsweek* 56 (August 8, 1960): 76.
4. "*La Dolce Vita* blazes subtitled paths." *Variety*, November 1, 1961, p. 19.
5. Bosley Crowther. "Subtitles must go." *New York Times*, August 7, 1960, sec. 2, pp. 1, 3.
6. Bosley Crowther. "Dubbing (continued)." *New York Times*, August 21, 1960, sec. 2, pp. 1, 6.
7. Robert Hatch. "Films." *The Nation* 191 (September 3, 1960): 119–120.
8. Bosley Crowther. "On doing dubbing." *New York Times*, December 3, 1961, sec. 2, p. 1.
9. Bosley Crowther. "Hearing voices again." *New York Times*, September 20, 1964, sec. 2, p. 1.
10. Arthur Knight. "The great dubbing controversy." *Saturday Review* 43 (October 29, 1960): 28.
11. Stanley Kauffmann. "Foreign languages in foreign pictures." *New Republic* 143 (December 12, 1960): 27–28.
12. "Days of subtitled foreign films for U.S. market nearly over." *Variety*, June 7, 1961, p. 14.

13. Vincent Canby. "N.Y. art houses: Anglo-Yank." *Variety*, July 5, 1961, p. 11.

14. Vincent Canby. "N.Y.'s art house explosion." *Variety*, August 29, 1962, p. 5; Mike Wear. "21 arty situations in Manhattan." *Variety*, October 24, 1962, p. 24.

15. Vincent Canby. "N.Y. foreign art film time up." *Variety*, October 23, 1963, pp. 1, 21.

16. Vincent Canby. "U.S. majors lead N.Y. arties." *Variety*, September 9, 1964, pp. 3, 25.

17. Vincent Canby. "N.Y. arties favoring U.S. pix." *Variety*, September 8, 1965, pp. 3, 70.

18. Bosley Crowther. "Speaking of foreign films." *New York Times*, June 13, 1965, sec. 2, p. 1.

19. "Slow-going uphuild of foreign film directors in U.S." *Variety*, December 13, 1961, p. 5.

20. "Parochial uproar in Ft. Lee; panics before foreign art films." *Variety*, February 24, 1960, pp. 3, 24.

21. *Ibid.*

22. "Ft. Lee, on holier-than-thou binge, proposes anti-foreign art film law." *Variety*, March 2, 1960, p. 15.

23. "Foreign art films imaginary danger, importers assure nervous Fort Lee." *Variety*, March 16, 1960, p. 19.

24. "Ft. Lee, N.J. police fingerprint exhib as requisite for art house license." *Variety*, March 23, 1960, pp. 1, 62.

25. Arthur L. Mayer. "Myth of the less virtuous foreign film." *Variety*, April 20, 1960, p. 25.

26. "An art house is not a home." *Variety*, August 30, 1961, p. 18.

27. "Filthy French pix sparking D.C. probe into moral tone of all film imports." *Variety*, August 23, 1961, pp. 1, 53.

28. "Film importers politely decline offer for ad-code okay of sell-copy." *Variety*, March 9, 1960, p. 21.

29. Murray Schumach. "Role of studios showing change." *New York Times*, January 9, 1962, p. 22.

30. "Legion of Decency data." *Variety*, December 20, 1961, p. 11.

31. Robert J. Landry. "Yankee prudes and foreign films." *Variety*, April 29, 1964, p. 31.

32. Hollis Alpert. "Britain's angry young director." *Saturday Review* 43 (December 24, 1960): 48–49.

33. "Foreign film producers scan terms and house expenses with more care as market improves." *Variety*, December 28, 1960, p. 3.

34. "Majors brush art for big b.o." *Variety*, February 5, 1963, pp. 5, 18.

35. "Moscow to halt U.S. film imports." *New York Times*, March 2, 1963, p. 5.

36. Jack Hoffberg. "Sees distribution of art film market as undeserved bonanza for theatres." *Variety*, January 5, 1966, p. 33.

37. Murray Schumach. "Film study sees import increase." *New York Times*, September 20, 1960, p. 46.

38. Lenny Litman. "Even tiny towns get foreign pix." *Variety*, May 8, 1963, p. 34.

39. Robert Rees. "Non-alike twin cities; St. Paul resists Le sexy." *Variety*, May 8, 1963, p. 34

40. Sam Lucheese. "10 years of art house operation in Atlanta; British easy favorites." *Variety*, May 8, 1963, p. 33.

41. Eugene Archer. "*Tom Jones* is due to earn record." *New York Times*, April 4, 1964, p. 15.

42. Vincent Canby. "Foreign films' U.S. jackpots." *Variety*, April 20, 1960, pp. 1, 78.

43. Vincent Canby. "British humor scores in U.S." *Variety*, April 26, 1961, pp. 1, 170.

44. Vincent Canby. "O'seas films' $69,000,000 in U.S." *Variety*, May 2, 1962, pp. 1, 18.

45. Vincent Canby. "Film imports on a seesaw." *Variety*, May 8, 1963, pp. 1, 34.

46. Vincent Canby. "Foreign rentals in U.S." *Variety*, April 29, 1964, pp. 30, 32.

47. Vincent Canby. "Britons top U.S. pix imports." *Variety*, May 12, 1965, pp. 1, 30.

48. Joseph Phillips. "Film conglomerate blockbusters." *The American Movie Industry: The Business of Motion Pictures.* Ed. Gorham Kindem. Carbondale, Ill.: Southern Illinois University Press, 1982, p. 33.

49. Kerry Segrave. *American Films Abroad: Hollywood's Domination of the World's Movie Screens.* Jefferson, N.C.: McFarland, 1997, p. 230.

CHAPTER 7

1. "Most fans think Antonioni is a cheese—Levine." *Variety*, May 24, 1967, p. 7.

2. "Japan (494), India (308), Italy (301), U.S. (300), Taiwan (246) most active." *Variety*, May 12, 1971, p. 37.

3. Hank Werba. "Italo film biz invading U.S." *Variety*, July 16, 1969, pp. 33, 36.

4. "Carlo Ponti's credo: Italy and U.S. need one another's feature films." *Variety*, January 20, 1971, p. 24.

5. "Lack of a theater forces Italians to lower N.Y. flag." *Variety*, June 15, 1988, p. 7.

6. Lawrence Cohn. "Two new films herald return of Italo pix to U.S. screens." *Variety*, February 7, 1990, p. 22.

7. Deborah Young. "Italo pic biz wrangles U.S. export declaration." *Variety*, August 16, 1999, p. 19.

8. Gene Moskowitz. "Raymond Danon: I don't believe French films unacceptable to U.S." *Variety*, May 10, 1972, p. 4.

9. Tom Allen. "Why are we so hard on French films?" *Village Voice*, March 29, 1976, p. 125.

10. "Gaumont's prod. head devises system for hits in U.S. market." *Variety*, November 23, 1977, p. 31.

11. Frank Segers. "Foreign pix seek key to U.S. masses." *Variety*, October 19, 1977, pp. 1, 40.

12. "Once upon a day Lelouche was hero of U.S. boxoffice." *Variety*, May 17, 1978, pp. 9, 127.

13. Gene Moskowitz. "Hopes stirring again in France for U.S. mkt. breakthrough." *Variety*, October 18, 1978, p. 242.

14. Ted Clark. "French see rebirth of interest by U.S. mkt." *Variety*, October 17, 1979, p. 298.

15. "Col & Gaumont at odds on Lido; overcoming U.S. tastes not easy." *Variety*, September 7, 1983, pp. 5, 32.

16. Louise Lief. "France's Gaumont takes aim at the American market." *Variety*, December 25, 1983, sec. 2, pp. 13, 15.

17. Fred Hift. "French renew fight for bigger slice of U.S. pie." *Variety*, November 26, 1990, pp. 3, 5.

18. Larry Rohter. "For foreign films, Vita is no longer Dolce." *New York Times*, April 11, 1991, pp. C15, C18.

19. John Baxter. "Ignorance as protectionism." *World Press Review* 43 (March, 1996): 44–45.

20. Ronald Holloway. "*Drum* might be the one." *Variety*, October 17, 1979, p. 12.

21. Ronald Holloway. "German pix finally score breakthrough in American market." *Variety*, January 9, 1980, pp. 1, 86; Ronald Holloway. "*Braun, Drum* help consolidate Germany's film Breakthrough in the United States market." *Variety*, May 7, 1980, pp. 420, 442.

22. "Teutonic films prove to be a tough sell overseas." *Variety*, December 5, 1994, p. 42.

23. Michael Silverman. "U.S.-Europe pic imbalance cuts two ways." *Variety*, September 10, 1986, pp. 5, 109.

24. Robert J. Landry. "Brazil woos U.S. film market." *Variety*, December 23, 1970, pp. 7, 40.

25. Sydney H. Schanberg. "New Delhi: pillage in the eyes of God." *New York Times*, August 30, 1971, p. 34.

26. "India's export earnings down." *Variety*, May 17, 1978, p. 90.

27. "Valenti to Russian film execs: stop thinking in reciprocity terms." *Variety*, July 25, 1973, pp. 1, 44.

28. Michael Thornhill. "Native accent of too many industries hampers export profit chances." *Variety*, May 10, 1978, p. 48.

29. Michael Silverman. "Indigenous Aussie features find U.S. market no piece of cake." *Variety*, May 7, 1986, pp. 347, 362.

30. Richard Gold. "*Ran* aims for wide audiences." *Variety*, December 18, 1985, p. 7.

31. Frank Segers. "Best customer for pics from Japan is U.S." *Variety*, December 9, 1987, pp. 1, 75.

32. Clavell (of *To Sir*) counsels British to make features more Yank style." *Variety*, April 24, 1968, p. 31.

33. "Danes shoot extra footage to meet U.S. market requirements on intelligibility." *Variety*, August 2, 1967, p. 13.

34. Addison Verrill. "Europe's key to U.S. sales." *Variety*, April 29, 1970, pp.1, 24.

35. Addison Verrill. "O'seas pix regaining U.S. audiences." *Variety*, May 8, 1974, pp. 1, 62.

36. "Aussie pix must think American, says Peter Weir." *Variety*, October 4, 1978, p. 61.

37. Peter Riethof. "Expert advice: dub with care if you expect to slip by in U.S." *Variety*, May 8, 1974, p. 170.

38. "How many foreign films get more revenue from U.S. mart?" *Variety*, May 7, 1975, p. 135.

39. Dan Yakir. "Cutting remarks." *Horizon* 28 (May, 1985): 78.

40. Lawrence Cohn. "Oft snubbed, dubbed Euro pix may make a comeback in U.S." *Variety*, August 10, 1992, pp. 72, 74.

41. Lawrence Cohn. "Apres Brigitte Bardot, whither dubbing?" *Variety*, December 13, 1993, p. 7.

42. Michael Williams. "Dub's the rub for Gallic pix in U.S." *Variety*, December 13, 1993, pp. 33, 35.

43. Leonard Klady. "H'wood foreign rub: join the dub club?" *Variety*, September 12, 1994, pp. 9, 17.

44. Stanley Kauffmann. "Books and the arts." *The New Republic* 213 (November 27, 1995): 28.

45. Terry Pristin. "Will dubbing fly in the U.S? Read my lips." *New York Times*, February 19, 1996, pp. D1, D4.

46. Leonard Klady. "Read their lips: Americans don't like dubbing." *New York Times*, August 29, 1999, sec. 2, p. 21.

47. Addison Verrill. "O'seas pix regaining U.S. audiences." *Variety*, May 8, 1974, pp. 1, 62; Lance Loud. "Illuminations." *American Film* 19 (January/February, 1992): 13.

48. Robert Koehler. "How auds learned to love the subtitles." *Variety*, January 14, 2002, p. A5.

49. Vincent Canby. "Foreign pictures

enjoyed big earnings in 1966." *New York Times*, January 18, 1967, p. 50.

50. Charles Schreger. "Hollywood checks directors from Europe as prone to flop in English language." *Variety*, May 17, 1978, p. 8.

51. "IFIDA films duck ratings." *Variety*, March 26, 1969, p. 18.

52. "International films key to success says Valenti." *Cinemag* no. 10 (September, 1978): 17.

53. Dan Yakir. "Cutting remarks." *Horizon* 28 (May, 1985): 73, 76.

54. Gregg Kilday. "Imported inspirations." *American Film* 14 (May, 1989): 14.

55. Josh Young. "The best French films you'll never see." *New York Times*, October 30, 1994, sec. 2, pp. 17, 22.

56. David Edelstein. "Remade in America: a label to avoid." *New York Times*, November 4, 2001, sec. 2A, p. 3.

57. "Foreign features show potential to become videocassette staple." *Variety*, October 13, 1982, p. 50.

58. Lauren Ptito. "Arts and leisure." *Europe* no. 338 (July/August, 1994): 46.

59. Terry Pristin. "Will dubbing fly in the U.S? Read my lips." *New York Times*, February 19, 1996, p. D4.

60. Harold Myers. "European producers big query: how U.S. figures the figures." *Variety*, May 8, 1968, p. 33.

61. "Another thing: Truffaut doesn't echo Godard's warnings against U.S. deals." *Variety*, July 3, 1968, p. 22.

62. "How U.S. distributors ranked in 1970." *Variety*, May 12, 1971, p. 35.

63. "Metro will test o'seas pickups before they get regular release." *Variety*, November 17, 1971, p. 5.

64. James Monaco. "Holding pattern." *Take One* 4 (no. 11, 1975): 38–39.

65. Tom Buckley. "At the movies." *New York Times*, January 13, 1978, p. C6.

66. Stanley Kauffmann. "Arts and lives." *New Republic* 179 (August 19, 1978): 28–29.

67. Frank Segers. "Foreign pix pick up more biz in U.S." *Variety*, May 9, 1979, pp. 1, 104.

68. Bruce Mallen. "Canadian features as export commodity." *Cinemag* no. 30 (January 21, 1980): 10–12.

69. "Indie distribs flocking to Hollywood." *Variety*, May 7, 1980, p. 11.

70. Dan Yakir. "The importance of being Dan Talbot." *American Film* 5 (April, 1980): 32–33.

71. *Ibid*.

72. Stephen Klein. "Prods. over-value U.S. art mart." *Variety*, May 4, 1983, pp. 1, 532, 542.

73. Harlan Jacobson. "How the classic kids snatched foreign film." *Village Voice*, November 22, 1983, pp. 74–76, 83.

74. Lawrence Cohn. "Overseas hits don't travel to U.S." *Variety*, May 9, 1984, pp. 1, 558.

75. Richard Gold. "U.S. buyers tough on subtitled pics." *Variety*, May 7, 1986, pp. 15, 506.

76. Linda Lee. "Nobody reads a good movie these days." *New York Times*, December 9, 1996, p. D9.

77. Stuart Klawans. "When the art film label is deadly." *New York Times*, November 18, 2001, sec. 2, p. 15.

78. Robert J. Landry. "Foreign showmen ask for more facts on U.S. market." *Variety*, May 8, 1968, p. 39.

79. Charles Teitel. "In Chicago, if you play a foreign pic, you could be tagged a Bolshevik." *Variety*, June 7, 1972, p. 7.

80. "Jerry Lewis sampler omits categories of foreign-language and porno films." *Variety*, June 7, 1972, p. 7.

81. "Southern New Jersey filmgoers find no foreign product on local screens." *Boxoffice* 114 (February 26, 1979): E1.

82. Harlan Jacobson. "It's still a thin market for foreign films in U.S." *Variety*, May 7, 1980, pp. 11, 344.

83. Jim Robbins. "U.S. market guide for imported films." *Variety*, February 3, 1982, pp. 43, 52.

84. Patricia Thomson. "Imports alive, not kicking." *Variety*, March 11, 1991, p. 44.

85. Ann Hornaday. "At many a multiplex, lots of screens but little choice." *New York Times*, August 4, 1996, sec. 2, pp. 18–19.

86. Jack Pitman. "British films too insular?" *Variety*, December 6, 1972, p. 27.

87. Richard Gold. "Foreign film disappointments at '85 boxoffice." *Variety*, January 8, 1986, p. 11.

88. Peter Besas. "How to crack U.S. with foreign pix." *Variety*, May 17, 1978, pp. 1, 90.

89. *Ibid*.

90. Frank Segers. "Foreign pix seek key to U.S. masses." *Variety*, October 19, 1977, pp. 1, 40.

91. "Survey for foreign producers measures response of U.S. auds." *Variety*, October 22, 1986, p. 14.

92. Don Groves. "Quality is the key to getting Euro pix into U.S., panel sez." *Variety*, July 5, 1989, pp. 22–23.

93. Paul Gardner. "Foreign films, popular in the U.S. in '60's, being treated like foreigners in '70's." *New York Times*, October 4, 1973, p. 56.

94. Vincent Canby. "Fans of foreign flicks— where are they now?" *New York Times*, February 17, 1974, sec. 2, pp. 1, 12.

95. Rob Medich. "Why foreign films founder." *Premiere* 2 (December, 1988): 30.

96. David Ansen. "Oscar looks abroad." *Newsweek* 115 (March 12, 1990): 86–87.

97. Christine Ogan. "The audience for foreign film in the United States." *Journal of Communications* 40 (no. 4, 1990): 58–60, 68, 74–75.

98. Patricia Thomson. "New generation tackles foreign film challenge." *Variety*, March 11, 1991, p. 42.

99. Richard Corliss. "Fellini go home." *Time* 149 (January 13, 1997): 68–70.

100. "Shall we, yawn, go to a film?" *The Economist* 342 (February 1, 1997): 85–86.

101. Andrew Sarris. "Why the foreign film has lost its cachet." *New York Times*, May 2, 1990, sec. 2A, pp. 15, 35.

102. Phillip Lopate. "When foreign movies mattered." *New York Times*, August 13, 2000, sec. 2, pp. 11, 20.

103. Patricia Thomson. "Int'l pix confront narrow coin margin." *Daily Variety*, July 30, 2001, p. 30+.

104. Box office receipts." *Variety*, May 12, 1971, p. 37.

105. Syd Silverman. "330 films above $100,000 rentals." *Variety*, May 12, 1971, p. 34.

106. "Hard going in the U.S. for foreign films." *Variety*, May 3, 1972, p. 31.

107. Kerry Segrave. *American Films Abroad: Hollywood's Domination of the World's Movie Screens*. Jefferson, N.C.: McFarland, 1997, pp. 230–231.

108. Rob Medich. "Why foreign films founder." *Premiere* 2 (December, 1988): 30.

109. "U.S. film imports vs. 1968." *Variety*, May 3, 1989, Cannes special issue, pp. 196+.

110. Kerry Segrave, op. cit., pp. 278–279.

111. Leonard Klady. "Legions of foreign-lingo pix colonize small market niche." *Variety*, April 29, 1996, pp. 11, 27; Leonard Klady. "Read their lips: Americans don't like dubbing." *New York Times*, August 29, 1999, sec. 2, p. 21.

112. Roger Smith. "Decannestruction." *Film Comment* 37 (July/August, 2001): 20–21.

113. Richard Corliss. "Handicapping the foreign Oscar." *Time* 125 (March 25, 1982): 72.

114. Howard A. Rodman. "The five nominees and how they grew." *Film Comment* 25 (March/April, 1989): 8, 80.

115. Benedict Carver and Dan Cox. "New lease on *Life* for foreign pix." *Variety*, March 29, 1999, pp. 36, 83.

116. "Top foreign films in U.S." *Variety*, August 31, 1992, p. 54; "All-time foreign-language films in North America." *Variety*, February 21, 2000, p. 16; "In just one weekend *Spider-Man* Jump-starts the whole summer for Hollywood." *New York Times*, May 7, 2002, pp. C1, C6.

117. Dalya Alberge. "Mike Leigh says British films are overexposed to U.S. influence." *Times* (London), May 18, 2002, p. 11.

Bibliography

Abel, Richard. *The Red Rooster Scare: Making Cinema American 1900–1910.* Berkeley: University of California Press, 1999.

"Abnormal bull market for foreign films in America not panning out well." *Variety,* December 28, 1938, p. 11.

"Acute shortage of features hits trade." *Variety,* April 21, 1922, p. 47.

Advertisement. *Variety,* January 12, 1907, p. 24.

Advertisement. *Variety,* February 22, 1908, p. 36.

Advertisement. *Variety,* March 7, 1908, p. 39.

Advertisement. *Variety,* December 12, 1908, p. 123.

Advertisement. *Variety,* February 27, 1909, p. 31.

Advertisement. *Variety,* December 26, 1919, p. 198.

"Adding American subjects." *Variety,* June 19, 1909, p. 11.

Ager, Cecelia. "Doug Fairbanks, Jr., now a producer." *Variety,* March 4, 1936, pp. 4, 39.

_____. "How U.S. and Europe differ." *Variety,* February 28, 1933, pp. 3, 41.

"Aggressive action possible by Mayor against pictures." *Variety,* March 5, 1910, p. 12.

"Agree on film tariff." *New York Times,* April 5, 1922, p. 15.

Alberge, Dalya. "Mike Leigh says British films are overexposed to U.S. influence." *Times* (London), May 18, 2002, p. 11.

"All Hollywood now lining up against German made films." *Variety,* May 20, 1921, pp. 1–2.

Allen, Tom. "Why are we so hard on French films?" *Village Voice,* March 29, 1976, p. 125.

"All-time foreign-language films in North America." *Variety,* February 21, 2000, p. 16.

"All-time top grosser." *Variety,* January 21, 1953, pp. 4, 20.

Alpert, Hollis. "Are foreign films better?" *Saturday Review* 43 (December 24, 1960): 43–45.

Alpert, Hollis. "Britain's angry young director." *Saturday Review* 43 (December 24, 1960): 48–49.

"America likes European films." *New York Times,* January 28, 1929, p. 22.

"American actors' parts in British films." *Times* (London), September 6, 1952, p. 6.

"American and British films coming to grips." *Literary Digest* 90 (August 28, 1926): 23.

"American film invasion abroad starting something." *Variety,* July 4, 1919, p. 3.

"American films got $26,500,000 in England last year." *Variety,* September 25, 1934, p. 21.

"American market for British films." *Times* (London), May 23, 1950, p. 5.

"Americans accused of British film bias." *New York Times,* February 11, 1956, p. 12.

"America's 40 foreign film importers: don't mistake us for plutocrats." *Variety,* April 15, 1959, p. 91.

Anderson, David. "Rising to the defense." *New York Times*, November 28, 1943, sec. 2, p. 3.
"Another thing: Truffaut doesn't echo Godard's warnings against U.S. deals." *Variety*, July 3, 1968, p. 22.
Ansen, David. "Oscar looks abroad." *Newsweek* 115 (March 12, 1990): 86–87.
"Aping Hollywood idea endangering foreigns' chance in U.S. market." *Variety*, September 13, 1932, pp. 14, 74.
Archer, Eugene. "*Tom Jones* is due to earn record." *New York Times*, April 4, 1964, p. 15.
"An art house is not a home." *Variety*, August 30, 1961, p. 18.
"Arties tabu on pix with 'C' rating may cue safe themes from o'seas." *Variety*, August 22, 1956, pp. 5, 12.
"Arty and foreign distribs see spurt in U.S. indie pix to make up shortage." *Variety*, September 6, 1939, p. 7.
"Aussie pix must think American, says Peter Weir." *Variety*, October 4, 1978, p. 61.
"Aver Anglo-U.S. film relations strained by Korda's television deal." *Variety*, May 5, 1948, p. 9.
"Average French or Italian film nets only 20–40G in U.S. market." *Variety*, November 17, 1948, p. 15.
Ayer, Douglas. "Self-censorship in the movie industry." *The American Movie Industry: The Business of Motion Pictures*. Ed. Gorham Kindem. Carbondale, Ill.: Southern Illinois University Press, 1982.
Bakshy, Alexander. "The German invasion." *The Nation* 132 (May 13, 1931): 538.
Balio, Tino. *Grand Design: Hollywood as a Modern Business Enterprise, 1930–1939 (History of the American Cinema, 5)*. New York: Scribner's Sons, 1993.
Baxter, John. "Ignorance as protectionism." *World Press Review* 43 (March, 1996): 44–45.
"BB vs. C: new boxoffice algebra." *Variety*, July 16, 1958, p. 15.
"Beautifully made but too few European films right for U.S." *Variety*, July 11, 1956, p. 5.
"Behind the G-B label." *New York Times*, December 29, 1935, sec. 9, p. 4.
"Berlin hears Ufa is sending high officials to liquidate U.S. ends." *Variety*, February 2, 1932, p. 11.
"Bernard Natan here viewing U.S. film methods intensively." *Variety*, July 19, 1934, p. 29.
Besas, Peter. "How to crack U.S. with foreign pix." *Variety*, May 17, 1978, pp. 1, 90.
"Better films in Europe." *New York Times*, September 11, 1913, p. 4.
"B.I.'s eye for eye here." *Variety*, October 1, 1930, pp. 7, 64.
Biery, Ruth and Eleanor Packer. "England challenges Hollywood." *Saturday Evening Post* 206 (July 29, 1933): 12–13.
"Big backlog on foreign films." *Variety*, November 6, 1940, p. 13.
"Biograph Co. licenses three manufacturers." *Variety*, February 22, 1908, p. 10.
Bowser, Eileen. *The Transformation of Cinema, 1907–1915 (History of the American Cinema, 2)*. New York: Scribner's Sons, 1990.
"Box office receipts." *Variety*, May 12, 1971, p. 37.
"Boycott of British films, because of Palestine, spreading in the U.S." *Variety*, August 11, 1948, pp. 1, 55.
"Boyer's caution." *Variety*, February 17, 1937, p. 4.
"Breen back; foreign particularly British, pix submit scripts." *Variety*, April 14, 1937, p. 7.
"Breen's nix on a number of British films straining Anglo-U.S. entente." *Variety*, May 7, 1947, pp. 9, 29.
Brill, Henry. "Will we gag films?" *The Nation* 175 (August 16, 1952): 132–133.
"Brit. pic trade no one-way street, sez Wilcox." *Variety*, March 28, 1956, p. 20.
"Brit. pix bloody but unbowed." *Variety*, May 5, 1948, pp. 15, 24.
"Brit. pix get 50% of coin o'seas but Rank's Davis unhappy over U.S. take." *Variety*, July 7, 1954, p. 13.
"Brit producers won't slant for U.S. market since TV is glad to get 'em." *Variety*, August 29, 1951, pp. 5, 14.
"Brit threatens U.S. pix imports." *Variety*, July 2, 1947, pp. 3, 48.

"Brit. unions' forced parity idea labeled unrealistic by Yanks." *Variety*, February 26, 1958, p. 5.
"Britain asks U.S. films made there carry Anglo-American identification." *Variety*, October 1, 1958, p. 1.
"British accent fine—if in U.S." *Variety*, December 28, 1955, pp. 7, 18.
"British B.O. in U.S. NSG—Blumberg." *Variety*, May 21, 1947, p. 5.
"British exhib prez sez producers should gear for U.S. market." *Variety*, February 2, 1955, p. 16.
"British film groups to fight Hollywood." *New York Times*, July 28, 1934, p. 16.
"British film industry organizing for concerted drive on U.S. market." *Variety*, February 23, 1927, p. 9.
"British filmmakers told U.S. still leads." *New York Times*, November 20, 1945, p. 21.
"British film men seek market here." *New York Times*, June 10, 1926, p. 28.
"British films earn $2,500,000 in U.S. in year." *Variety*, May 25, 1949, p. 19.
"British films in U.S." *Times* (London), June 1, 1950, p. 7.
"British in slow but sure headway; U.S. won't accept unknown stars." *Variety*, December 9, 1953, p. 10.
"British Lion goes a-huntin' for foreign markets." *Variety*, October 12, 1955, p. 7.
"British Nat'l wants stars to make pictures in England." *Variety*, June 15, 1927, p. 9.
"British pix finally click in U.S." *Variety*, September 11, 1946, pp. 3, 27.
"British pix industry blamed for lack of U.S. interest in product." *Variety*, June 6, 1956, p. 14.
"British prefer opportunity to play U.S. market, revenue incidental, Rank stresses to Yank distribs." *Variety*, July 2, 1947, pp. 3, 16.
"British producer's views." *New York Times*, May 18, 1930, sec. 8, p. 6.
"Britishers' U.S. take only $6,000,000?" *Variety*, March 17, 1948, pp. 4, 18.
Buckley, Tom. "At the movies." *New York Times*, January 13, 1978, p. C6.
"Buy British." *Time* 31 (April 11, 1938): 23.
"*Caligari* barred by Albany crowd." *Variety*, December 2, 1921, p. 47.
"Calls British film unworthy product." *New York Times*, July 10, 1926, p. 5.
"Camouflaging German pix for U.S." *Variety*, May 1, 1934, p. 1.
"Canada largest importer for American films in 1923." *Variety*, February 14, 1924, p. 19.
Canby, Vincent. "British humor scores in U.S." *Variety*, April 26, 1961, pp. 1, 170.
_____. "Britons top U.S. pix imports." *Variety*, May 12, 1965, pp. 1, 30.
_____. "Fans of foreign flicks—where are they now? *New York Times*, February 17, 1974, Sec. 2, pp. 1, 12.
_____. "Film imports a seesaw." *Variety*, May 8, 1963, pp. 1, 34.
_____. "Foreign films' U.S. jackpots." *Variety*, April 20, 1960, pp. 1, 78.
_____. "Foreign pictures enjoyed big earning in 1966." *New York Times*, January 18, 1967, p. 50.
_____. "Foreign rentals in U.S." *Variety*, April 29, 1964, pp. 30, 32.
_____. "N.Y. art houses: Anglo-Yank." *Variety*, July 5, 1961, p. 11.
_____. "N.Y. arties favoring U.S. pix." *Variety*, September 8, 1965, pp. 3, 70.
_____. "N.Y. foreign art film time up." *Variety*, October 23, 1963, pp. 1, 21.
_____. "N.Y's art house explosion." *Variety*, August 29, 1962, p. 5.
_____. "O'seas films' $69,000,000 in U.S." *Variety*, May 2, 1962, pp. 1, 18.
_____. "U.S. majors lead N.Y. arties." *Variety*, September 9, 1964, pp. 3, 25.
"Careless errata weaken British side of case." *Variety*, February 15, 1956, p. 16.
"Carlo Ponti credo: Italy and U.S. need one another's feature films." *Variety*, January 20, 1971, p. 24.
Carver, Benedict and Dan Cox. "New lease on *Life* for foreign pix." *Variety*, March 29, 1999, pp. 36, 83.
Cassady, Ralph Jr. "Monopoly in production and distribution, 1908–1915." Ed. Gorham Kindem. *The American Movie Industry: The Business of Motion Pictures*. Carbondale, Ill.: Southern Illinois University Press, 1982.

"Caution on any concerted action curbs U.S. majors from jointly agreeing to book British films." *Variety*, May 28, 1947, p. 9.

"Chicago expects lively times." *Variety*, February 29, 1908, p. 10.

Clark, Ted. "French see rebirth of interest by U.S. mkt." *Variety*, October 17, 1979, p. 298.

"Clavell (of *To Sir*) counsels British to make features more Yank style." *Variety*, April 24, 1968, p. 31.

"Code and Legion again loom high as foreign pix seek commercial coin." *Variety*, March 16, 1955, p. 16.

"Code seal to 305 during 1955." *Variety*, January 25, 1956, p. 7.

Cohn, Lawrence. "Apres Brigitte Bardot, whither dubbing." *Variety*, June 21, 1993, p. 7.

_____. "Oft snubbed, dubbed Euro pix may make a comeback in U.S." *Variety*, August 10, 1992, pp. 72, 74.

_____. "Overseas hits don't travel to U.S." *Variety*, May 9, 1984, pp. 1, 558.

_____. "Two new films herald return of Italo pix to U.S. screens." *Variety*, February 7, 1990, p. 22.

"Col and Gaumont at odds on Lido: overcoming U.S. tastes not easy." *Variety*, September 7, 1983, pp. 5, 32.

"Columbia's special dept. to handle foreign features starts Sept. 15." *Variety*, July 27, 1955, pp. 3, 18.

"Comparative schedules for 3 years." *Variety*, July 15, 1942, p. 5.

Corliss, Richard. "Fellini go home!" *Time* 149 (January 13, 1997): 68–70.

_____. "Handicapping the foreign Oscar." *Time* 125 (March 25, 1982): 72.

Crowther, Bosley. "Changing voices." *New York Times*, September 7, 1958, sec. 2, p. 1.

_____. "Dubbing (continued)." *New York Times*, August 21, 1960, sec. 2, pp. 1, 6.

_____. "Hearing voices again." *New York Times*, September 20, 1964, sec. 2, p. 1.

_____. "On British films." *New York Times*, November 17, 1946, sec. 2, p. 1.

_____. "On doing dubbing." *New York Times*, December 3, 1961, sec. 2, p. 1.

_____. "Snows of yesteryear." *New York Times*, February 29, 1948, sec. 2, p. 1.

_____. "Speaking of foreign films." *New York Times*, June 13, 1965, sec. 2, p. 1.

_____. "Subtitles must go." *New York Times*, August 7, 1960, sec. 2, pp. 1, 3.

_____. "Touting foreign films." *New York Times*, September 16, 1956, sec. 2, p. 1.

"Cut rate war may follow independents' aggressions." *Variety*, March 13, 1909, p. 13.

"Danes shoot extra footage to meet U.S. market requirements on intelligibility." *Variety*, August 2, 1967, p. 13.

"Davis gives figures on how Brit pix fail to get fair return out of U.S." *Variety*, November 17, 1954, pp. 5, 8.

"Days of subtitled foreign films for U.S. market nearly over." *Variety*, June 7, 1961, p. 14.

"Delighted sums up reaction to aliens' U.S. sell." *Variety*, December 5, 1956, pp. 3, 7.

"Deluge of film productions compels an amalgamation." *Variety*, January 21, 1916, p. 19.

Dent, Arthur. "British films and the American market." *Variety*, January 4, 1939, pp. 5, 30.

"Despite beefs to Uncle Sam, German pix (oldies) are being shown here." *Variety*, February 18, 1942, p. 7.

"*La Dolce Vita* blazes subtitled paths." *Variety*, November 1, 1961, p. 19.

"Don't fear German films." *New York Times*, May 29, 1921, p. 14.

"Don't like Europeans' contract terms" *Variety*, April 24, 1957, p. 4.

"Drop U.S. isolationist anti–British pic exhib policy, pleads O'Brien." *Variety*, September 1, 1954, pp. 5, 22.

"Dubbing of foreign pix still a moot point among distribs in U.S. market." *Variety*, April 9, 1952, p. 13.

Edelstein, David. "Remade in America: a label to avoid." *New York Times*, November 4, 2001, Sec. 2A, p. 3.

"$8,500,000 British B.O. in U.S." *Variety*, November 20, 1946, pp. 3, 38.

"Emphasize English-language films in foreign prod. With eye to U.S. B.O." *Variety*, October 3, 1951, p. 18.

"England and the tariff." *New York Times*, August 7, 1921, sec. 6, p. 2.

"English bankers surveying American industry for world-wide films." *Variety*, January 6, 1926, p. 27.

"English film opportunities." *New York Times*, July 12, 1926, p. 18.

"English-made American films novel idea by Geo. Ridgwell." *Variety*, December 24, 1924, p. 23.

"English maker's lesson on B'way enough—foreign no go at Cohan." *Variety*, December 10, 1930, p. 5.

"English producers bidding for American film stars." *Variety*, June 30, 1922, p. 38.

"English producers to exploit British films in this country." *Variety*, October 3, 1919, p. 61.

"English to study filmmaking here." *New York Times*, July 18, 1920, p. 22.

"Entertainment." *News-Week* 4 (August 18, 1934): 23.

"Equity aiding fight for American films." *New York Times*, June 4, 1921, p. 14.

"Estimates 850 film features scheduled for '25–'26 season." *Variety*, September 2, 1925, p. 25.

"Europe needs advice." *Variety*, March 7, 1928, p. 3.

"Europe needy—for U.S. facts." *Variety*, February 22, 1956, p. 7.

"European producers should aim to please families—Eric Johnston." *Variety*, July 4, 1956, p. 7.

"Europe's '53 remittables, $78,200,000; British take $4,400,000 from U.S." *Variety*, April 21, 1954, p. 11.

"Europe's new H'wood accent." *Variety*, October 28, 1953, pp. 1, 54.

"Europe's show window." *Variety*, March 14, 1928, pp. 5, 26.

"Ever-hopeful distribs think maybe slump might help foreign films." *Variety*, December 7, 1955, p. 25.

"Exhibit independent films." *Variety*, February 27, 1909, p. 13.

"Export union to boost German product in U.S." *Variety*, July 15, 1959, p. 18.

Fabian, S. H. "A money picture is American-made." *Variety*, April 15, 1959, p. 28.

"Feature film men fearful over the road next season." *Variety*, June 12, 1914, p. 18.

"Few foreign films." *Variety*, September 10, 1930, p. 7.

"'51 top prod. year since '44." *Variety*, May 7, 1952, p. 5.

"Fight foreign films tax." *New York Times*, August 26, 1921, p. 8.

"Fight importation of foreign films." *Variety*, June 18, 1920, p. 36.

"Fight moving-picture rate." *New York Times*, September 13, 1908, pt. 2, p. 6.

"Film center planned." *New York Times*, June 8, 1955, p. 26.

"Film competition." *New York Times*, April 20, 1921, p. 12.

"Film importers politely decline offer for ad-code okay of sell-copy." *Variety*, March 9, 1960, p. 21.

"Film imports for five years." *Variety*, January 6, 1937, p. 33.

"Film producers ask double tariff duty." *Variety*, December 28, 1921, p. 7.

"Film reciprocity." *Times* (London), July 10, 1926, p. 15.

"Film renters meet in convention." *Variety*, February 15, 1908, p. 10.

"Film shortage opens way for foreigns here." *Variety*, March 21, 1933, p. 4.

"The film situation in America." *Times* (London), August 10, 1920, p. 8.

"The film situation in America." *Times* (London), August 13, 1920, p. 8.

"Film tariff fight under way as German imports increase." *Variety*, April 22, 1921, p. 46.

"Film time increase is sought by Rank." *New York Times*, October 5, 1948, p. 31.

"Films across sea." *Business Week*, July 21, 1945, pp. 32, 34.

"Filthy French pix sparking D.C. probe into moral tone of all film imports." *Variety*, August 23, 1961, pp. 1, 53.

"555 first-line features with 219 indie full lengths." *Variety*, May 30, 1928, p. 4.

"506 releases in 1948; up 39." *Variety*, November 19, 1947, p. 5.

"Flaud repeats same points, ignores Mayer." *Variety*, March 21, 1956, pp. 5, 48.

"Flaud's theories, not facts, denied; U.S. importers think French fail to evaluate market chances." *Variety*, February 15, 1956, p. 16.

"Flood of German features starts action for protection." *Variety*, April 15, 1921, p. 45.
"Foreign art films imaginary danger, importers assure nervous Fort Lee." *Variety*, March 16, 1960, p. 19.
"Foreign features show potential to become videocassette staple." *Variety*, October 13, 1982, p. 50.
"Foreign film bubble bursts." *Variety*, August 31, 1949, pp. 3, 22.
"Foreign film coin in '36 at record high." *Variety*, September 8, 1937, p. 3.
"Foreign film imports show slight increase." *Variety*, August 12, 1925, p. 22.
"Foreign filmmakers combine to press fight." *Variety*, March 21, 1908, p. 14.
"Foreign filmmakers combining for break into this market." *Variety*, October 15, 1924, p. 21.
"Foreign film producers scan terms and house expenses with more care as market improves." *Variety*, December 28, 1960, p. 3.
"Foreign filmers form own trade assn.; 50 indies." *Variety*, March 15, 1950, pp. 4, 61.
"Foreign filmmakers need handbook to warn and guide 'em on U.S." *Variety*, April 7, 1954, pp. 1, 56.
"Foreign films glut U.S. market; B.O. clicks rare, most of 'em weakies." *Variety*, May 11, 1938, p. 12.
"Foreign films' new year for color adds to U.S. importers' hazards." *Variety*, June 30, 1954, p. 7.
"Foreign films nominated for Oscar never seen in America." *Variety*, December 30, 1959, p. 5.
"Foreign films over here." *Variety*, December 29, 1931, pp. 13, 178.
"Foreign films' sales out." *Variety*, August 8, 1933, pp. 17, 48.
"Foreign governments plan to break into U.S. market." *Variety*, August 29, 1919, p. 73.
"Foreign lingo pix in U.S. wane." *Variety*, November 14, 1951, pp. 7, 10.
"Foreign market vital to French pix producers; 20% yearly loss." *Variety*, May 10, 1950, pp. 12–13.
"Foreign pix debacle." *Variety*, January 7, 1942, p. 91.
"Foreign pix hope for more U.S. dates with curtailment of 'B' productions." *Variety*, September 20, 1953, pp. 3, 8.
"Foreign pix spurt toward peak U.S. dates; play half N.Y. arties." *Variety*, April 9, 1952, p. 12.
"Foreign pix worst year since '45." *Variety*, January 21, 1953, pp. 4, 20.
"Foreign producers advised by Brandt to develop, not borrow, stars." *Variety*, October 19, 1955, p. 16.
"Foreigners losing pull for U.S. screen." *Variety*, September 13, 1932, pp. 14, 74.
"Foreigners sing censor blues." *Variety*, September 8, 1954, pp. 11, 20.
"Foresee reciprocity in quota." *Variety*, January 26, 1938, p. 13.
"Ft. Lee, N.J., police fingerprint exhib as requisite for art house license." *Variety*, March 23, 1960, pp. 1, 62.
"Ft Lee, on holier-than-thou binge, proposes anti-foreign art film law." *Variety*, March 2, 1960, p. 15.
"Forty-one filmmakers to consider European merger." *Variety*, January 30, 1909, p. 12.
"47% of films lack code seal." *Variety*, December 29, 1954, pp. 5, 55.
"400 aliens in U.S. films." *Variety*, June 22, 1927, pp. 1, 10.
"405 films from 11 distribs." *Variety*, January 1, 1947, p. 3.
"France and pictures." *Variety*, December 27, 1918, p. 183.
Frankel, Dan. "Casting the distribution dice." *New York Times*, October 20, 1957, sec. 2, p. 5.
"Free access to U.S. market." *Variety*, October 6, 1954, p. 16.
"French actor asserts French films not seen here." *Variety*, February 24, 1922, p. 37.
"French demands." *Variety*, March 8, 1939, p. 23.
"French film problem in United States." *Variety*, March 21, 1956, p. 7.

"French film producers aiming new product at U.S. market." *Variety*, November 22, 1932, p. 11.

"French, Italian delegates see their product's acceptance far off in U.S." *Variety*, May 31, 1950, p. 7.

"French prods. hit by export mkt. slump, lagging domestic amortizing." *Variety*, June 25, 1952, p. 12.

"French producers over here promoting sale of French-made films." *Variety*, January 23, 1929, p. 6.

"French producers see American market waning for their pictures." *Variety*, March 8, 1939, p. 23.

"French producers with eye on Yank market, strive for U.S. pix slant." *Variety*, December 7, 1955, p. 17.

"French-Yanks in two-year deal; subsidizes French office in U.S." *Variety*, December 16, 1953, p. 7.

"From 400 to 500 foreign pictures made abroad in '28–'29 cutting down U.S. grosses." *Variety*, May 23, 1928, p. 10.

Gardner, Paul. "Foreign films, popular in the U.S. in '60's, being treated like foreigners in '70s." *New York Times*, October 4, 1973, p. 56.

"Gaumont printing plant goes over to independents." *Variety*, June 25, 1910, p. 8.

"Gaumont's prod. head devises system for hits in U.S. market." *Variety*, November 23, 1977, p. 31.

"GB washes up own U.S. selling org." *Variety*, December 14, 1938, p. 5.

"Geo. Kleine leaves G.F. Co. but holds on to his stock." *Variety*, June 26, 1914, p. 17.

"German chains smothering foreign film operation in U.S." *Variety*, June 2, 1931, p. 7.

"German director, Lubitsch, regarded unkindly, he says." *Variety*, February 3, 1922, p. 46.

"German 08/15 distrib calls imports fated for plush art house ghetto." *Variety*, April 24, 1957, pp. 4, 18.

"German film aide here." *New York Times*, April 10, 1957, p. 39.

"German film feeling reported dying out." *Variety*, June 3, 1921, p. 47.

"German films get a setback in city." *New York Times*, May 9, 1933, p. 20.

"German-made films now found to be heavy drug on market." *Variety*, June 24, 1921, pp. 1–2.

"German regulations for issuing of 50 picture export premium permits." *Variety*, March 27, 1929, pp. 2, 60.

"Germans are wise." *Variety*, August 14, 1914, p. 19.

"Germans daydream: What Italians, French do in U.S., we can, too." *Variety*, June 9, 1954, pp. 4, 16.

"Germans latest to see U.S. video as film market; easier dubbing problem." *Variety*, July 27, 1955, p. 18.

"Germany looks this way." *New York Times*, July 17, 1927, sec. 7, p. 5.

"Germany's latest triumph." *New York Times*, April 19, 1921, p. 16.

"G.F. fighting Pathé." *Variety*, March 20, 1914, p. 22.

"GI's in England develop British films and stars for U.S. audiences." *Variety*, June 6, 1945, pp. 1, 28.

Gold, Richard. "Foreign film disappointments at '85 boxoffice." *Variety*, January 8, 1986, p. 11.

_____. "*Ran* aims for wide audiences." *Variety*, December 18, 1985, p. 7.

_____. "U.S. buyers tough on subtitled pics." *Variety*, May 7, 1986, pp. 15, 506.

Golden, Herb. "Yanks steam at British chill." *Variety*, January 22, 1947, pp. 3, 18.

"Goldenson to urge German, British pix slanted for American market." *Variety*, May 19, 1954, pp. 3, 325.

Gould, Jack. "Prelate praises radio and video." *New York Times*, December 13, 1957, p. 29.

Green, Abel. "Nix exhib stand vs. British pix." *Variety*, February 6, 1946, pp. 3, 57.

_____. "World's screen and stage." *Variety*, July 30, 1930, pp. 3, 18.

Griffith, Richard. "European films and American audiences." *Saturday Review* 34 (January 13, 1951): 52–54+.

Groves, Don. "Quality is the key to getting Euro pix into U.S., panel sez." *Variety*, July 5, 1989, pp. 22–23.

"Hand kisses spoil films." *New York Times*, February 21, 1926, sec. 2, p. 10.

"Hard going in the U.S. for foreign films." *Variety*, May 3, 1972, p. 31.

"Hartlieb: Reich must move fast in U.S. market." *Variety*, October 17, 1956, pp. 3, 15.

Hatch, Robert. "Films." *The Nation* 191 (September 3, 1960): 119–120.

"High film duty reported out of new tariff bill." *Variety*, October 14, 1921, p. 46.

Higson, Andrew and Richard Maltby. *Film Europe and Film America: Cinema, Commerce and Cultural Exchange 1920–1939.* Exeter: University of Exeter Press, 1999.

"Hitler thing deadly." *Variety*, July 18, 1933, p. 31.

Hoffberg, Jack. "Sees distortion of art film market as undeserved bonanza for theatres." *Variety*, January 5, 1966, p. 33.

Hollinger, Hy. "Foreign pix gain by racy tags." *Variety*, June 30, 1954, pp. 7, 18.

Holloway, Ronald. "*Braun, Drum* help consolidate Germany's film breakthrough in the United States market." *Variety*, May 7, 1980, pp. 420–442.

_____. "*Drum* might be the one." *Variety*, October 17, 1979, p. 12.

_____. "German pix finally score breakthrough in American market." *Variety*, January 9, 1980, pp. 1, 86.

Hornaday, Ann. "At many a multiplex, lots of screens but little choice." *New York Times*, August 4, 1996, sec. 2, pp. 18–19.

"How may foreign films get more revenues from U.S. mart?" *Variety*, May 7, 1975, p. 135.

"How U.S. distribs ranked in 1970." *Variety*, May 12, 1971, p. 35.

Hift, Fred. "Again issue of Hollywood code." *Variety*, August 27, 1958, pp. 7, 16.

_____. "British films have best chance; all foreign product handicapped." *Variety*, April 24, 1957, pp. 5, 18.

_____. "Censorship by U.S. Customs." *Variety*, April 8, 1959, p. 7.

_____. "Deny foreign film prejudice." *Variety*, March 28, 1956, pp. 3, 20.

_____. "Europe's a code for a code." *Variety*, October 6, 1954, pp. 1, 16.

_____. "Foreign films arrive in U.S." *Variety*, January 30, 1957, pp. 1, 62.

_____. "Foreign films catering more to U.S. taste." *Variety*, January 6, 1954, pp. 5, 48.

_____. "Foreign films find U.S. gold." *Variety*, April 9, 1958, pp. 1, 119.

_____. "Foreign films in America: up from zero." *Variety*, April 9, 1958, p. 25.

_____. "Foreign stars invade U.S." *Variety*, April 3, 1957, pp. 1, 94.

_____. "French puzzling out U.S. ways." *Variety*, June 9, 1954, pp. 5, 18.

_____. "French renew fight for bigger slice of U.S. pie." *Variety*, November 26, 1990, pp. 3, 5.

_____. "French resent American code; taking $10,000,000 globally but almost nothing from U.S.A." *Variety*, June 8, 1955, pp. 5, 24.

_____. "German films too inbred." *Variety*, September 21, 1955, pp. 7, 18.

_____. "Italy triples foreign market take but hopes to do better in U.S.A." *Variety*, September 29, 1954, pp. 7, 18.

_____. "Mystery of Yank market." *Variety*, October 17, 1956, pp. 5, 78.

_____. "One world—of film headaches." *Variety*, January 4, 1956, p. 53.

_____. "Pals no get what USSR got." *Variety*, October 22, 1958, p. 17.

_____. "Pro-U.S. and it's tough—Schwarz." *Variety*, July 11, 1956, pp. 5, 22.

_____. "Time favors foreign films in U.S. but Yank theatre men notably timid." *Variety*, April 15, 1959, p. 28.

_____. "U.S. buildup of film imports." *Variety*, April 15, 1959, pp. 1, 30.

_____. "Yanks pick stories for world appeal, British don't, and lose, but squawk." *Variety*, October 12, 1955, p. 7.

"H'wood more 'n' more fills openings for unknowns from overseas." *Variety*, July 16, 1958, p. 15.

"H'wood whips foreign threats." *Variety*, October 25, 1950, pp. 1, 16.

"If the British are too British for American film tastes how explain Guinness' popularity?" *Variety*, March 21, 1956, pp. 5, 18.

"IFIDA films duck ratings." *Variety*, March 26, 1969, p. 18.

"Import license, remittance ratio increasingly used by foreigners to force their pix on America." *Variety*, March 24, 1954, pp. 5, 24.

"Importers in burn at Johnston." *Variety*, October 21, 1959, p. 15.

"Imports and exports." *New York Times*, January 15, 1922, sec.6, p. 3.

"Imports $1,000,000; exports $300,000,000." *Variety*, April 28, 1926, p. 2.

"In ducking Japan's code, U.S. film men echo Europe's peeve vs. H'wood seal." *Variety*, September 28, 1955, p. 7.

"In the mail bag." *New York Times*, April 23, 1922, sec. 6, p. 1.

"In the meantime." *Time* 70 (November 18, 1957): 112–114.

"In U.S. Frenchmen go it alone; money doesn't justify cooperation." *Variety*, December 15, 1954, p. 10.

"Independents cleaning house." *Variety*, February 19, 1910, p. 14.

"Independents still convening." *Variety*, June 25, 1910, p. 8.

"India latest foreign land to badly misunderstand U.S. film economics." *Variety*, February 27, 1957, p. 10.

"India's export earnings down." *Variety*, May 17, 1978, p. 90.

"Indie channel or major company poses distrib question in U.S." *Variety*, August 3, 1955, pp. 7, 61.

"Indie distribs flocking to Hollywood." *Variety*, May 7, 1980, p. 11.

"Indie exhibitors want German and Italian pix kept out of the U.S." *Variety*, March 26, 1941, p. 1.

"Inside stuff—pictures." *Variety*, February 25, 1921, p. 44.

"International film co. has novel distributing scheme." *Variety*, February 20, 1909, p. 13.

"International films key to success says Valenti." *Cinemag* no. 10 (September, 1978): 17.

"International resume." *Variety*, September 8, 1931, pp. 5, 30.

"Issue-and-costs of dubbing foreign films for States again examined." *Variety*, December 4, 1957, p. 24.

"Italian Cines out." *Variety*, August 15, 1908, p. 11.

"Italian film invasion." *Life* 33 (October 20, 1952): 107–113.

"Italo *Open City* freak B.O. in U.S." *Variety*, June 19, 1946, p. 4.

"Italo-U.S. pact may pour $6,000,000 in U.S. pix purse, hamstring IFE." *Variety*, April 1, 1950, pp. 5, 20.

Jacobson, Harlan. "How the classic kids snatched foreign film." *Village Voice*, November 22, 1983, pp. 74–76, 83.

Jacobson, Harlan. "It's still a thin market for foreign films in U.S." *Variety*, May 7, 1980, pp. 11, 344.

Jahrblum, Charles. "With English subtitles." *New York Times*, June 27, 1937, sec. 10, p. 3.

"Japan (494), India (308), Italy (301), U.S. (300), Taiwan (246) most active." *Variety*, May 12, 1971, p. 37.

"Jerry Lewis sampler omits categories of foreign-language and porno films." *Variety*, June 7, 1972, p. 7.

"Johnston appraises state of film biz on foreign and domestic fronts." *Variety*, July 28, 1948, p. 17.

"Johnston denies U.S. movie curbs." *New York Times*, October 16, 1948, p. 8.

Kauffmann, Stanley. "Arts and lives." *The New Republic* 179 (August 19, 1978): 28–29.

_____. "Books & the arts." *The New Republic* 213 (November 27, 1993): 28.

_____. "Foreign languages in foreign pictures." *The New Republic* 143 (December 12, 1960): 27–28.

Kilday, Gregg. "Imported inspiration." *American Film* 14 (May, 1989): 14.

Klady, Leonard. "H'wood foreign rub: join the dub club?" *Variety*, September 12, 1994, pp. 9, 17.

_____. "Legions of foreign-lingo pix colonize small market niche." *Variety*, April 29, 1996, pp. 11, 27.

_____. "Read their lips: Americans don't like dubbing." *New York Times*, August 29, 1999, sec. 2, p. 21.

Klawans, Stuart. "When the art film label is deadly." *New York Times*, November 18, 2001, sec. 2, p. 15.

Klein, Stephen. "Prods. over-value U.S. art mart." *Variety*, May 4, 1983, pp. 1, 532, 542.

"Kleine Co. answers Edison." *Variety*, February 29, 1908, p. 12.

Knight, Arthur. "The great dubbing controversy." *Saturday Review* 43 (October 29, 1960): 28.

Koehler, Robert. "How auds learned to love the subtitles." *Variety*, January 14, 2002, pp. A5+.

Korda, Alexander. "Is the screen really free?" *New York Times*, December 1, 1946, sec. 2, p. 5.

"Korda's TV threat to exhibs." *Variety*, October 6, 1948, p. 3.

Kuttner, Alfred B. "A tariff for the movies?" *New York Times*, April 24, 1921, sec. 7, p. 6.

"Lack of a theater forces Italians to lower N.Y. flag." *Variety*, June 15, 1988, p. 7.

Landry, Robert J. "Brazil woos U.S. film market." *Variety*, December 23, 1970, pp. 7, 40.

_____. "Foreign showmen ask for more facts on U.S. market." *Variety*, May 8, 1968, p. 39.

_____. "Unsold in the land of sell." *Variety*, April 24, 1957, p. 5.

_____. "Yankee prudes and foreign films." *Variety*, April 29, 1964, p. 31.

Lee, Linda. "Nobody reads a good movie these days." *New York Times*, December 9, 1996, p. D9.

"Legion of Decency data." *Variety*, December 20, 1961, p. 11.

"Leon Gaumont tells why Europe can't compete with U.S." *Variety*, October 27, 1926, p. 59.

Lief, Louise. "France's Gaumont takes aim at the American market." *Variety*, December 25, 1983, Sec. 2, pp. 13, 15.

Litman, Lenny. "Even tiny towns get foreign pix." *Variety*, May 8, 1963, p. 34.

"Little films." *New York Times*, March 1, 1931, p. 1.

"London has big film supply that lacks American mart." *Variety*, February 12, 1915, p. 21.

Lopate, Phillip. "When foreign movies mattered." *New York Times*, August 13, 2000, sec. 2, pp. 11, 20.

Loud, Lance. "Illuminations." *American Film* 19 (January/February, 1992): 13.

"Lubin has a reason." *Variety*, February 29, 1908, p. 10.

Lucheese, Sam. "10 years of art house operation in Atlanta; British easy favorites." *Variety*, May 8, 1963, p. 33.

MacCormac, John. "London film notes." *New York Times*, December 9, 1928, sec. 10, p. 7.

"Made-in-Europe-for-America." *Variety*, December 24, 1958, pp. 5, 15.

"Mail bag memos." *New York Times*, December 21, 1947, sec. 2, p. 7.

"Majors brush art for big b.o." *Variety*, February 6, 1963, pp. 5, 18

Mallen, Bruce. "Canadian features as export commodity." *Cinemag* no. 30 (January 21, 1980): 10–12.

"Manufacturers assume control of all moving pictures." *Variety*, January 16, 1909, p. 13.

"Many imports fail to score." *Variety*, May 21, 1920, p. 35.

Marshall, Ernest. "London screen notes." *New York Times*, June 18, 1933, sec. 10, p. 2.

Maxwell, John. "Can reciprocity pay?" *Variety*, January 2, 1929, p. 5.

Mayer, Arthur. "From Bernhardt to Bardot." *Saturday Review* 42 (June 27, 1959): 8–10+

Mayer, Arthur L. "Myth of the less virtuous foreign film." *Variety*, April 20, 1960, p. 25.

Meadow, Noel. "French pictures gain in popularity." *New York Times*, June 8, 1947, sec. 2, p. 5.

_____. "TV no threat to film imports." *Variety*, January 24, 1951, pp. 7, 55.

_____. "U.S. market on foreign films says due to bad quality." *Variety*, June 24, 1953, pp. 17, 20.

Medich, Rob. "Why foreign films founder." *Premiere* 2 (December, 1988): 30.

"Méliès has Patent license." *Variety*, August 7, 1909, p. 13.

"Méliès suspends releases." *Variety*, December 18, 1909, p. 15.

"Menace of German films." *Literary Digest* 69 (May 14, 1921): 28–29

"Metro will test o'seas pickups before they get regular release." *Variety*, November 17, 1971, p. 5.

Monaco, James. "Holding pattern." *Take One* 4 (no. 11, 1975): 38–39.

"Moscow to halt U.S. film imports." *New York Times*, March 2, 1963, p. 5.

Moskowitz, Gene. "Hopes stirring again in France for U.S. mkt. breakthrough." *Variety*, October 18, 1978, p. 242

_____. "Raymond Dannon: I don't believe French films unacceptable to U.S." *Variety*, May 10, 1972, p. 4.

"Most fans think Antonioni is a cheese—Levine." *Variety*, May 24, 1967, p. 7.

"Movie house with a past." *New York Times Magazine*, March 28, 1954, p. 39

"Movie missionary." *Fortune* 32 (October, 1945): 148–151+.

"The moving picture industry." *Variety*, December 11, 1909, pp. 33, 125

"Moving picture peace strongly rumored about." *Variety*, August 15, 1908, p. 11.

"MPAA vs. foreign retaliation." *Variety*, October 22, 1952, pp. 3, 16.

Musser, Charles. *The Emergence of Cinema: The American Screen to 1907 (History of the American Cinema, 1)*. New York: Scribner's Sons, 1990.

Myers, Harold. "East Berlin can't get U.S. playdates." *Variety*, July 15, 1959, p. 17.

_____. "European producers' big query: how U.S. figures the figures." *Variety*, May 8, 1968, p. 33.

"Natan tells what's wrong with U.S." *Variety*, August 14, 1934, pp. 2, 47

"Need special approach budget to sell British pix in U.S., sez U exec." *Variety*, August 12, 1953, p. 16.

"New Italian-U.S. film pact drops principle of subsidy." *Variety*, June 9, 1954, p. 11.

"Newsreelers' switch to foreign pix seen as big lift to imported films." *Variety*, May 21, 1947, pp. 5, 20.

"No cash advances for foreign films." *Variety*, August 19, 1921, p. 38.

"No foreign pictures, new Famous Players sales slogan." *Variety*, December 8, 1922, p. 38.

"No foreign pix blackout." *Variety*, February 7, 1940, p. 11.

"No room for us in U.S." *Variety*, January 20, 1937, pp. 3, 31.

"Nothing to it, says Ince." *Variety*, August 14, 1914, p. 19.

Nugent, Frank S. "How fared the English visits last year?" *New York Times*, March 3, 1935, sec. 8, p. 3.

"Of all foreign-mades over here only German talkers standing up on showings in New York City." *Variety*, April 29, 1931, p. 7.

"Of 73 'C' (condemned) films only two with a major distrib." *Variety*, November 10, 1954, p. 7.

Ogan, Christine. "The audience for foreign film in the United States." *Journal of Communications* 40 (no. 4, 1990): 58–77.

"Once dud, N.J. house reaps profits, protests on foreign film policy." *Variety*, November 2, 1955, p. 10.

"Once upon a day Lelouche was hero of U.S. boxoffice." *Variety*, May 17, 1978, pp. 9, 127.

"100 German cinemas in U.S. drop to 6." *Variety*, May 23, 1933, p. 13.

"135 blockbusters: $311,950,000." *Variety*, January 6, 1954, pp. 5, 66.

"Ostrer and Hagen join the C. M. Wolf wailing wall." *Variety*, January 27, 1937, p. 7.

"Par pledges more bookings for Rank but indie circuits still skeptical." *Variety*, June 4, 1947, pp. 3, 22.

"Paris paper warns." *Variety*, November 20, 1909, p. 12.

"Parochial uproar in Ft. Lee; panics before foreign art films." *Variety*, February 24, 1960, pp. 3, 24.

"Pash and pinko pix peeve." *Variety*, March 31, 1937, p. 7.

"Patents Co. sues independent." *Variety*, September 4, 1909, p. 12.
"Pathé alarmed." *Variety*, March 1, 1918, p. 49.
"Pathé farming stars." *Variety*, April 12, 1918, p. 48.
"Pathé in Mutual." *Variety*, October 31, 1914, p. 25.
"Pathé in new quarters." *Variety*, February 1, 1908, p. 11.
"Pathé to quit?" *Variety*, February 18, 1916, p. 29.
Phillips, Joseph D. "Film conglomerate blockbusters." *The American Movie Industry: the Business of Motion Pictures*. In Ed. Gorham Kindem. Carbondale, Ill.: Southern Illinois University Press, 1982.
"Picture-making abroad." *New York Times*, December 17, 1922, sec. 7, p. 2.
"Picture sensational draw." *Variety*, December 17, 1920, pp. 1, 45.
"Picture service prices on the downward slide." *Variety*, February 20, 1915, p. 22.
Pitman, Jack. "British films too insular?" *Variety*, December 6, 1922, p. 27.
"Plenty of foreign film production but not enough qualify for the U.S." *Variety*, November 15, 1939, p. 14.
"Point up continued foreign films failure to seek American seal." *Variety*, April 3, 1957, p. 12.
"Poor handling hurts French films in the U.S." *Variety*, October 29, 1920, p. 47.
Pristin, Terry. "Will dubbing fly in the U.S.? Read my lips." *New York Times*, February 19, 1996, pp. D1, D4.
"Producers' batting averages." *Variety*, November 13, 1909, p. 13.
"Producers' batting averages." *Variety*, December 4, 1909, p. 13.
"Protest film invasion." *New York Times*, July 16, 1919, p. 13.
"Protest U.S. actors in British film roles." *New York Times*, June 29, 1950, p. 36.
Pryor, Thomas M. "Breen's mission to London." *New York Times*, August 18, 1946, sec. 2, p. 3.
_____. "Foreign film distributors organize." *New York Times*, March 19, 1950, sec. 2, p. 5.
_____. "Johnston decries foreign film bar." *New York Times*, January 9, 1954, p. 11.
Ptito, Lauren. "Arts & leisure." *Europe* no. 338 (July/August, 1994): 46.
"Quota ups Brits., hits U.S." *Variety*, June 15, 1938, p. 13.
"Rank combine hits by B.O. dip in U.S., '47 take only 40% of $10,000,000 dream." *Variety*, December 17, 1947, pp. 4, 18.
"Rank thinks Yank distribs never did their best to sell his pix in U.S." *Variety*, March 17, 1948, pp. 3, 22.
"Rank-Yank hits Schine bias." *Variety*, February 26, 1958, p. 5.
"Rank-Young interviewers evidence that U.S. press seems plenty sold on British pix superiority to H'wood." *Variety*, May 14, 1947, pp. 6, 22.
"Rank's prestige pix unit for U.S." *Variety*, June 26, 1946, p. 4.
"Rank's retreat." *Time* 54 (October 24, 1949): 96–97.
"Rank's $2-mil for American dig-in." *Variety*, June 19, 1957, p. 4.
"Reciprocity scheme criticized." *Times* (London), July 15, 1926, p. 13.
Rees, Robert. "Non-alike twin cities; St. Paul resists Le sexy." *Variety*, May 8, 1963, p. 34.
"Retaliatory action deemed certain if tariff passes." *Variety*, August 19, 1921, p. 38.
Riethof, Peter. "Expert advice: dub with care if you expect to slip by in U.S." *Variety*, May 8, 1974, p. 170.
_____. "Future of the dubbed film." *Variety*, January 12, 1955, p. 24.
"Riot over German feature picture." *Variety*, May 13, 1921, p. 47.
Robbins, Jim. "U.S. market guide for imported films." *Variety*, February 3, 1982, pp. 43, 52.
Rodman, Howard A. "The five nominees and how they grew." *Film Comment* 25 (March/April, 1989): 8, 80.
Rohter, Larry. "For foreign films, vita is no longer dolce." *New York Times*, April 11, 1991, pp. C15, C18.
Rotha, Paul. *The Film Till Now*. London: Vision, 1960.
"Rowland and Cippico's deal with great Italian film co." *Variety*, June 13, 1919, p. 54.

"Russians cool to pix deal with Yanks; ideas on reciprocity a stalemate." *Variety*, September 11, 1957, p. 11.

"Sales of British films in U.S." *Times* (London), November 8, 1962, p. 11.

"Sales resistance to British films in the United States." *Times* (London), December 2, 1955, p. 3.

"Sapene, French quota author, coming to U.S. with ultimatum 'buy film or take exclusion.'" *Variety*, January 30, 1929, p. 6.

"Sapene utters downright boycott threat against American trade unless French films are shown." *Variety*, March 27, 1929, pp. 2, 60.

Sarris, Andrew. "Why the foreign film has lost its cachet." *New York Times*, May 2, 1999, sec. 2A, pp. 15, 35.

Schanberg, Sydney H. "New Delhi: pillage in the eyes of God." *New York Times*, August 30, 1971, p. 34.

Schreger, Charles. "Hollywood checks directors from Europe as prone to flop in English language." *Variety*, May 17, 1978, p. 8.

Schumach, Murray. "Film study sees import increase." *New York Times*, September 20, 1960, p. 46.

_____. "Role of studios showing change." *New York Times*, January 9, 1962, p. 22.

"Screen: film circulation." *New York Times*, August 6, 1922, sec. 6, p. 3.

"Screen: the public be served." *New York Times*, July 30, 1922, sec. 6, p. 3.

"Screen: the public rejects." *New York Times*, August 27, 1922, sec. 6, p. 3.

"2nd British film invasion." *Variety*, May 1, 1935, p. 5.

"Secret move for French subsidy to push Gallic films in America." *Variety*, June 12, 1934, p. 20.

"Security check on foreign pix." *Variety*, January 14, 1953, pp. 3, 61.

"See dangers in aiming European films for mass Yank audience." *Variety*, March 8, 1950, p. 15.

"See Spanish-language pix as solution to the foreign product slack in U.S." *Variety*, May 15 1950, p. 15.

Segers, Frank. "Best customer for pics from Japan is U.S." *Variety*, December 9, 1987, pp. 1, 75.

_____. "Foreign pix pick up more biz in U.S." *Variety*, May 9, 1979, pp. 1, 104.

_____. "Foreign pix seek key to U.S. masses." *Variety*, October 19, 1977, pp. 1, 40.

Segrave, Kerry. *American Films Abroad: Hollywood's Domination of the World's Movie Screens.* Jefferson, N.C.: McFarland, 1997.

"Seidelman again warns U.S. must up $ for British films, or else." *Variety*, April 30, 1947, pp. 11, 22.

Seldes, Gilbert. "Are the foreign films better?" *Atlantic Monthly* 184 (September, 1949): 49–52.

"Selling, not sharing new foreign method." *Variety*, June 14, 1932, p. 13.

"$71,000,000 from foreign sales." *Variety*, August 17, 1927, p. 8.

"Sexacious selling best B.O. slant for foreign language films in U.S." *Variety*, June 9, 1948, pp. 2, 18.

"Shall we, yawn, go to a film?" *The Economist* 342 (February 1, 1997): 85–86.

Shelton, Robert. "Movie men of few words." *New York Times*, June 15, 1958, sec. 2, p. 8.

"Shortages vs. closed minds." *Variety*, June 9, 1954, pp. 5, 18.

Silverman, Michael. "Indigenous Aussie features find U.S. market no piece of cake." *Variety*, May 7, 1986, pp. 347, 362.

_____. "U.S.-Euro pic imbalance cuts two ways." *Variety*, September 10, 1986, pp. 5, 109.

Silverman, Syd. "330 films above $100,000 rentals." *Variety*, May 12, 1971, p. 34.

"Sir Oswald panning us." *Variety*, October 5, 1927, pp. 3, 10.

"Sir Oswald sailing: leaves wonder behind." *Variety*, October 12, 1927, p. 3.

"Sked Cockney, clean up in U.S." *Variety*, January 30, 1963, pp. 7, 18.

"Slow-going upbuild of foreign film directors in U.S." *Variety*, December 13, 1961, p. 5.

Smith, Roger. "Decannestruction." *Film Comment* 37 (July/August, 2001): 20–21.

"Something of a boom for foreign pix into Americanese impends." *Variety*, February 19, 1937, p. 4.

"Southern New Jersey filmgoers find no foreign product on local screens." *Boxoffice* 114 (February 26, 1979): E1.

Spoor, George K. "Judging film subjects for the American market." *Variety*, December 12, 1908, p. 29.

"A square deal for all is Thomas Edison's promise." *Variety*, June 20, 1908, p. 12.

"State not refunding censor fees." *Variety*, April 8, 1959, p. 7.

"Stix still nix British pix." *Variety*, June 18, 1947, pp. 1, 16.

"Stress lack of foreign pix with broad aud appeal for America." *Variety*, January 14, 1953, p. 4.

"Stresses French inability to compete with British in pitch for U.S. market." *Variety*, January 29, 1947, p. 16.

"Survey for foreign producers measures response of U.S. auds." *Variety*, October 22, 1986, p. 14.

"Swede on Yanks' prudery." *Variety*, November 19, 1958, p. 3.

"Swedish-Biograph planning appeal only to Swedes here." *Variety*, December 9, 1921, p. 37.

Talbot, Hayden. "Rank making serious mistake trying to pressure U.S. exhibs into playing his pix, says Wilby." *Variety*, January 22, 1947, pp. 3, 52.

"Tear bombs injure 9 at foreign films here." *New York Times*, May 7, 1939, p. 1.

Teitel, Charles. "In Chicago, if you play a foreign pic, you could be tagged a Bolshevik." *Variety*, May 12, 1971, pp. 35, 206.

"Testing Okla. City's taste for foreign features; 8 for $4." *Variety*, October 12, 1955, p. 7.

"Teutonic films prove to be a tough sell overseas." *Variety*, December 5, 1994, p. 42.

"That import tax." *New York Times*, August 28, 1921, sec. 6, p. 3.

Thomson, Patricia. "Imports alive, not kicking." *Variety*, March 11, 1991, p. 44.

_____. "Int'l pix confront narrow coin margin." *Daily Variety*, July 30, 2001, pp. 30+.

_____. "New generation tackles foreign film challenge." *Variety*, March 11, 1991, p. 42.

Thornhill, Michael. "Native accent of too many industries hampers export profit chances." *Variety*, May 10, 1978, p. 48.

"Those English subtitles." *Newsweek* 56 (August 8, 1960): 76.

"3 banned unseen." *Variety*, October 6, 1954, p. 16.

Tilley, Frank. "Variety called vitriolic on British films by Beaverbrook's daily." *Variety*, September 26, 1928, p. 6.

"Tobis making another attempt to crash Anglo-American markets." *Variety*, April 29, 1936, p. 4.

"Top foreign films in U.S." *Variety*, August 31, 1992, p. 54.

"Trust and independent line-up for season in picture division." *Variety*, September 10, 1910, p. 12.

"Truth about U.S. boycott of British productions." *Variety*, April 14, 1922, p. 43.

"20th-Fox's 4-year deal to distribute Korda's product is another step forward for Anglo-U.S. film accord." *Variety*, July 2, 1947, pp. 3, 16.

"UFA plans to open theatre on Broadway." *New York Times*, November 29, 1927, p. 31.

"UFA's future in U.S. is dubious." *Variety*, April 23, 1930, p. 7.

"Ultimately the war will make U.S. more foreign film-minded—Rosener." *Variety*, August 21, 1940, p. 4.

"Universal assigns sales talent to push British (Rank) features." *Variety*, January 27, 1954, pp. 5, 24.

"Urges special code class for imports." *Variety*, June 30, 1954, p. 7.

"U's sales accent on British films for big U.S. keys." *Variety*, July 28, 1948, pp. 4, 17.

"U's sales on Rank pix in U.S. to be highly selective." *Variety*, August 18, 1948, pp. 3, 21.

"U.S. exhibs resist Metro's foreign imports, claiming OK for arties only." *Variety*, March 5, 1947, pp. 3, 22.

"U.S. exhibs scored by Jarratt, Korda aide, for shunning British product." *Variety*, December 18, 1946, pp. 1, 29.

"U.S. film imports 1988 vs. 1968." *Variety*, May 3, 1989, Cannes special issue, pp. 196+.
"U.S. films' peak foreign b.o." *Variety*, February 19, 1947, pp. 3, 48.
"U.S. interest in foreign revives." *Variety*, October 24, 1933, p. 12.
"U.S. life-or-death to Brit pix." *Variety*, December 25, 1946, pp. 9, 22.
"U.S. picture firms null distribution of Latin-American product." *Variety*, February 19, 1941, p. 13.
"U.S. pix on world scale." *Variety*, June 17, 1953, p. 3.
"U.S. sees first Japanese movie." *Literary Digest* 123 (April 10, 1937): 28.
"U.S. to combat invasion?" *Variety*, March 18, 1936, pp. 7, 58.
"Valenti to Russian film execs: stop thinking in reciprocity terms." *Variety*, July 25, 1973, pp. 1, 44.
"Variety and the foreign-mades." *Variety*, September 11, 1929, p. 7.
Verrill, Addison. "Europe's key to U.S. sales." *Variety*, April 29, 1970, pp. 1, 24.
_____. "O'seas pix regaining U.S. audiences." *Variety*, May 8, 1974, pp. 1, 62.
"Wait for fall: can TV put talky British feature over with American public?" *Variety*, July 20, 1955, p. 5.
"Warners enforce block booking on entire output of talk films." *Variety*, September 19, 1928, p. 24.
"Warnings vs. foreign pictures come through." *Variety*, November 1, 1950, pp. 3, 23.
"Warns that unions may reform films." *New York Times*, June 9, 1926, p. 25.
Wear, Mike. "Foreign pix in U.S." *Variety*, January 5, 1938, p. 57.
_____. "21 arty situations in Manhattan." *Variety*, October 24, 1962, p. 24.
"Welcome mat for imports." *Variety*, September 29, 1954, pp. 3, 18.
Werba, Hank. "Italo film biz invading U.S." *Variety*, July 16, 1969, pp. 33, 36.
"What British M.P.'s actually said." *Variety*, February 15, 1956, p. 16.
"Who likes foreign films." *Variety*, September 29, 1954, p. 3.
"Wholesale attempt to corral all exhibitors with Chaplin." *Variety*, June 11, 1915, p. 3.
"Why American films are best." *New York Times*, May 20, 1923, sec. 7, p. 2.
Williams, Michael. "Dub's the rub for Gallic pix in U.S." *Variety*, December 13, 1993, pp. 33, 35.
"With Berlin foreign center: Famous shuffling directors." *Variety*, November 25, 1921, p. 44.
"Wm. Fox to drop all the foreign feature films." *Variety*, July 24, 1914, p. 17.
Yakir, Dan. "Cutting remarks." *Horizon* 28 (May, 1985): 73–78.
_____. "The importance of being Dan Talbot." *American Film* 5 (April, 1980): 30–34+.
"Yank distribs increasingly handle foreign pix outside U.S. market." *Variety*, March 16, 1955, p. 15.
"Yank-exhibs criticize British films." *Variety*, December 14, 1955, p. 3.
"Yank exhibs still cool on imports, as Europe strains for U.S. favor." *Variety*, June 1, 1955, pp. 4, 20.
"Yankee fans star fixation retards upbuilding of imported films." *Variety*, March 13, 1957, p. 5.
"Yanks see quota cry, other angles; view M.P. cracks as muddled logic." *Variety*, February 15, 1956, p. 16.
Young, Deborah. "Italo pic biz wrangles U.S. export declaration." *Variety*, August 16, 1999, p. 19.
Young, Josh. "The best French films you will never see." *New York Times*, October 30, 1994, sec. 2, pp. 17, 22.
"Zukor has bought so far 129 German features for Famous." *Variety*, April 29, 1921, p. 45.

Index

247